G. A. Cohen

Key Contemporary Thinkers series includes:

Lee Braver, *Heidegger*
John Burgess, *Kripke*
Filipe Carreira da Silva, *G. H. Mead*
Claire Colebrook and Jason Maxwell, *Agamben*
Jean-Pierre Couture, *Sloterdijk*
Gareth Dale, *Karl Polanyi*
Oliver Davis, *Jacques Rancière*
Gerard de Vries, *Bruno Latour*
Reidar Andreas Due, *Deleuze*
Stuart Elden, *Canguilhem*
Neil Gascoigne, *Richard Rorty*
Graeme Gilloch, *Siegfried Kracauer*
Lawrence Hamilton, *Amartya Sen*
M. G. Hayes, *John Maynard Keynes*
Rachel Jones, *Irigaray*
S. K. Keltner, *Kristeva*
Steven Knepper, Ethan Stoneman and Robert Wyllie, *Byung-Chul Han*
Matthew H. Kramer, *H.L.A. Hart*
Moya Lloyd, *Judith Butler*
Ronald Loeffler, *Brandom*
James McGilvray, *Chomsky, 2nd Edition*
Dermot Moran, *Edmund Husserl*
Marie-Eve Morin, *Jean-Luc Nancy*
Timothy Murphy, *Antonio Negri*
Daniel H. Neilson, *Minsky*
James O'Shea, *Wilfrid Sellars*
William Outhwaite, *Habermas, 2nd edition*
Ed Pluth, *Badiou*
Reiland Rabaka, *Du Bois*
J. Toby Reiner, *Michael Walzer*
Neil G. Robertson, *Leo Strauss*
William Scheuerman, *Morgenthau*
Severin Schroeder, *Wittgenstein*
Anthony Paul Smith, *Laruelle*
James Smith, *Terry Eagleton*
Felix Stalder, *Manuel Castells*
Christine Sypnowich, *G. A. Cohen*
Christopher Zurn, *Axel Honneth*

G. A. Cohen

Liberty, Justice and Equality

Christine Sypnowich

polity

Copyright © Christine Sypnowich 2024

The right of Christine Sypnowich to be identified as Author of this Work has been asserted in accordance with the UK Copyright, Designs and Patents Act 1988.

First published in 2024 by Polity Press

Polity Press
65 Bridge Street
Cambridge CB2 1UR, UK

Polity Press
111 River Street
Hoboken, NJ 07030, USA

All rights reserved. Except for the quotation of short passages for the purpose of criticism and review, no part of this publication may be reproduced, stored in a retrieval system or transmitted, in any form or by any means, electronic, mechanical, photocopying, recording or otherwise, without the prior permission of the publisher.

ISBN-13: 978-1-5095-2993-3
ISBN-13: 978-1-5095-2994-0(pb)

A catalogue record for this book is available from the British Library.

Library of Congress Control Number: 2023939926

Typeset in 10.5 on 12pt Palatino
by Fakenham Prepress Solutions, Fakenham, Norfolk NR21 8NL
Printed and bound in Great Britain by TJ Books Ltd, Padstow, Cornwall

The publisher has used its best endeavours to ensure that the URLs for external websites referred to in this book are correct and active at the time of going to press. However, the publisher has no responsibility for the websites and can make no guarantee that a site will remain live or that the content is or will remain appropriate.

Every effort has been made to trace all copyright holders, but if any have been overlooked the publisher will be pleased to include any necessary credits in any subsequent reprint or edition.

For further information on Polity, visit our website:
politybooks.com

For David

Contents

Preface		viii
1	The Political is Personal: G. A. Cohen's Philosophical Journey	1
2	'No-Bullshit Marxism' and the Fate of Historical Materialism	32
3	Rescuing Freedom from Nozick	56
4	Rescuing Justice from Rawls	80
5	Taking Responsibility for Egalitarianism	106
6	Rescuing Existing Value – For or Against Socialism?	137
7	Conclusion: Paradox and Legacy	164
Notes		176
References		216
Index		244

Preface

I first met Jerry Cohen in Hilary term in the winter of 1985, when he arrived in Oxford to take up the Chichele Chair in Social and Political Theory at All Souls College. I was already embarked on my doctoral dissertation, which sought to use the resources of liberal legal and political philosophy to make a case for a theory of socialist law. It was a topic proximate to Cohen's interests and I was excited by the prospect of him being in Oxford. My prior academic background was in the domain of critical theory and, with the exception of my acquaintance with C.B. Macpherson's incisive work on the theory of 'possessive individualism', I was quite unschooled in analytical philosophy. I was therefore bowled over by Cohen's combination of sharp-eyed precision and ardent radical commitment. It is perhaps unsurprising then, that as a huge admirer of his work and in awe of his compelling lectures, I feared looking a fool in a personal encounter. Meeting him both confirmed and dispelled my worries – he was as tough-minded an interlocutor as I anticipated, but also a delightful person, kind and tremendous fun.

Cohen's tragic death in 2009 occasioned an outpouring of esteem and affection. This is due in part to Cohen's unusual background that, as he frequently noted, shaped his scholarly pursuits. It was also due to the exceptional humanity he displayed in his dealings with others; he was not just 'widely admired but loved'.[1] I believe Jerry Cohen therefore makes for a specially interesting and compelling subject in the 'Key Contemporary Thinkers' series. Who could not be intrigued by the story of the young Jerry growing up in a Jewish

Communist community in working-class Montreal, then finding dazzling success on the British philosophical scene, and ultimately holding a prestigious chair in Oxford? The life-long socialist whose philosophy was the fruits of 'explicit political engagement' and conviction? The 'amazingly gifted political philosopher' with an 'inimitable voice' who, though fiercely austere in his philosophical standards, could make 'instant friendships with strangers', who had a 'contagious tenderness' and could make people laugh 'to the point of tears'?[2]

With such a rich background to draw upon, I chose to include much more of Cohen's personal narrative than is customary in books of this kind. Cohen himself made so many references to his family background and politics that incorporating this material seemed the obvious thing to do. I hope readers will agree that the result exemplifies the way the 'personal is political' and makes for an illuminating read.

I found writing this book a daunting task. 'What would Jerry think?' I often pondered as I tried to articulate a complicated thought, wondered whether to include an anecdote, or made philosophical judgements about his work. I feel so fortunate to have known Jerry and enjoyed his friendship. I wanted to do justice to his place in the canon of political philosophy, but also to him, the person. Moreover, I've been acutely conscious of the scrutiny this book will receive, not just from philosophers, but also from Jerry's family, colleagues and the many, many friends he made around the world and throughout his life.

Though daunting, working on this book has been an enormous pleasure in so many ways. Chief among them was the chance to spend time in Jerry's world, to get to know and talk with so many people who knew and loved him. I am deeply grateful to the Cohen family. Jerry's children, Gideon, Miriam and Sarah were wonderful in sharing their memories. I am very thankful to Miriam for the warm welcome to her family home so that I could pore over her father's papers and engage her in discussion. His rusty filing cabinet was a treasure trove of materials that greatly enhanced the narrative I tell here. Jerry's brother Michael kindly spent a day with me, gave me a vivid personal picture of his brother, and showed me around the 'Jerry landmarks' in Montreal. Maggie Cohen was good enough to speak with me at length about her marriage to Jerry and their life together raising a young family in London. I've been lucky enough to know Michèle Cohen for many years, and I am grateful to her for sharing memories of her beloved husband. Arnold Zuboff was enormously generous and enthusiastic in talking to me about his dear friend. I am also grateful to those Analytical Marxists, good friends of Jerry, who shared their memories and ideas: John Roemer, Hillel Steiner and Philippe Van Parijs. I thank Jo Wolff who met with me at a busy time for a very valuable conversation.

I started work on this book as a Visiting Fellow in the Department of Politics and International Relations at the Australian National University in spring 2018. I am grateful to the ANU faculty and graduate students for their interest in my research, and particularly Keith Dowding, my generous and supportive host.

I am indebted to the Warden and Fellows of All Souls, whose gracious and warm welcome enhanced the unique privilege of my Visiting Fellowship in Trinity term in 2022. Postponed for two years due to the Covid pandemic, my sojourn at All Souls was magical. The chance to spend time in Jerry's cherished community, among his colleagues and friends, in such superb accommodations, was such a gift. I am truly grateful. I also thank the College staff – domestic, library, administrative, IT – who were all enormously helpful.

The deep connections Jerry forged with the fellows of All Souls meant many were forthcoming with stories and anecdotes. I thank John Vickers, Lucia Zedner, Avner Offer, David Gellner, David Addison, Santanu Das, Peregrine Hordin, Ian Rumfitt, Dame Marina Warner, Margaret Bent, Robin Briggs, Edward Hussey, Ian Maclean, David Parkin, Dan Segal, Sir Keith Thomas, Sarah Bufkin and Paul Seabright. A special thank you to Cécile Fabre who guided me during my time at All Souls, generously spoke to me at length about her former supervisor, and who became a good friend.

I am immensely grateful to Paula Casal, who organized a workshop at Pompeu Fabra University in Barcelona to discuss a draft of the book. Paula was a great advocate for the project, put together a wonderful programme of speakers, offered excellent advice, and was a superb host. Many thanks also to Nicholas Vrousalis, Mike Otsuka, Anca Gheaus and Zosia Stemplowska for their exceptionally acute and constructive commentaries and to Tom Parr, Serena Olsaretti, Andrew Williams and other participants at the Barcelona workshop for their tremendously valuable insights. I am also very grateful for the exceedingly helpful feedback from the anonymous reviewers of the proposal and manuscript, whose identities were later kindly disclosed to me: Mike Otsuka, Tom Parr, Matthew Clayton, Nicholas Vrousalis and Colin Macleod. I'm grateful to George Owers, the Polity editor who commissioned the book, and his unfailingly patient and sympathetic successor, Ian Malcolm, who was such an excellent source of support, guidance and enthusiasm. Thanks also to associate editor Ellen MacDonald-Kramer for all her assistance and Ian Tuttle for his helpful copyediting.

Many of the ideas in this book were shared at seminars and workshops. I thank the hosts and audiences at the Warwick Philosophy Department; the All Souls Visiting Fellows Colloquium; the University College Dublin Equality Studies Programme; the Political Philosophy Reading Group, and the Saturday Club speaker series, both at Queen's University, Kingston; the Ralph Miliband Lecture Series at the London School of Economics; the University of Arizona Centre for Philosophy of Freedom; the Halbert Centre for Canadian Studies at the Hebrew University of Jerusalem; the Social Justice Centre at Concordia University; the Oxford-Queen's Politics/Philosophy/Law Workshop at St. John's College, Oxford; the Department of Philosophy at Havana University; the Prague Spring Interdisciplinary Workshop in Prague; the National Trust National Conference in Fredericton, New Brunswick; the University of Melbourne Legal Theory Workshop; the Moral, Social and Political Theory Seminar at the Australian National University in Canberra; the Montréal meetings of the European Consortium of Political Research; the Philosophy Seminar at the Institute of Education, University College London; the Nuffield Political Theory Workshop in Oxford; and the annual conference of the Philosophy of Education Society of Great Britain at New College, Oxford.

Many conversations contributed to my understanding of Jerry, his life and work, and how best to approach this project. I am grateful to Will Kymlicka, Adam Swift, David Miller, Margaret Moore, Andrew Lister, Jeff Collins, Colin Farrelly, Alistair Macleod, Elliot Paul, Shlomi Segall, Keith Dowding, Henry Laycock, Rahul Kumar, Sue Donaldson, Kerah Gordon-Solmon, Ben Ewing, Robin Archer, Wendy Webster, Cheryl Misak, David Dyzenhaus, Pablo Gilabert, Igor Schoikhedbrod, Glen Coulthard, Lois McNay, Sudhir Hazareesingh, Patrick Tomlin, Alice Crary, Michael Kremer, David Brink, Daniel Weinstock, Jeroen Knijff and Lois McNay.

I must also mention the political philosophy graduate students at Queen's, several of whom attended the Political Philosophy Reading Group or were members of my 'Justice League' research group, for their invaluable insights. Among them are Owen Clifton, Michael Luoma, Arthur Hill, Yuanjin Xia, Aidan Testa, Josh Mosely, Jessica McMullin, Jordan Desmond, Kyle Johannsen, Jeremy Butler,

Ryan McSheffrey, Omar Bachour, Brennen Harwood, Eden Elliot, Xiaojing Sun, Katie Jourdeil and Xinyuan Liang.

The challenges of writing this book were compounded by my being Head of Department, at a particularly challenging time for universities. I thank our wonderful office staff – Marilyn Lavoie, Susanne Cliff-Jüngling, Jen McLaren and Sheena Wilkinson – who provided invaluable administrative support.

Family was for me, as it was for Jerry, the precondition of my labours. My work, often done very early in the morning before others have stirred, was made more enjoyable by the company of my Siamese companions, Luna and Felix. More important, I owe a special thanks to my husband, David Bakhurst, to whom this book is dedicated. David generously read parts of the manuscript, unstintingly gave comments and advice, and kept up my spirits when they risked being low. Jerry was fond of David, an expert on Soviet Marxism, and he often addressed the two of us as 'Baknowich' or 'Sypnohurst', in a nod to 'unity in diversity' as Hegelian Marxists would say. My beloved children, Rosemary and Hugh, and now Rosemary's husband, James, helped remind me that the personal isn't just political. I am so fortunate to have all these dear Bakhursts in my life. My siblings and their partners, Paula and Martin, Catherine Mary and Claudio, John and Laure, were a great source of kind support. I have been fortunate to have wonderful parents, Marcia and Peter, who took an interest in this project. My mother was instantly charmed by Jerry's wit and hospitality at a dinner at All Souls many years ago. My father, who sadly passed away when I was in the final stages of preparing this manuscript, was an intellectual force, and his inculcation of socialist ideals in me as a young child have always stayed with me (though not with him – he became quite conservative in his old age, and not just in Jerry's sense of valuing existing things!).

Finally, I must thank Jerry Cohen himself. I know my approach to philosophy is no match for his in analytical acuity, but his standard inspires. And certainly, Jerry's socialist convictions, the belief in equality, to be argued for as honestly and forcefully as one can, is an ideal that I strive to realize. The last time I saw Jerry was in the spring of 2009, just a few months before he suddenly died. He had spent a few days in Kingston giving talks at Queen's. The trip had been an immense success. I was dropping him off at the station and felt overcome with sentiment about saying goodbye. He laughed at me and said, 'I love you too'. How Jerry. I hope this book is worthy.

1

The Political is Personal:
G. A. Cohen's Philosophical Journey

It 'was like a lollipop', Jerry Cohen said of his first acquaintance with the word 'philosophy' when, as a young boy, he tried to pronounce the 'tongue-loving word' on the cover of his babysitter's textbook.[1] Though that first sense that philosophy was both mysterious and delectable inspired the young Jerry, it would be some time before philosophy took a hold on his ambitions and pursuits. His earliest influence, rather, was a strong set of political convictions. How his politics generated a philosophy guided by a 'clear, distinctive and demanding ideal of equality' is key to the compelling story of his life and work.[2]

Gerald Allan Cohen (1941–2009) was a philosopher who produced writings of depth and insight on the most fundamental ideas of political theory: liberty, justice and equality. Moreover, his intellectual career was unusually wide-ranging, exploring Marxist, liberal and even conservative traditions of political thought. An outstanding scholar and an exemplary teacher, Cohen enjoyed an exceptional international reputation for his rigorous socialist political philosophy. His book, *Karl Marx's Theory of History: A Defence*, inaugurated the school of 'Analytical Marxism' and irrevocably changed the character of left-wing political thought.

Cohen's distinctive political philosophy grew out of his fascinating personal history that, as he often remarked, so shaped his philosophical career. This lends his thought a specially compelling character. As was remarked in the Preface, Cohen's story is especially compelling, from his childhood in a Jewish communist community in working-class Montreal, to making his mark on the

British philosophical scene, to his appointment to a prestigious chair in Oxford. But understanding Cohen's unique contribution is not just a matter of tracing the story of his political convictions and how they shaped his stirring political philosophy. The high regard for Cohen was also due to his personality, his sense of humour, and his rare ability to connect with people, all of which shines through in his writings. Cohen's impact must therefore be understood in light of Cohen the person: charismatic, witty, humane, loveable and loved.

Montreal Origins: Communist Community, Repression and Disappointment

Cohen's communist community

Gerald Allan was born in 1941 in Montreal, Canada, to Bella (née Lipkin) and Morris (Morrie) Cohen. He spent the first eight years of his life in a small apartment on Montreal's Park Avenue above Shiveck's jewellery store. His parents had met in Montreal as workers in the garment trade. Bella's life was characterized by downward mobility. Born in Kharkov (Kharkiv), Ukraine, in 1912, she grew up in a well-off, secular Jewish family. Her father was a timber merchant who, after the Russian Revolution of 1917, continued to prosper under the New Economic Policy. However, by 1930 Soviet politics had become hostile to the business class and Bella's parents, along with Bella and her sister, emigrated to Canada, thereby experiencing an inevitable decline in economic and social position. Yet for the young Bella – a committed Bolshevik since her youth – entry into the proletariat was not unwelcome. It was as a sewing machine operator that she met her future husband, a dress cutter with 'an impeccably proletarian pedigree' as the son of a poor tailor from Lithuania. Bella and Morrie's courtship took place amidst long days in the factory and trade union struggles, punctuated by respite at the summer camp outside of town established by and for radical Jewish workers.[3] Cohen's younger brother Michael recounts a vivid memory of Bella in a corner of the living room operating her electric sewing machine. The sewing machine was on the same circuit as the television and running it caused frequent interruptions to the Ed Sullivan Show or the hockey game, much to the protestations of her menfolk.[4]

Bella, a charismatic, articulate and passionate woman, was an active member of the Canadian Communist Party, whilst her husband, a quiet, diffident and shy man, pursued his left-wing political convictions in the more low-key United Jewish People's Order (UJPO). The family was resolutely working class, socialist, anti-religious and politically engaged. In the Cohen family, ideas mattered and were to be discussed any time and any place. Jewish holidays were celebrated in terms of the general theme of resistance to oppression. Thus Jerry and Michael, nine years Jerry's junior, grew up in this politically charged atmosphere and it permanently shaped their outlook, ideals and careers. Looking back on his childhood, Cohen likened the beliefs he grew up with to those of a religious creed. Though he held them firmly, on well-reasoned grounds, he also was convinced that it was 'an accident of birth and upbringing' that he had them.[5]

Jerry's schooling

The young Jerry went to a school run by the UJPO: the Morris Winchevsky School, named after a Jewish proletarian poet. Mornings were devoted to standard curriculum, taught by non-communist gentile women teachers (antisemitic discrimination in the teaching profession meant there were no Jewish candidates for such positions). Afternoon lessons, in Yiddish, were devoted to Jewish history and Yiddish language and literature, all with a decidedly Marxist inflection. Jerry recalled with pride that he got a straight A in 'History of Class Struggle' in 1949.[6]

As Cohen reminds us, the 1940s were characterized by harmonious relations between the western capitalist countries and the USSR, a consequence of their alliance in the Second World War. This was evidenced, he notes, by a special issue of *Life* magazine in 1943 which celebrated Soviet achievements, with vivid photos and testimonials. For Jerry and his classmates, communism and democracy were inextricably intertwined – people's control of their destinies required both. And for the young Cohen, to be Jewish was to be communist. The belief that 'all people are equal, all people are capable of good, there is tremendous potential in the human spirit' pervaded their lives.[7] Thus, the election of a Montreal Jew from the Communist Party to the Canadian Parliament in 1943 seemed part of the natural order of things.

Anti-communism and Khrushchev's speech

That order ended abruptly in 1952 when, under the aegis of the anti-communist Padlock Law and on the orders of conservative Quebec premier Maurice Duplessis, the Anti-Subversive (Red) Squad stormed the Morris Winchevsky School along with the offices of the UJPO. Although the school was allowed to remain open, enough fearful parents withdrew their children to make its continued existence untenable, and so the students were forced to venture into the non-communist world for the rest of their schooling. Jerry, now age 11, went to Alfred Joyce School. There his education was entirely in the hands of anglophone protestants, and though the students were almost all Jewish, Christmas carols and daily incantations of the Lord's Prayer were de rigueur. To this there was not 'even a mild squeak of protest', perhaps in part, Cohen mused, because of the assumption that a more explicitly antisemitic Catholic school would have been worse.

The young Jerry continued to be active in communist organizations, delivering pamphlets and making speeches at youth groups. He was widely recognized as an intellectual leader by his comrades.[8] However, he kept these activities secret at school, not just to avoid detection by the police, but to ward off the disapprobation of his classmates who, though they were almost all Jewish, were certainly not all, or even mostly, communist. The young Jerry thus lived in 'two Jewish worlds', one anti-Zionist and communist, the other Zionist and anti-communist. But left-wing society could still be found at the Jewish summer camp, and of course in the Cohen home.[9]

This was profoundly shaken, however, in 1956, with the release of Soviet premier Nikita Khrushchev's 'secret speech', discrediting Stalin and indicating the extent of the horrors of his authoritarian regime. Canadian communists were devastated. After the difficult years of postwar anti-communism, where they were sustained by camaraderie and 'a sense of oneness', to suddenly discover that everything said by your enemies – and some friends – was true, hit like a thunderbolt.[10] In Montreal the sense of betrayal was compounded by the realization that the news had been concealed by the national delegates from Toronto. The Communist Party split into hardliners and revisionists, with Bella as one of the leaders of the latter. Some months later, a vote regarding the Canadian Party's leadership was contrived to ensure the hardliners retained power, and Jerry's mother, along with other revisionists, feeling disenfranchised, fell away from the party.[11]

Brothers

Bella and Morrie had personal challenges too. Bella gave birth to another boy, David, who tragically died of an asthma attack at age 3. Bella never fully recovered from the heartache, and this early loss deeply affected Jerry too.[12] However, joy followed sorrow with the arrival of Michael in 1950. Jerry was delighted to have a brother again, and the bond between the two was strong, despite the nine-year age gap. Michael remembers fondly his older brother's kindnesses. Jerry took him to the amusement park, to baseball games and, when Michael was 13 and Jerry home on holiday from Oxford, they hitchhiked together to Cornell University to visit one of Jerry's friends. When Jerry got engaged, he brought his little brother to London to meet his bride-to-be, and the two brothers went on a trip to Paris. The then 15-year-old Michael was thrilled by such filial attentions. Michael recalls that, although he was often compared to his more academically successful brother, there was 'zero sibling rivalry'.

Michael grew up in a very different time when the communist community so dear to Jerry had largely fallen apart. Moreover, Michael had his own path; he was a star athlete in high school, attended a different Montreal university, and ended up pursuing a successful career in labour law in Montreal, allying not so much with East European Jewish communists, but the French-Canadian working class.[13] Fighting for justice in the world, rather than conceptualizing it in philosophy, garnered tremendous respect from his big brother. All their lives the two men would spend time together, their last meeting a glorious autumn weekend in the Saguenay in Quebec two years before Jerry's death.[14]

Despite the Moscow revelations, Cohen family politics remained pro-Soviet and this put Jerry at odds with the now 'pale pink' summer camp where he had worked as a counsellor for many years. So, as a university student at age 19 he found himself a new summer job at Wooden Acres, a mainstream, non-communist Jewish children's camp run by B'Nai Brith, which, Cohen recalled, 'led to my closest encounter ever with the Jewish religion'. For a time at Wooden Acres Jerry participated in a Hebrew prayer group, finding himself more receptive than he expected.[15] It would not be until much later in his life, however, that Cohen would seriously reflect on spiritual matters.

Academic Success: Strathcona, Outremont High, McGill, Oxford

Jerry takes flight

The young Jerry excelled in high school, first at Strathcona Academy and then for his final year at Outremont High. He placed ninth in the entire province of Quebec, made public in the academic ranking published in the *Montreal Gazette*.[16] In 1957 Jerry began his studies at McGill, aware that the university had until recently imposed higher academic requirements for Jews as part of an antisemitic quota system. He embarked on a four-year Arts degree which involved a diversity of subjects. Though Jews were a minority, it was a sizable enough one at McGill, and it was to Jews he gravitated. The gregarious and entertaining Jerry made many friends, keeping in touch with a close circle all his life.

For his elective at McGill, under the influence of the family's economic determinist creed (or as Bella put it, 'everything is economic'), Jerry planned to study economic history. However, the fact that, as he put it, 'the bourgeois, suit-wearing Zionist boys' took economic history swayed him to study philosophy and political science instead.[17] He could always switch to economics later, and political science enabled him to retain some connection to the real world, though he wittily observed 'at least with the super-structure, since by doing philosophy I was depriving myself of the economic base'.[18]

As it happened, Cohen 'fell in love with philosophy', a discipline he took to be one of ideas and ideals, forms and beauty, a subject where, in contrast to the empirical studies of politics, 'one could fly free'.[19] At that point his philosophy education was without the rigorous methods that might have clipped his wings, though McGill's focus on great texts did not invite many flights of fancy either. But Cohen was in his element, writing papers that his professors declared were 'monumental' or 'bristled with ideas',[20] and he excelled, winning the McGill Gold Medal.

Oxford

Graduate studies beckoned, in particular, a B.Phil. at Oxford,[21] though his McGill professors warned against the 'new form of philosophy' there, dismissing it as 'talk about talk'. In the autumn of 1961, Cohen, keen for a European adventure, but wary of Paris due to unease about his French language skills, set sail for New College, Oxford. For their part, Bella and Morrie, always tremendously proud of their son, felt their hearts would burst as Jerry set off.[22]

It was not, however, an easy transition, if only because Cohen finally found himself in a 'non-Jewish world'.[23] Many who come to Oxford for graduate studies are beset by fears that they might not be good enough, often compounded for international students who are regarded as 'colonials' by their British peers and teachers. These feelings would have been amplified further by Cohen whose Jewishness, if not a cause of outright discrimination, would have set him further apart.[24] Yet hard though it is to believe, it was intellectual anxiety especially that afflicted the high-achieving Jerry. He recalls his worries when attending a seminar led by David Wiggins and Michael Woods: 'I was confident I could not master this difficult thing' – Oxford philosophy – in the two years available.[25] Cohen was fortunate to find a kindred spirit in Marshall Berman, another Jewish socialist from North America who found Oxford forbidding; the two young men became very close.[26]

Mentors

However, Cohen encountered Gilbert Ryle, and, under his 'benign guidance', steeped himself in the rigour and discipline of an Oxford philosophical training. Ryle, he says, was wonderful, 'in the sense to be wondered at' – eccentric and inspiring.[27] Ryle was a pioneering figure in Oxford, one of the founders of ordinary language philosophy. Committed to demystifying philosophical inquiry, Ryle was convinced that the task of the philosopher was to clarify how language sheds light on everyday experience.[28] If that meant the discipline had to be 'taken several pegs down its once exalted sense of itself', so be it.[29]

Cohen took to analytical philosophy like a duck to water, proving able at spotting foibles in arguments, breaking down weak defences and marshalling forces towards alternative, warranted conclusions.[30] As his former doctoral student Nicholas Vrousalis put it, Cohen was 'a mastermind of guerrilla warfare' in the world of philosophy.[31] Yet Cohen the argumentative tactician was also enchanted with philosophy's trove of questions and ideas. Indeed, the notes he compiled in those years, written in messy black fountain pen in small, lined booklets, provide a window into his almost obsessional enthusiasm: for instance, he tallied a list of 183 topics, for each of which he wrote a few philosophizing paragraphs. Topics include: do men make their own history?; driving on left or right; career ambitions; intrinsic evil of lying; anti-philosophy; on historical materialism; worrying about worrying; freedom is the recognition of necessity; 'Good'.[32]

Nonetheless, for all his burgeoning talent for Oxford philosophy, Cohen decided to play it safe and got permission from Ryle to sit his examinations in subjects he had first studied at McGill, principally moral and political philosophy, and to write a thesis on Marxism. Political philosophy, let alone Marxism, was not much in favour in Oxford, and Ryle sent him elsewhere for guidance. And thus came another formative influence on his philosophical career, Isaiah Berlin, the Chichele Professor of Social and Political Theory, famed for his 'bracing' lectures on Marx.[33]

Berlin became Cohen's teacher, mentor and friend. As it turned out, Cohen did not write his B.Phil. thesis on Marx after all; his analytical training ultimately won the day. But Cohen contends it was not their mutual interest in Marx, but his and Berlin's 'common Jewishness', and Berlin's erudite views on the role of Jews in western intellectual history, which really drew Cohen in. He 'basked in' being accepted by the great man, and admired, even if he did not emulate, Berlin's capacity to reveal the rich historical context of ideas. The two men thereafter kept in frequent touch, in a relationship characterized by considerable regard and affection.[34]

A surprising friendship

Cohen strongly disagreed with Berlin's negative views of Marx and Marxism and was adamant that Berlin was wrong to deny that lack of money 'carries with it lack of freedom'.[35] Moreover, Cohen was much more of an analytical philosopher than Berlin, the historian of ideas. Yet these disagreements caused no rift between the two friends. Their closeness is striking; one would expect there to be some political and personal bite to their philosophical differences. Berlin was an anti-communist Cold War figure, and the Cohen family's experience of McCarthyite repression could have set Jerry against Isaiah.[36]

True, Berlin abhorred McCarthy, but he also penned his famous 1958 essay on positive and negative liberty to defend 'capitalist civilization' in the 'open war' between 'two systems of ideas'.[37] Over time, Berlin made many revisions to that essay, and one reviewer claimed that the alterations in the 1969 version owed a lot to the fact that Marxism had become 'less intellectually disreputable' in the intervening years.[38] Unhappy with this review,[39] Berlin wrote to Cohen for support, with Cohen kindly nursing his friend's wounded ego.[40]

In retrospect, what might have divided the two men was the fact that Berlin had actively sabotaged the appointment of the Marxist Isaac Deutscher at the University of Sussex, a fact that, given Berlin's 'embarrassed coverup',[41] only came fully to light after the death of both Berlin and Cohen.[42] Ironically, Cohen's book on Marx won the Isaac Deutscher Memorial Prize, and this helped secure Cohen the Oxford chair once held by Berlin. That irony is further compounded by Cohen's lecture on the occasion of the award, in which he took a rather different view from that of his mentor, praising Deutscher for showing that 'scrupulous scholarship was compatible with political engagement'.[43]

Although the Berlin–Cohen friendship was surprising, Cohen felt nurtured and probably flattered by the eminent Berlin's attentions; in a 1979 letter Cohen refers, gratefully, to 'your strong interest in my welfare'.[44] And in 1984, after Cohen had news that he was appointed to the chair that Berlin had once held, Cohen wrote to his mentor with gratitude. Recognizing the role Berlin had played in promoting his candidacy, Cohen wittily notes on the other side of an art postcard depicting Lowry's 'Industrial Landscape', 'The productive forces and I are deeply grateful for everything you have done which contributed to our recent unexpected recognition'.[45] After Berlin's death, Cohen dedicated an essay to him, proclaiming how his love for his teacher was 'imperishably present'.[46]

London: Work, Family and Comradeship

At University College London

In 1963 Cohen took up a lectureship at University College London (UCL), where he spent over 20 happy years.[47] His head of department, Richard Wollheim, was fair and open minded, 'famously hospitable to radical and unconventional ideas',[48] unusual at a time when

British philosophy was dominated by the analytical creed. Cohen thrived under his leadership. Among Cohen's colleagues was Myles Burnyeat, who began as a graduate student when Cohen joined the department and then became his colleague; Burnyeat and Cohen were later colleagues again at All Souls. Also at UCL was fellow Canadian Ted Honderich, who lived near the Cohen family in Hampstead. Honderich's relationship with Cohen was friendly though competitive, the two often sparring on issues philosophical, political and personal.[49]

At UCL Cohen met an Englishwoman a year younger than him, Margaret (Maggie) Pearce, who was studying philosophy. The daughter of a shopkeeper from a small town, Maggie was not Jewish, nor from a progressive background, but she and Jerry shared socialist convictions and fell in love. They married in 1965 and a year later Gideon was born, to be followed by Miriam in 1970, and Sarah in 1975. Like the feminist husbands he touted as 'moral pioneers' in his later work on personal obligations and justice,[50] Cohen took on additional childcare responsibilities when Maggie embarked on postgraduate training as a psychotherapist, tackling the cooking with his limited culinary repertoire.[51]

At the same time, Cohen's work ethic at UCL was legendary, and he juggled his various duties by going into his College office on Saturdays to continue his philosophical research.[52] Maggie Cohen recollects how her husband spoke of the courage needed for academic work, to confront that blank page and get on with it. He would invoke the climb to his study on the top floor of the family home as a metaphor for the challenge of both pushing oneself to work and surmounting conceptual obstacles in the arduous task of writing philosophy.[53]

The bonds of family

Although his children recall that Cohen's work was sacred and 'uninterruptable', that applied also to family life. He was a devoted father, tremendous fun, concerned to guide and advise, but respecting his children's intellect and autonomous choices.[54] Time alone in conversation with Dad was always treasured, and Cohen made such opportunities a priority, despite the hectic pace of life in the busy Cohen family. As an adult, Sarah discussed with her father the merits of the spiritual ideal of enlightenment from Eastern religions, her father adamant that one should not aspire to love all equally, but rather adhere to a hierarchy of love, with family at the apex. That her father wouldn't budge on the matter was touching for Sarah: 'he was so vehemently attached and also attached to being attached, to his particular family. When someone loves like that, you feel it.'[55]

The children grew up in an atmosphere set by both parents of progressive political convictions, ruthless honesty about ideas and arguments, irreverence and fun, music and singing. They were often in the company of friends and colleagues from London and around the world, for example, the communist lawyer Michael Seifert (who provided legal counsel to striking mineworkers, the African National Congress and others)[56] and the Canadian socialist philosopher John McMurtry and his family.

If possible, summers were spent back in Canada, in the Laurentian mountains, with Morrie, Bella and Michael, as well as uncles, aunts and family friends who had shared the heady times of the old days, including Sam Carr, a prominent officer of the Communist Party who had served time in prison for being a Soviet spy.[57] Bella, effervescent and full of intellectual energy, in high heels and beautiful homemade dresses, could be intimidating. Certainly, for the young English wife and mother from a quiet, conservative background, it took some adjustment. But Maggie, like her children, relished the times away from London with this fascinating extended family in the beautiful Quebec landscape.[58] To this day Maggie can sing the socialist hymns she learned at those gatherings.

Heartbreaking news from Montreal, comradeship in London

However, tragedy struck. Bella's mental health had been precarious ever since the Khrushchev revelations. She and Morrie had lost comrades who had abandoned the socialist cause for careers in business, swapping communist Russia for Zionist Israel as the object of their political loyalty. But especially hard for Bella was the loss of friends who preferred to move in more privileged social circles than the Cohens. Though she had a strong, outgoing personality, there were also bouts of significant anxiety and low moods. Her mental health declined and in June 1972, age 60, she took her own life. Jerry, always close to his mother, was heartbroken. With his father's financial help, it was resolved that the family should make annual trips back to Canada.[59]

In 1974 Arnold Zuboff, a doctoral student at Princeton University, joined the UCL department as a young lecturer and a friendship with Cohen quickly formed. Also hailing from a North American Jewish family, and a talented if diffident philosopher himself, Zuboff became Cohen's intellectual interlocutor, sounding board and unfailing admirer. The two spent hours in Cohen's study at the family's Agincourt Road house delighting in each other's company and discussing Cohen's projects, be they his philosophical arguments or his latest comedy routines. For Zuboff, that small room was a 'magical place', full of intellectual excitement; it was exhilarating to subject Cohen's work to sustained criticism and play a part in its craft, as well as to receive Cohen's phone calls the next morning reporting his progress on the problems they had discussed.[60]

As Cohen's career thrived, Zuboff took pleasure in each triumph and felt that in some small way he shared in them. He too, wanted his pal to 'knock 'em dead', whatever the occasion. Cohen repeatedly credited Zuboff in his publications, grateful that 'his fertile and razor-sharp mind' was 'always at my disposal'.[61] Unmarried and childless until later in life, Zuboff was virtually a family member, often babysitting and enjoying time with the Cohens. He was indeed, as Cohen wrote in a book dedication, 'brilliant critic, devoted friend'.[62]

Time to philosophize about Marx

Not long after arriving at UCL, Cohen decided to draw upon the tools forged in his Oxford education to mount a rigorous, sustained defence of Marx's historical materialism. Prior to that, he had contended 'with the complacent self-endorsement of youth' that, insofar as he was a Marxist, he was not a philosopher, and insofar as he was a philosopher, he was not a Marxist. This influenced his attitude to graduate studies in philosophy: 'I came to Oxford already steeped in Marxism, and so, unlike most of my politically congenial contemporaries, I did not look to university philosophy to furnish me with ideas that mattered.'[63] Cohen's political views were so deeply personal and impregnable, they needed no defence. Philosophy, on the other hand, was all about testing arguments and finding them wanting. Cohen was good at it, worked hard and enjoyed it, but until he wrote the Marx book, in the end maybe it was just a job. Or perhaps the contrast could be put another way – politics was serious stuff; philosophy was the confection portended by that lollipop-sound all those years ago.

Cohen remained pro-Soviet, even after Khrushchev's revelations, though seeds of doubt had been sown. In 1968, however, the invasion of Czechoslovakia cemented his disillusion.[64] Cohen was highly conscious of the damage done by Soviet 'actually existing socialism' to Marxist theory. Increasingly, though, he also became preoccupied with the undisciplined way in which the Marxist doctrine had been defended. By the late 1960s Cohen became convinced that the creed with which he had grown up should be tackled with the best resources he had at his disposal, rigorous analytical philosophy, and he set out to produce a book defending Marx's historical materialism.

Cohen published two essays that presaged his opus on Marx, tackling the interface between a Marxist tenet and a philosophical concern. His very first published essay considered the impact of social roles on a person's identity. Another posed the question of whether the material causes of ideas were relevant to their truth.[65] A third essay, in 1970, defended the economic determinism of Marx directly, making the ingenious and elegant argument that would be the heart of the Marx book, that is, that the superstructural, non-material realm which emerges out of economic relations, though it owes its existence to the material realm, can yet cause changes within it.[66]

Cohen's progress on the Marx book was slow, in part because of his exacting standards, but also because this work was interrupted when, in 1975, he made a trip to Princeton. Three years earlier his friend Gerald Dworkin had drawn his attention to the work of the libertarian Robert Nozick and Cohen resolved this would be the focus of his Princeton lectures. Cohen was shaken by the commonality between Nozick's self-ownership argument about the exploitation inflicted by the state and the Marxist theory of the exploitation of workers by capital. So Cohen resolved to delay work on his book to tackle the problem of freedom and capitalism. The result was several acute critical essays on the place of liberty in libertarianism. In Princeton, Cohen also got to know the philosophers Thomas Scanlon and Thomas Nagel, who were less convinced about the threat posed by Nozick. Cohen noted the paradox that Nozick's challenge looms larger the further left one's politics.[67]

Historical Materialism and 'No-Bullshit Marxism'

Karl Marx's Theory of History

In 1978 Cohen finally published his monograph, *Karl Marx's Theory of History: A Defence*, widely acknowledged to be a masterpiece for its incisive analysis of historical materialism. The book was an immense success and won the esteemed Deutscher Prize. Cohen was thrilled by the impact of his book, writing to his mentor:

> Frankly, Isaiah, I have to tell you that my cup runneth over with the reception my book is getting, by which I largely mean what people privately tell me, but also the review by Hobsbawm … which you may have seen. I feared him because he's a real historian and an acerbic personality. But he called my book 'formidable'. I find it extremely difficult to accept the truth of that, being so conscious, as no one else can be, I suppose, of the weaknesses and evasions in it.[68]

There were many critical responses, often sent directly to Cohen with an admiring note, and Cohen would reply, expressing appreciation for astute criticism, disputing points, graciously thankful for the engagement.[69] As he wrote to Maurice Mandelbaum, 'I'm a glutton for attention, including being refuted'.[70] Cohen annotated reviews with comments, affirming a point, expressing irritation, making a joke. In a pleasing sense of things coming full circle, the Hobsbawm review was reprinted in April 1979 in *Canadian Jewish Outlook* (a socialist Jewish periodical supported by the United Jewish People's Order), with a note applauding Cohen's academic success and observing that the review had originally appeared in the 'prestigious' *New Statesman*.[71]

Cohen returned to the book's themes to defend his functionalist account in several articles thereafter (including an essay co-authored with his Canadian doctoral student Will Kymlicka whom he credited with 'breaking a logjam in my thinking').[72] But Cohen felt a weight had been lifted. He wrote in a letter to Berlin:

> I realised a surprising thing after I'd finished the Marx book. It was that the book was, unconsciously, a kind of homage to my communist parents and upbringing, and, consequently, having paid that homage, I am now free for the first time to say what I alone think, never mind whether Marx thought it too. I now see what an enormous labour it was to think in double harness, when whatever

I put into the book had to be both inherently OK <u>and</u> attributable to Marx. Now I can say whatever I like about Marx and this is immensely liberating. I had not realised how unliberated I was. Still, I'm sure you'll agree that it was a good thing to be unliberated in that way – well, I'm not <u>sure</u> you'll agree, but you should – since the enormous labour in double harness is what made that book good. It was quite right to be like that, but it would be absurd to continue to be like that.[73]

'No-Bullshit Marxism' is born

The success of the Marx book meant invitations and opportunities. A pivotal moment in Cohen's life was meeting Jon Elster at a conference on exploitation. Both men were determined to reinvigorate Marxism by deploying exacting analytical methods. They delighted in the meeting of minds and Maggie fondly recalls the excitement of the time: 'it was a bit like falling in love'.[74] The two thinkers resolved to meet regularly, and in Paris in September 1978, they were joined by the left-wing economist John Roemer.[75]

Thence began the 'No-Bullshit Marxist' group, later dubbed the Analytical Marxists, or the September Group.[76] Canadian and left-libertarian political theorist Hillel Steiner, as well as Belgian political philosopher Philippe Van Parijs with his freshly minted Oxford D.Phil., were then invited to join.[77] Parijs later proclaimed that 'no one could have a more formidable impact on my intellectual life' than Cohen; and indeed, Cohen wanted Van Parijs to succeed him in the All Souls chair.[78] The group also came to include: Pranab Bardhan, Samuel Bowles, Robert Brenner, Joshua Cohen, Robert Van der Veen and Erik Olin Wright. Cohen and Wright emerged as the group's most dedicated members.[79]

The group met annually thereafter, often inviting other scholars whose work engaged with its critical Left, analytical project. The new approach attracted suspicion from other Marxists. For his part, Cohen said, 'I don't know, or care, whether it is still right to call me a Marxist. But I am certainly to the left of both Rawls and Dworkin, who have complicated ways of defending capitalist inequality that I continue to condemn.'[80] Members of the group, all male, became close friends, and doubtless there was something of a boys' club about their social interactions. Nonetheless, they all considered themselves feminists and were embarrassed about the lack of women, making a point of inviting women guests, including Susan

Moller Okin, hoping that they would join the group. Seana Shiffrin (one of Cohen's former doctoral students) and Debra Satz became the first women members in the 1990s.[81]

Tensions among the Analytical Marxists

The membership of the September group stayed constant for some time, but in the mid-1980s there was a move to oust Hillel Steiner when it became known that he had signed a manifesto calling for the dismantling of the welfare state. Elster, among others, believed that someone with such views, even a left libertarian, did not belong in a Marxist or semi-Marxist group.[82] In the end the group decided to ask him to stay, and Cohen reassured Hillel that 'your particular intellectual contribution is invaluable'.[83]

Such controversies notwithstanding, the group enjoyed remarkable stability in those early years, with Cohen as its 'moral and intellectual centre'[84] and disciplined coordinator.[85] The high regard all had for Cohen also provided cohesion, Roemer ruminating retrospectively that 'Jerry was a genius; the rest of us were merely talented'.[86] In any case, the group offered a unique opportunity to engage in productive exchange on key radical questions; it also catalysed lifelong friendships. The group stayed in touch with letters, postcards, faxes, even telegrams, to discuss meeting plans, share news about family and career, but also to engage in long, substantive intellectual exchanges. Brilliant, witty, and charismatic, the 'bullshitphobes'[87] looked forward to their meetings and thoroughly enjoyed each other's company.[88]

In 1991 Jon Elster and Adam Prezworski left the group, perhaps because of the bleak climate for Marxism with the collapse of the Soviet Union, or because they felt that the main purposes of the group had been accomplished, or that some of its members were too deferential to Marxism.[89] Cohen was very disappointed, particularly to lose the group's co-founder. Roemer took the view that the group was united by a commitment to good social science in the pursuit of left-wing ideals, and to the extent it succeeded it would no longer be necessary. That commitment might be said to have been realized; their clarification of Marxist ideas was integrated into social scientific literature to a significant extent, even if it did not result in widespread endorsement, as Roemer had optimistically hoped, of the view that humanity undoubtedly has a socialist future.[90]

The Analytical Marxists continued to meet over the years, though with less gusto after the passing of Cohen and then Wright. In 2021 John Roemer resigned, proposing that the other 'oldsters' follow suit, so that the group could continue uninhibited. Some original members continue to attend on occasion, but now as guests.[91] Thus the group continues, no longer Marxist but still opposed to bullshit (as might also be said of all the original members still alive).

All Souls: Fellowship, Opportunities and Challenges

The Chichele Chair

It was Amartya Sen who suggested to Cohen that he apply for the Chichele Professorship of Social and Political Theory,[92] one of the most important positions in the world of political philosophy. Cohen was hesitant at first and, when offered the post, deliberated about whether to accept, worrying about the commute from London, about moving, officially at least, from philosophy to politics, and also whether he would fit in at All Souls.[93] Cohen would not be the first left-winger in the job; Charles Taylor, another progressive Montrealer, was the incumbent, and indeed the guild socialist G. D. H. Cole had been the first to hold the chair.

Although it has been said that it was 'proof of the catholicity and openness of British philosophy' that it would give one of its highest honours to a maverick such as Cohen,[94] the appointment came as a surprise to many. Discussed in the national press, the choice of a Marxist who beat out 'inside' candidates was much remarked on. *Private Eye* speculated that Cohen overcame the competition in part because he was 'a raconteur of immense wit and charm who will be an asset to any High Table confabulation'.[95] So in 1985, at the relatively young age of 43, Cohen took up the Chichele Professorship and became a fellow of All Souls College.

Cohen's first lecture in the role was on a crisp morning of the first week of Hilary term. Undergraduates, graduate students and dons filled a large lecture hall. The excitement was palpable. All hushed when a short, sharp-eyed man with shock of grey hair entered, took his place at the podium and presented a Marxist account of individual freedom. The lecture, as incisive as it was amusing, disabused everyone of their prejudices – analytical philosophers who had doubted whether socialist thought could be more than dogma, and Leftists wary of submitting their deepest convictions to analytical scrutiny. Cohen's performance, like many more to come, was a tour de force.[96]

In the bosom of All Souls

All Souls College, Cohen's academic home for the next 23 years, is a curious place. Founded in 1438, it is one of the most illustrious of Oxford's colleges. It has no students, undergraduate or postgraduate. Yet the lack of student fees is not an issue – the college is wealthy, as Cohen later noted, a 'self-funding institution, which lives on its own endowment, and which is consequently unbeholden to any outside institutions'.[97] All Souls is physically beautiful, its distinctive spires a prominent feature on the Oxford skyline; it has extensive grounds and well-appointed common rooms. The fellows are treated to fine meals served in exquisite surroundings.[98]

Cohen was given a Jacobean panelled study and small bedroom. He was also allocated the part-time assistance of a secretary whom he shared with Peter Pulzer. Pulzer was the newly appointed Gladstone Professor of Government and Public Administration, an expert on the history of Jewish people in Germany, and an Austrian refugee from the Nazis. Although they had very different backgrounds, the two men shared their Jewishness, their opposition to Thatcher's government,[99] and a progressive and humane outlook.

Cohen delighted in how far he had come from Mile End, his working-class neighbourhood in Montreal. Notwithstanding All Souls' reputation as a stuffy conservative institution,[100] Cohen quickly got over whatever unease he might have felt. He breathed life into the place and his outgoing, entertaining personality won people over. He forged connections with everyone, from the Warden at the college's helm to the 'scout' who cleaned his rooms.[101] Among his close college friends was the philosopher Derek Parfit, and Cohen became Parfit's 'closest All Souls intellectual confidante'.[102] Cohen was in awe of Parfit, but found in him much kindness.[103] Parfit, for his part, said of Cohen that he was 'the most acute critic of arguments I know'.[104]

Cohen threw himself into college life, serving on committees, pressing for measures to conserve the college's infrastructure and traditions, and partaking of the pleasures of its traditions and rituals. Cohen's familiar scrawl in black fountain pen can be found in the college betting book, wagering about whether the song 'Chattanooga Choo Choo' was first performed before 1940; it was not, Cohen won. Just over a year after his arrival, when Hillel Steiner came to dine in college and asked how Cohen was adjusting, Sen, also an All Souls fellow at that time, retorted, 'well – too well!'[105] The camaraderie and sense of collective purpose struck a chord with Jerry. It was like being at camp again, Maggie recalled, and Cohen sometimes referred to the college as 'my kibbutz'.[106]

Moreover, the college evolved, in part due to Cohen's progressive influence. Cohen's friend and fellow political philosopher, Susan Hurley, the college's first woman fellow, had been appointed in 1981. Over the years more women and people of colour joined the fellowship and the gentlemen's club atmosphere diminished. 'All Souls changed, but so did Dad', recall his children, marvelling over how he even came to enjoy giving the Christian grace, said in Latin, when presiding at college dinners.[107]

Comedy and charisma

Cohen's humour and sense of fun, his joy in the 'solidarity of hilarity',[108] were legendary, as noted with great fondness in the many reminiscences, tributes and obituaries upon his death. His brand of humour would arguably land him in trouble today,[109] but his jokes were always affectionate.[110] Arguably humour was the mode in which he was most confident, and it was his default orientation in social encounters.[111] Often to his family's embarrassment, he would jump at the opportunity to engage in mischief and fun with strangers, joking around in restaurants with staff and patrons at nearby tables.[112] His parents and brother delighted in his impersonations and routines, calling upon him to perform whenever he was back in Canada.[113] (It is ironic that Cohen had found Bella's showing off embarrassing, when he turned out to be such an inveterate performer himself.) As a student at McGill, Cohen took opportunities to do stand-up comedy. At UCL he wrote a musical which poked fun at his colleagues and the discipline and in the late 1970s he was one of three participants in an evening of impersonations.[114] His connection with Montreal friends was evident in a compilation of skits he put together near the end of his life for a high school reunion.

Cohen so enjoyed perfecting his routines[115] and cataloguing his repertoire that he often wondered, wistfully, if he ought to have pursued a career in comedy. (The idea filled Maggie and

Gideon with 'abject horror'.[116]) Nonetheless, humour inflected his intellectual work, evident in the pages of his writings and his reputation as the 'funniest political philosopher in the world'.[117] One of Cohen's students at UCL was the comedian and actor Ricky Gervais. At a recent encounter with Miriam and Sarah in North London, Gervais said his former teacher 'was a very funny guy'.[118] Cohen would have treasured that praise as much as any regarding his philosophical prowess. The YouTube videos of his jokes and impersonations – where his unique combination of astute political commentary, progressive conviction, keen observation of human foibles, ribald humour and irony are all in evidence – are a part of Cohen's legacy.

Cohen was a towering personality in Oxford; students flocked to him, often jostling for his approval and attentions. His arrival meant that the renowned 'Star Wars' seminars with Dworkin, Parfit and Sen had a new, invigorating participant, prepared to introduce ideas about Marx, socialism and revolution. In the Thatcher era, when questions about the future of the Left and the fate of the welfare state were top of mind, graduate students found these philosophical discussions thrilling.[119] Though loved by many, Cohen's impact also felt like a 'pebble in the shoe' for some of his less charismatic male colleagues who worked in his shadow.[120]

Cohen's focus on the details of argument, and his hostility to the vague and woolly affected his mindset in other ways too. Maggie recalls calling her husband to ask him to get dinner started and being pressed for each step (get out the pot, fill it with water, put the gas on …). But he was not a rigid thinker. Cohen was impressively capable of changing his mind, be it about the predictive power of Marxism, or the value of the idea of self-ownership. And in many more mundane matters he would dismiss something as of no interest, then be persuaded to give it a try and change his mind utterly, becoming thoroughly absorbed and knowledgeable, be it about George Eliot's fiction, historic architecture or Renaissance art.[121]

The toll of Oxford life

In addition to the Star Wars seminars, Cohen joined other discussion groups, formal and informal. He was active in the high-powered, invitation-only Tuesday Group of philosophers, established by A. J. Ayer back in 1960. Apparently some new invitees were so intimidated, it took them a year to pluck up the courage to speak.[122] Cohen was no doubt not so reticent. There was no question of his ability of course – his mind was outstandingly sharp and creative. He had a tremendous eye for detail and a prodigious memory,[123] his thinking charged by deep political convictions, humanity and compassion. Yet the deep pond of Oxford political philosophy, and the elite sensibilities of All Souls, could easily give rise to self-doubt, even in the apparently confident Cohen. Thus, although he was at the pinnacle of his career, going from triumph to triumph, there remained insecurity. Cohen was famously competitive and concerned about his standing relative to other philosophers. He often expressed worries about whether a lecture hall would be full, what philosophers he admired thought of him, and his place in the pantheon of greats in contemporary political philosophy.[124]

Cohen often expressed the opinion that 'women are nicer',[125] a view that might seem condescending, especially for his female graduate students. However, Cohen may have been indicating an understandable need for gentler, less aggressive encounters as a balm for the very Oxford expectation of 'effortless superiority' in his largely male world.[126] Such feelings were not uncommon in the Oxford pressure cooker, even among the most accomplished scholars.[127] A self-described 'obsessional perfectionist',[128] Cohen would write, rewrite, respond to objections, rewrite again, his work going through multiple drafts. His Oxford colleague Michael Rosen recollects, 'if an objection struck him as having the slightest merit, he absolutely refused to leave it unanswered', and he was his own fiercest critic.[129] Cohen was diffident about his work, often stating that his corpus was largely interpretive, rather than original,[130] surely an absurdly modest appraisal of his philosophy.

The celebrated Marx book, his subsequent engagement with libertarianism, and the excitement sparked by Analytical Marxism meant Cohen was much sought after as a progressive sage. When the *New Left Review* was in danger of imploding due to political conflict, both sides wanted him to intervene on their behalf; Cohen, no doubt wisely, demurred.[131] In Oxford, he helped mentor the fledgling Oxford Socialist Discussion Group.[132] Cohen was invited to give talks around the world. His few trips to the USSR confirmed his disappointment in 'actually existing socialism'. Interestingly, the journey that most affected him was a trip to India, and Cohen wrote a wonderful essay, humorous and moving, about all his encounters there, from Cohenites in the academy to beggars on the streets.[133]

Although he insisted that 'the question for political philosophy is not what we should do but what we should think, even when what we should think makes no practical difference',[134] Cohen was politically engaged. In his Hampstead neighbourhood he defended the interests of residents when it came to a campaign from a neighbouring street (with higher property values) to divert traffic onto theirs. Cohen 'single-handedly' won the day.[135] He appended his name to many petitions, went on marches, canvassed for the Labour Party and for nuclear disarmament (often with children in tow), and spoke on BBC radio about the Vietnam War.[136] Once back in Oxford, Cohen applied his philosophical acumen to the political issues of the day[137] and took on the role of activist. At All Souls, Cohen and some other fellows urged that the college's holdings be scrutinized for unethical investments.[138] He became a central figure in the 'Oxford Academics Against Apartheid' group with Tony Holiday and Michael Dummett, pressing the Rhodes Trust to address the paucity of Black South African Rhodes Scholars,[139] and in the *London Review of Books* he engaged in a lively debate about racism in Britain.[140]

Egalitarianism and the Egalitarian Conscience

Dworkin's liberal egalitarianism

In 1989 Cohen published 'The Currency of Egalitarian Justice', a pivotal article tackling themes in Ronald Dworkin's political thought. Dworkin was Chair in Jurisprudence at Oxford and his importance – in general, but for Cohen in particular – is hard to overstate. His defence of rights as individuals' 'trumps' against social goals, his theory of equality, and his forays into public philosophy on social issues such as pornography or affirmative action meant that his influence in political philosophy was second only to that of Rawls.

Certainly, Dworkin had considerable impact on Cohen's intellectual trajectory. Cohen and Dworkin were often in each other's company, teaching seminars together, but also discussing each other's work in progress in informal discussion groups. A fellow North American Jew, but bourgeois, poised and patrician in style, Dworkin loomed large in Cohen's psyche. He was a colleague and friend, but also Cohen's nemesis, prompting feelings of competitiveness that often manifested in sharply funny jokes about Dworkin's vanity or other foibles.

Cohen focused on developing a powerful case against his colleague's 'expensive tastes' argument. Whereas Dworkin contended that the principles of egalitarianism should not cater to people's costly preferences, Cohen likened tastes to unchosen needs, hearkening to Marx's distributive credo, 'to each according to his needs'. Moreover, Cohen developed a richer understanding of what it is that should be made equal – not resources or welfare, but something in between, 'access to advantage'. However, to the surprise and disappointment of some, the approbation of others, Cohen endorsed Dworkin's luck egalitarianism.[141] Some thought Cohen's 'man crush' on Dworkin[142] had an unfortunate impact on his philosophy, causing issues about desert and choice to displace his more traditionally socialistic ideas of need and community.[143]

Cohen tackles Rawls

Themes in liberal egalitarianism dominated Cohen's philosophical preoccupations for the rest of his career. His contributions made for a unique, trenchant and powerful voice elaborating a new understanding of the ideals of socialism with which he began his intellectual journey. Cohen's paper on the injustice of incentives, sparked by the Thatcher tax cuts, ingeniously linked the policy to arguments in Rawls's *Theory of Justice*. Cohen maintained that the idea that productivity requires giving higher rewards to some was at odds with the concept of justice. A revised version of the paper opened Cohen's masterful *Rescuing Justice and Equality*.[144]

Cohen reflected on the problem of selfishness, remaining convinced that a world beyond the 'greed and fear' of capitalism was not beyond human capacity.[145] Cohen's view that the 'personal is political', invoking the 1970s feminist slogan, is found in his general outlook of 'sympathetic curiosity', his urge to connect with others. For him, justice involved, not just institutions, but interactions between individuals.[146] His story of his father's callous treatment at the hands of his factory boss evokes this powerfully.[147] Justice was something personal for Cohen in other ways too. He felt some responsibility for the failures of real-world communism, providing an apologetic preface to his 'Why Not Socialism?' paper in his presentation to a Prague audience whose memory of Soviet tanks in the streets inevitably coloured their engagement with communist ideals. 'We thought equality and community were good, we tried to achieve them, and produced disaster', he confessed.[148]

The Soviet legacy

Prague 1968 had disabused Cohen of his pro-Soviet loyalties, and in spring 1972 Cohen engaged in an exchange of letters with his uncle, Sam Carr, who in contrast remained resolutely pro-Soviet until his death. Cohen sought to explain why his socialist position involved opposing Soviet authoritarianism and defending certain 'bourgeois' freedoms.[149] For all that, the collapse of the USSR in 1989 was nonetheless shattering for Cohen. He put it poignantly: 'It is true that I was heavily critical of the Soviet Union, but the little boy who pummels his father's chest will not be glad if the old man collapses.' He explained that although he had had little hope for Soviet socialism, 'there is a vast difference between nourishing little hope and giving up all hope'. His small hope was 'an immense thing', if only for ensuring 'a non-capitalist mental space in which to think about socialism'.[150]

Cohen was insistent that disappointment in socialist practice should not lead one to give up on socialism because it is difficult to realize.[151] Because the Soviet era made clear that socialism would not issue inevitably from the laws of history, ethical reflection was crucial. For Cohen, this entailed fidelity to objective moral ideals such as justice which 'just is',[152] a view he traced to Marx's critique of capitalism, even if Marx's historicism dissembled this. If history is not on your side,[153] then socialism will need to be inspired by an ambitious ideal of people furthering equality, not just by obeying the rules of just institutions, but by acting justly in their personal lives.

Morrie dies, children come of age

In 1985, at age 75, Cohen's father Morrie died of a heart attack in Montreal. The loss of this quiet, dignified man, who Jerry perhaps never fully understood,[154] in some ways brought to a close the communist world of Jewish Montreal for the Cohens.

There were unexpected turns of events closer to home: Gideon, the first-born 'brilliant' child and only boy,[155] surprised his parents with his path in life, turning to Rastafarianism as a teenager. He went on to earn a PhD in the London School of Oriental and African Studies, and moved to Africa where he lives with his family and works on development and food policy.

At age 16 Miriam returned from a holiday in Greece with a new boyfriend, a labourer who then became her husband. The Cohens welcomed the self-described 'love refugee' into the family, and Cohen counted among his friends fishermen in his son-in-law's village in Greece. Though shyer and wary of being known as Jerry's daughter, Miriam recalls that she and her father 'shared a way of thinking'.[156] After an undergraduate degree at UCL, she embarked on a doctorate in philosophy under Derek Parfit, focusing on Dworkin's political thought, finding she could no longer avoid her father's work. Now teaching philosophy in schools, it is pleasing to see her father in her vocation, combining philosophy with a talent for connecting with children. Miriam and her family live in the Agincourt Road house among her father's books and with his desk now serving as a dining room table, finding that holidays with her husband's Greek family evoke the delightful, exuberant time with her father's family when she was a child.

Like Miriam, Sarah also studied philosophy at UCL, and an interest in ideas remained with her too, though like Gideon, in a more spiritual direction. Her life is dedicated to AMMA the 'Hugging Saint', and she has worked for years at her Ashram in Southern India. She also lives partly in Greece.

These were not directions that Cohen had expected his children to take, but he offered unfailing support, engaged them in discussion of their choices, and was quick to reappraise his earlier views ('Did I say that? I was an idiot!' he'd exclaim).[157] He was proud of their achievements[158] and a loving grandfather to his seven grandchildren. As he said to his brother, what mattered most was not that his children be successful, or even that they be good; rather, that they be happy.[159]

Sarah affirms that though her Dad, like many men of his generation, might not have been immediately attuned to emotional matters, 'if the need was made known, he would always be there for us'.[160] As it happens, all three, happy in their chosen paths, share their parents' progressive politics and laugh at the thought of how their father would have reacted if they had become right-wing. They feel Jewish, though not only Jewish, and grew up assuming that to be Jewish was to be progressive; when they were young, they were shocked to discover Jews who were bourgeois and conservative.[161]

Love lost and found

Jerry and Maggie's marriage had been fraught over the years, with more than one separation. Although both were devoted to their family's wellbeing, the children were affected by their parents' unhappiness.[162] With their final parting in the early 1990s, Cohen was particularly despondent, at times homeless apart from his (albeit splendid) All Souls digs, though he admirably reflected on his 'glass half-full' and determined to be more positive.[163] In 1996 the couple divorced, though they remained good friends, gathering with their children and partners for family celebrations, and Jerry, in his inimitable playful way, introduced Maggie's new partner as his 'lover-in-law'.[164] Indeed, throughout all the marital ups and downs, Maggie remained a part of Jerry's life, good friends with his brother and Arnold Zuboff, and keen to continue her role as the host of the social evening on the September Group gatherings for some years after the breakup. The group honoured her with a pewter bowl engraved 'with thanks for ten years of culinary delights'.[165]

Cohen found love again with Michèle Jacottet, his Swiss administrative assistant at All Souls. After many years together they married in the Warden's Lodgings at All Souls in 1999. They set up house, not in one of the posh neighbourhoods in north Oxford, but in a terrace off the Cowley Road – Cohen 'wanted to live where it felt real', as Miriam put it.[166] There the happy couple entertained family and friends, with fondue the specialty of the house, often hosting members of the September Group. Jerry helped raise Michèle's two children, enjoying loving relationships with both, and providing indispensable support in times of crisis.[167]

Intimately connected with Jerry's work, dispatching letters, helping translate materials into French, and discussing his philosophical ideas with him, Michèle played a formative role in shaping his thought. Cohen's former doctoral student Paula Casal likened Michèle to Harriet Taylor, John Stuart Mill's radical wife, a reference presumably to Michèle's progressive feminist influence.[168] Jerry and Michèle enjoyed many happy times, such as travel around the globe, with India becoming a special place for them both. Cohen declared that, without her, he would be 'a ship without a sail on a stormy sea, with no harbour in sight'.[169] To have their time together cut short so soon after Cohen's retirement was devastating for Michèle.

Cohen the teacher

Cohen's strong sense of ethical duty as a practice, not just a political philosophy, was evident in his professional interactions in Oxford. For all the lustre of his post at All Souls, it included significant administration for the Department of Politics, which he discharged faithfully and without complaint.[170] More significantly, Cohen was a truly exceptional teacher. His intense analytical thinking in the service of deeply held political ideals was exciting, and he was much sought after as a supervisor. His former doctoral student, Cécile Fabre, recalls his 'amazing' detailed and incisive criticisms on thesis drafts, although she notes that the criticism could be daunting and that Cohen was best attending to the particular; when it came to guiding a project in a more overarching way, his students were on their own.[171]

Certainly Cohen's commitment to analytical standards often had an intimidating fierceness. It was difficult to follow the wise counsel he gave his diffident students: 'a bad way to never make a mistake is to shut up and say nothing'[172] if one feared that what one would say would not meet his high standards. Even his All Souls colleagues who shared his progressive outlook felt uneasy engaging with him on philosophical matters, fearing that they might turn out to be the fool who wouldn't be suffered gladly. It was said that his methodology was forbidding, so dissonant with his commitment to do well by the ordinary person.[173] But Cohen's 'take-no-prisoners' approach to academic discourse set a standard that inspired students, even if it may have scared some of them a little.[174] 'Completely lacking in inhibition', Cohen could be riotously funny if also disconcerting in personal conversation, where 'nothing was too inappropriate, private, bizarre, or embarrassing to be suddenly brought into' the discussion.[175] That capacity to speak his mind with zero embarrassment was also key to his utter candour in philosophical contexts, his unrelenting drive to get an argument right.[176]

Moreover, Cohen was also encouraging, supportive and affectionate, providing help, often of the most practical kind, when students needed it.[177] He sought to enable the full development of, as he recalled upon his retirement, the 'halting, tripping anxious youngsters struggling to get a foothold' who sought his guidance.[178] Although from a generation which too often mistook the overthrow of Victorian prudishness to license chauvinistic libertinism, Cohen was exceptionally perceptive about sexism, and a feminist ally to his women students making their way in the largely male, and masculine, Oxford world.[179] The significant philosophical contributions and impressive careers of so many of his students suggest his tutelage – tough but kind – worked.[180] And the affection his students had for him was unmistakeable. Although Cohen was happiest if he was the comic and others the appreciative audience, his sense of fun prompted an inspired riposte. At one of Cohen's final talks in Oxford, his students unfurled a banner from the balcony that proclaimed, 'retired professors of the world unite, you have nothing to lose but your pre-phylloxera claret', a reference to Dworkin's expensive taste argument that had so exercised Cohen. It was a delightful moment on a bittersweet occasion.

An ethical life

Although it is well known that Cohen had a range of minor vices: indiscretion, an occasional callousness about intellectual blunders, competitiveness, and an over-fondness for marijuana, he also demonstrated an uncommon humanity and lived an ethical life. He loved human diversity and had unique friendships with a seemingly endless number of people.[181] John Roemer said Cohen was his closest friend, quickly adding that 'quite a few people would say that'.[182] Cohen gave to beggars in his Cowley Road neighbourhood, donated to charity and political causes, and as noted by Gideon, forged connection with people from other social classes and communities, be it the Southeast Asian shopkeepers in his neighbourhood, who enthusiastically joined his 'double or quits' game at the till, or the 'scouts' and staff of All Souls.[183] According to his old friend Marshall Berman, though Cohen's 'stardom' meant he could make a difference to people, he felt 'intensely guilty' because he had got there, he thought, 'only by radically separating himself from "the people"'.[184] But this was hardly the case.

Cohen's insights about relating to beggars are powerful. He states that 'if I project pity at them, I am demeaning them'. Though they pretend to want pity, this is just 'the language of beggary'. What they want is money; 'they are right to ask for it, and I am happy to give it'. What makes the encounter moving, Cohen says, 'is that our eyes meet with a certain mutual understanding and with unexaggerated gratitude from them. You can open to each other'.[185] That commitment to treating others as equals meant, as his children recall, he would give generous amounts to beggars and say, outrageously, 'you must spend this on alcohol', flouting the usual paternalism that goes with charity.[186]

Cohen showed an openness to spirituality at the end of his life, embarked on a careful reading of the New Testament, and even penned a paper on spiritual themes, the latter the essay that meant the most to Gideon and Sarah. This might suggest Cohen turned away from his communist roots, which were after all atheistic. But for him there was a consistent thread. The social ethos that animated his idea of an egalitarian community involved personal reflection, gratitude and grace. One of his discussions of overcoming capitalist greed quoted the Bible: 'For what shall it profit a man, if he shall gain the whole world, and lose his own soul?'[187] His spiritual offspring felt vindicated by this openness to the non-material as part and parcel of the socialist ideal.

Looking back

The importance of connection with others figured centrally in a surprising essay Cohen wrote near the end of his career defending a conservative attitude to change. Cohen was throughout his life loyal to people, but also to the past, to his family and the community in which he was born and raised, to the education he received in his Yiddish communist elementary school, in public school, and the halls of McGill and Oxford. At a conference celebrating his career Cohen surprised everyone at the end when he read aloud the imperialistic poems he learned in high school, but these too could be understood as 'a modest and self-mocking assertion of loyalty to his former self'.[188] As Cohen admitted at the time, 'my errant heart was drawn forward by their celebration of sacrifice and of virtue in community with others in the service of a noble cause'.[189]

Cohen died, tragically, just a few months after his retirement, in 2009, at the age of 68. He never saw the advance copies of his last book, *Why Not Socialism?*, which had arrived at All Souls that day. The news was 'like an earthquake', Fabre recalls. Expressions of shock, grief, affection, and esteem came from close friends, students and colleagues from all over the world, but also from those who had met him but once, or whose encounters were limited to hearing him speak in crowded lecture halls or reading his writings.

When Cohen took his leave of the Chichele chair just a few months before his passing, he reflected on the satisfaction of seeing his students come into their own. Although he had at first feared his retirement, he welcomed the next phase of his life as a kind of 'harvest time'.[190] He had achieved what he had set out to do in philosophy and still had projects to finish: the desk-cum-dining table installed at the Agincourt Road house still has taped to its corner a list of 'back burner' and 'front burner' topics he was working on.[191] Both Cohen's funeral and the memorial service many months later were held at his cherished college. They were joyous occasions, for all the deep grief felt by so many people he had touched, as all remembered with philosophical tributes, personal recollections, humour and song, the inimitable, brilliant and beloved, Jerry Cohen.

The Paradoxes of Cohen

This book brings to life the richness of Cohen's philosophy by focusing on several fascinating paradoxes in his career. This enables the exploration of surprising features of his thought, its many strengths and unresolved tensions.

Chapter 2 tackles the paradox of how Cohen, the young dogmatic Communist, came to embrace the rigours of 'bourgeois' analytical philosophy and to use it to test and develop his Marxist politics, inaugurating the school of Analytical Marxism. It considers the arguments of his famous work, *Karl Marx's Theory of History*, and how best to understand their meaning and significance.

Chapter 3 examines the paradox that while most progressives found right-wing libertarianism so uncongenial that they largely ignored it, Cohen's first foray into political philosophy engaged with Robert Nozick's argument for liberty and private property. For Cohen, the libertarian's conception of 'self-ownership' bore a startling similarity to Marx's ideas of exploitation, calling for a thoroughgoing understanding of the place of freedom and equality in the socialist enterprise.

Chapter 4 focuses on a paradox in Cohen's critique of John Rawls. Cohen criticized Rawls for being inegalitarian in his countenancing of incentive-based disparities of wealth. Cohen argued that theories of justice should not be hamstrung by empirical considerations about human motivation or practical matters of implementation. This chapter seeks to understand this move which, though radical in its import, flies in the face of what many would take to be the canonical left-wing premiss that political theory should be rooted in an understanding of the material situation of society.

Chapter 5 considers a paradox that bears on the whole of Cohen's thought: the tension between his preoccupation with individual responsibility and his idea of a socialist ethos. Cohen endorses the 'luck egalitarianism' of liberals like Ronald Dworkin, in which justice requires mitigation only of the disadvantages that accrue from unchosen circumstances. This move seems in tension with Cohen's larger commitment to a radical socialist ideal where principles of community obligate one to forgo the opportunity to accumulate wealth.

The final paradox is how Cohen, socialist critic of liberal theories of justice, turned to conservatism late in his career. Chapter 6 examines his argument for the importance of 'existing value' and the need to appreciate the conservative insight that change can mean loss. It remains to be seen whether Cohen's defence of these conservative values can be squared with his egalitarian commitments and the spirit of social change that informs so much work in the socialist tradition.

These paradoxes in Cohen's thought provide a fascinating avenue into the complexities of his various positions. I will suggest that some paradoxes can be resolved, demonstrating the richness of Cohen's position; others, however, point to inconsistencies that are vulnerable to powerful critiques, raising profound questions about the egalitarian ideal and the socialist project. Throughout, the book will demonstrate Cohen to be an incisive, powerful and highly relevant philosopher in his outstanding contribution to a number of fundamental questions in political theory.

2

'No-Bullshit Marxism' and the Fate of Historical Materialism

Does a radical critique of social, political and economic institutions necessitate a particular philosophical method? Karl Marx famously contended that his theoretical approach, historical materialism, was uniquely qualified to understand and explain the ills of capitalism, and moreover, to equip revolutionaries in planning and executing its downfall. Close to 200 years later, the question continues to attract controversy. Some argue today that continental European philosophical schools, drawn from existentialism, German idealism, the Frankfurt School, poststructuralism or French postmodernism, can better express radical thought than the philosophical idiom of mainstream anglophone philosophy.

This conviction about the superiority of 'continental philosophy' for radical political thought dates to the 1960s and 1970s, and G. A. Cohen, like many on the Left, found it seductive, however briefly. Nevertheless, he famously came to reject this view, marshalling the analytical tools of the Anglo-American tradition for an unabashedly radical project in political theory. Cohen undertook a systematic investigation of Marx's economic determinism in a celebrated book and in several key essays. How Cohen drew on Oxford philosophy to couch a distinctive 'Analytical Marxist' philosophical method is the subject of this chapter. In this, the focus is what might be deemed a methodological paradox in Cohen's thought: the use of conventional philosophical tools for radical argument.

Postwar Analytical Philosophy: Metaphysical, not Political

Philosophy without Marxism

When the young Jerry arrived as a B.Phil. student at New College, Oxford, he was in his personal life an avowed communist, but this had not influenced his philosophical studies in any significant way. As we saw in the last chapter, initially Cohen was alarmed by how the historical focus of his studies at McGill in Montreal had not prepared him for Oxford philosophy, prompting him to seek to avoid its rigours.[1] However, in time Cohen became keen to acquire the analytical techniques deployed by his teachers. Michael Rosen describes Cohen's 'innate talent and temperament' and 'extraordinary gift for precision and sensitivity to differences of meaning', which meant that Cohen came to find himself well suited for the rather 'austere kind of analytical philosophy that was practised in Oxford at that time'.[2] He accordingly focused his studies on non-normative subjects then prominent, working with the 'ordinary language' philosopher of mind, Gilbert Ryle, who was his B.Phil. supervisor. That a communist should so choose was unusual; left-wing students tended to reject Oxford philosophy, regarding it, Cohen recalled, as 'bourgeois, or trivial, or both'.[3]

Looking back on the early days of his academic career, Cohen contended that he felt no need to interpolate his Marxist views in his work as a philosopher and was therefore quite comfortable within the analytical milieu of mainstream Oxford philosophy. Accordingly, Cohen kept his politics and philosophical pursuits separate during his graduate studies. When he took up an appointment as a lecturer at University College London, he continued to work on issues outside of the domain of ethics. His first published paper was 'Beliefs and Roles', a topic with some relationship to Marxism, but not a direct one, where Cohen stressed that to be free involves forming beliefs as a human being rather than an occupier of a social role.[4]

But Cohen's lack of interest in deploying the resources of philosophy to elaborate his radical views was due to other factors besides the solidity of his Marxist belief. The methodology of postwar British philosophy defined what kinds of topics counted as philosophically relevant, and normative philosophy tended to be excluded. Cohen recalls: 'almost all B.Phil. candidates chose at least one of Epistemology and Metaphysics and Logic and Scientific Method, since those subjects were thought to constitute the centre of philosophy, and they were, moreover, ones in which Oxford was preeminent'. Cohen notes that, 'almost no one' among his contemporaries chose to study political philosophy.[5]

Political philosophy's malaise

These trends in Oxford reflected how, due to the dominance of logical positivism for much of the twentieth century, questions of value were understood as not properly philosophical. Logical positivism distinguished between empirical and conceptual inquiry – matters of fact as opposed to matters of logic – and tended to regard anything outside those two camps as philosophically suspect, literally non-sense. Normative questions were accordingly deemed outside the purview of philosophy. As a branch of philosophy seeking to direct rather than merely to understand human practices, political theory was essentially cast as a non-subject. Such scientific ideas lingered in the ordinary language philosophy that succeeded logical positivism (of which, as noted above, Cohen's supervisor Ryle was a renowned exponent). Ordinary language philosophy, in limiting its investigation to the use of current vocabularies, also rejected normative questions as not truly philosophical ones.

Indeed, political questions were particularly disadvantaged. Ethics could be construed as a meta-discipline concerned with the scope and limits of moral concepts that might be otherwise taken for granted. However, the intrinsically controversial nature of political questions – Should wealth be equally distributed? What is the rationale for government? – meant that no such convenient transformation was available for political theory. Political philosophy could consist only of threadbare exercises of linguistic usage that interrogated how speakers use political terms. This was a long way from the original and ambitious questions Plato and Aristotle posed about the good life and how we ought to live in common – ideas that had inspired the young Jerry as an undergraduate at McGill University. The one notable exception in Oxford was the work of Isaiah Berlin, who held the Chichele Chair in Social and Political Theory whilst Jerry was a student. However, Berlin's work was largely within the tradition of the history of ideas, and he himself concluded that 'no commanding work of political philosophy has appeared in the twentieth century'.[6] Small wonder that Iris Murdoch, lamenting the state of left-wing thought in 1958, said that political philosophy had 'almost perished'; John Plamenatz, a previous Chichele professor, declared it 'widely presumed to be dead' in Oxford.[7] Thus arguably Cohen came to decide not to pursue political philosophy when he arrived in Oxford because he deemed there was none, or none that was worthwhile, to be found.

'Bullshit' and the Left

Marxism and the Cold War

The diminished role of political philosophy as a normative inquiry reflected not just the empiricism of contemporary philosophical method, but also arguably a certain smugness about the empirically given in the liberal capitalist West. The Cold War dogmatism that infected the political culture of the postwar period fuelled a sense that there were no political questions that needed to be addressed, that the communist alternative was not worth considering and thus politics was in a sense beyond the realm of philosophical deliberation. And Cohen too, coming from the other camp in the Cold War, his communist creed beyond question, felt no need to engage in a world-historical debate about the relative merits of two warring ideologies.

It is interesting that when Cohen began considering Marxist themes as a philosopher, it was at first unaffected by the analytical approach in which he had been schooled. When Cohen was in his early twenties, like many on the Left at the time, he was attracted to the work of the French Marxist Louis Althusser, whose grand statements seemed 'exciting and suggestive', if difficult to pin down.[8] Althusser, a member of the Communist Party who taught at the École normale supérieure in Paris, sought to reconceive Marx's theoretical project by excising its philosophical aspects to render it properly scientific – not in the positivist sense which invoked the conventional norms of the natural sciences – but by devising a new, uniquely radical method. In particular, Althusser and the poststructuralists invoked an 'epistemological break' between the young and the late Marx, the latter having rightly disposed of philosophical concerns under the supposed deleterious influence of Hegel about human beings' capacity to labour and find self-realization.⁹ It was perhaps not surprising that in searching for a philosophical home for his steadfast communist convictions, Cohen should be tempted by what one critic describes as the 'abstruse Marxism, dogmatic and almost theological' of a 'philosopher-cleric'.¹⁰

Looking back on Althusser's philosophy in the 'Complete Bullshit' essays of the early 2000s, Cohen contended that he did not end up 'succumbing to its intoxication, because I came to see that its reiterated affirmation of the value of conceptual rigor was not matched by conceptual rigor in its intellectual practices'. Just as he was honest about his philosophical insecurities upon arriving in Oxford, Cohen is also refreshingly candid about his experience reading French poststructuralism. Finding these new, purportedly scientific writings about Marx hard to understand, and knowing that they were 'attracting a great deal of respectful, and even reverent, attention', he was 'inclined to put the blame for finding the Althusserians hard to understand entirely on myself'. Moreover, he noted, when he did extract a kernel of sense from Marxist poststructuralism, he attributed much more interest and importance to it than it had, a symptom of a psychological mechanism of 'cognitive dissonance reduction' or 'adaptive preference formation' where one does not want to have wasted one's time:

> Someone struggles for ages with some rebarbative text, manages to find some sense in it, and then reports that sense with enthusiasm, even though it is a banality that could have been expressed in a couple of sentences instead of across the course of the dozens of paragraphs to which the said someone projected herself.¹¹

Diagnosing 'Bullshit'

Nonetheless, Cohen came to conclude that Althusser's work was in fact not worth his time. Such ideas, Cohen decided, should be consigned to the category of 'bullshit', a term elaborated by the philosopher Harry Frankfurt.¹² However, Cohen contended Althusser's bullshit was not that diagnosed by Frankfurt, as indifference to the truth values of one's statements. Rather, Althusser's bullshit was that of 'unclarifiable unclarity', a conception that makes no claims about the motives of the bullshitter – for example, insincerity or bluffing – but rather focuses on the bullshit itself, as a kind of nonsense.[13] Cohen does suggest some dishonesty is manifest when it comes to philosophical debate with the bullshitter, who responds to criticism, not by taking 'precise measure of the force of the assault in order to alter his position in a controlled and scientifically indicated way', but rather, 'simply shifts to another unthought-through and/or obscure position, in order to remain undefeated'.[14]

Further, Cohen agrees with his former doctoral student and good friend Michael Otsuka that sometimes an academic is disposed to, though not aiming for, bullshit, when the aim is profundity, and unclarifiable clarity can mask the failure to achieve it.[15] According to Cohen, that was at work in the case of Althusser's writings, and why it took some time before Cohen ultimately 'resisted its intoxication'. Moreover, in the case of the school of postmodernism, Cohen points out, there is also a trend to expressly disparage truth, a consummation he wittily calls, after Hegel, 'bullshit risen to consciousness of itself'.[16]

Moreover, Cohen impugned the character of the bullshitter in his musings on what he took to be a distinctively French propensity for bullshit, with the benefit of the insights of his graduate students from continental Europe, Paula Casal and Cécile Fabre.[17] Cohen speculated that there are cultural factors – the broader influence of intellectuals, the premium put on style, the emphasis on passion and non-conformity – at work that mean intellectuals in some societies are more likely to engage in and produce bullshit.

The cultural context of bullshit is particularly interesting in the case of radical thought. For it may be that progressive thinkers are particularly prone to bullshit; they are pushing against conventional understandings, pursuing radical political ideals, convinced of their urgency and importance, which might tempt them to take conceptual shortcuts. In the spirit of the end justifying the means, a deep personal investment in the stakes, as well as a strong sense of moral certainty, if not self-righteousness – all this encourages murky thinking in order to reach the right (Left) conclusions. Recent debates about being 'woke' or 'political correctness' (the latter being for earlier radical generations a self-mocking pseudo-Stalinist ascription) revolve around the worry that a 'party line' is dictated whereby certain questions are impermissible, or uncomfortable findings to be buried. Cohen, in contrast, in his critique of bullshit, takes the view that 'the premium should always be on truth' in the doing of philosophy.[18] In this, Cohen has much to teach us.

Historical Materialism and Functional Explanation

Interrogating communist belief

The pursuit of truth for a postwar communist is a dangerous business, however, as it forces a confrontation with the limitations of one's political beliefs in their relationship to the world, not just in the arguments of abstract philosophy. As we saw in the last chapter, by the late 1960s Cohen's communist creed was in need of the robust engagement for which the tools of analytical philosophy looked well suited. In fact, one might say that as a young man Cohen himself had been guilty of bullshit, not principally because of his foray into French philosophy, but in his evasion of the political realities of Soviet communism. As a teenager Jerry had accepted the Soviet invasion of Hungary in 1956 as necessary in the fight against fascism, but by 1968 the invasion of Czechoslovakia, he contended, served to 'thoroughly rid me of my pro-Sovietism' though he made no public declaration.[19]

It was time for Cohen's political allegiances to undergo some philosophical elucidation and, disillusioned after his Althusserian phase, the obvious choice was the analytical school in which he had been trained. This shift was marked by his 1968 paper, 'The Workers and the Word', which argued that though the claim that ideas owe their origins to material circumstances impugns their truth, this is the case for all social classes but the proletariat, the one class whose ideas are universal in their normative scope.[20]

From the late 1960s onwards, Cohen wrote many articles on Marxist themes, deploying his Oxford training to defend central tenets of historical materialism. His work of greatest distinction in this period was his 1978 book, *Karl Marx's Theory of History: A Defence*, winner of the Isaac Deutscher Memorial Prize, a project which germinated in the 1960s after a trip to McGill University to give lectures on Marx. Cohen subsequently described the volume as 'homage to the milieu in which I learned the plain Marxism which the book defended'. It 'reflected gratitude to my parents, to the school which had taught me, to the political community in which I was raised'.[21]

But this was no work of dogma or apologetics; it was an incisive, hard-headed argument for the plausibility of Marxist ideas. The book thus sought to honour Cohen's family in the best possible way – by treating with respect the ideas by which they had lived their lives, honestly and critically assessing their value. In a discussion of multiculturalism, the celebrated political philosopher Charles Taylor (a fellow Montrealer and Cohen's immediate predecessor in the Chichele Chair in Social and Political Theory) contends it is a refusal of a 'genuine act of respect' to consider some paradigms of thought 'no-go' areas for intellectual engagement.[22] Cohen accordingly undertook to self-consciously rethink Marxist method in a way that scrupulously avoided the obfuscation of his poststructuralist phase. The book on Marx was thus, not just a tribute to the politics of his family, but also how, as he put it, he 'settled accounts' with his 'Althusserian flirtation'.[23]

Economic determinism and functional explanation

Cohen's prodigious volume delves into several themes in Marxist political philosophy. Among them are commodity fetishism, that is, the ways in which under the distorted social relationships of capitalism we endow our creations with magical properties, as well as the problem of exchange value, or how goods' market value is distinct from their utility. The book's overarching theme, however, is a defence of economic determinism, the central claim of Marx's historical materialist theory.

Marx understood non-economic phenomena as determined, or caused, by economic phenomena. His theory advances a materialist position insofar as it emphasizes the causality of the material for the non-material, that is, how productive capacity shapes our economic relations, and how our economic relations in turn shape the political, legal and social dimensions of society. This is not a biological materialism: the fact that human beings are natural creatures who must eat to survive is why we engage in relations of production, but our biological nature is not, according to Marx, a matter of history. Marx's materialism is historical because it focuses on the dynamic character of economic forces, and their corresponding economic and social relations.

A canonical passage in Marx's 'Contribution to the Critique of Political Economy' lays out the central claims that are at the heart of Cohen's study:

> In the social production of their life, men enter into definite relations that are indispensable and independent of their will, relations of production which correspond to a definite stage in the development

of their material productive forces. The sum total of these relations of production constitutes the economic structure, the real basis, on which arises a legal and political superstructure and to which correspond definite forms of social consciousness. The mode of production of material life conditions the process of social, political and intellectual life process in general. It is not the consciousness of men that determines their being, but, on the contrary, their social being that determines their consciousness. At a certain stage of their development, the material productive forces of society come in conflict with the existing relations of production, or – what is but a legal expression of the same thing – with the property relations within which they have been at work hitherto. From forms of development of the productive forces these relations turn into their fetters. Then begins an epoch of social revolution. With the change of the economic foundation the entire immense superstructure is more or less rapidly transformed.[24]

The precise character of these economic forces, economic relations and non-economic relations, and how they are connected, was ripe for analytical scrutiny. Historical materialism articulates a valuable insight with the general idea that economic matters influence non-economic matters. Marx, though, couched this more forcefully, as follows: At a certain point in history, technological development, access to resources and so forth have the potential to enable a certain amount of productive capacity. But for this potential to be realized, human beings must organize themselves into certain relationships – for example, the capitalist wage labour relation in large-scale factories. Moreover, one mode of production succeeds another, thus capitalism follows feudalism, due to the development of productive forces.

On this view, a particular set of productive forces means that society will tend to develop certain productive relations. These relations, in turn, will need specific kinds of political and legal institutions, such as the protection of economic freedom, the enforcement of contracts and the institution of property rights. Thus, a change in forces, that is technological change, will dictate a change in relations, which will cause a change in the non-material realm, that is government, law, culture and so forth.

Cohen illustrates this well with the point that producers in a society of computer technology could not be slaves, 'if only because the degree of culture needed in labourers who can work that technology would lead them to revolt, successfully, against slave status'. Furthermore, the degree of culture needed for computer technology would require that workers enjoy rights of autonomy, access to education and so forth, which would be impossible under conditions of slavery.[25] And thus, as Cohen puts it, the kind of class that is in ascendancy is dictated by the current economic relations: 'a class gains and possesses power because it marches in step with the productive forces'.[26] There is a progressivist story here insofar as each stage in history is succeeded by another, more advanced one. As Cohen's former graduate student Nicholas Vrousalis declares, Marx's (and Cohen's) account sets out why humanity is not 'bogged down into slavery, serfdom or indeed wage labour' throughout history.[27] Thus Marx and Cohen map out 'the trajectory of unemancipated humanity's career', a kind of 'primordial relay race to freedom', to socialism.[28]

The role of state and politics

How does a materialist account understand the nature of state institutions and the role they play governing society? After all, on this picture the nature of the state is determined by more fundamental relations, but this seems at odds with the important, active role the state is known to play in capitalist societies. Cohen notes that this deterministic story entails a claim about how the phenomenon that is determined nonetheless plays a supporting role for that which determined it. This 'feedback loop' looks perilously close to being a circular argument, oblivious to temporality.

For example, the view is understood to mean that capitalist economic relations determine the kind of political state that obtains in a capitalist society, so that it may provide property rights, laws about contract and so forth. Yet if the institutions of government are supporting the capitalist economy, they might also permit progressive reforms of the welfare state such as socialized medicine and unemployment benefits, in order to quell discontent from a radicalized working class. The state seems to be both capitalist and non-capitalist because of its relationship to the economy, and anything the state does is simply assumed to be determined or required by capitalism.

Cohen proposes that the best way to construe these theses is to understand them in terms of a functional mode of explanation. That is, something takes place because it would tend to produce a certain beneficial result. This kind of explanation is much like the typical logical explanation of an antecedent and consequent, but the difference is that the antecedent is hypothetical or dispositional, characterized by its tendency to produce a certain effect.[29] On this explication, we can understand why forces of production have primacy for relations of production, and relations of production have primacy for non-productive social, political and legal relations. This does not commit us to thinking that forces and economic relations, economic relations and non-economic relations, determine each other back and forth, willy-nilly. Cohen draws on the natural sciences to make his point: 'A species with camouflage might have developed a different camouflage in the same environment ... but this does not show that the species influences the environment'.[30]

Thus we can see what Cohen calls the 'primacy' of the base when it comes to the superstructure, even if we can at the same time see the complementary effect of the ideological superstructure on the economic base, the latter relationship only being possible because of the pre-eminence of the economic base.[31] What this account offers, according to Cohen, is the most plausible form of 'consequence explanation' by which it explains an event in terms of its propensity to have certain consequences.[32]

Praise for the book

Karl Marx's Theory of History was widely celebrated. In his review, Taylor saluted Cohen for rendering 'a great service' to readers of Anglo-American philosophy and to Marxism. Cohen, he said, had laid to rest 'some of the grosser confusions' current among Marxists and their critics, and helped 'to pose more clearly the basic questions and challenges that Marxism must meet'. Taylor captured the import of Cohen's project well when he noted that orthodox Marxists might be oblivious to this achievement, but 'a blow is nevertheless struck for civilization if somewhere in the universe an issue can be got clear'.[33]

Cohen's achievement was also acclaimed by other prominent philosophers, including those on the Marxist Left, one of whom said, 'while Althusserians talked a great deal about rigour, Cohen actually practised it'.[34] Alex Callinicos praised Cohen's 'elegant and ingenious' arguments for a 'highly orthodox version of historical materialism' that rightly, he said, 'dominated subsequent discussion' on the matter.[35] And, as we saw in the last chapter, the positive review from none other than the revered Marxist historian Eric Hobsbawm was gratifying indeed.[36] Particularly promising was the prospect of comradeship on such matters: Cohen was delighted to learn that a young philosopher from Belgium, Philippe Van Parijs, had been working out a similar approach.[37]

Critiques from the Left

Nonetheless, Cohen's argument was not without critics. Indeed, some fellow Marxists of an analytical bent were particularly pointed in their assessments, opposing functional explanation as 'untestable, inherently incomplete, and generally unsatisfactory for scientific purposes'.[38] The most prominent was Jon Elster, who eschewed functional explanations as a form of objective teleology that sets out a process with a goal but no subject, and no mechanism for why something that is favourable to an economic structure comes into being.[39] For Elster, Marxism is not akin to biology, and cannot therefore use the kinds of explanations biologists use, but must subscribe to the methodological individualist maxim that human agents are at the centre of social explanation.[40]

Other analytic philosophers sympathetic to historical materialism also worried about the plausibility of Cohen's functional account, noting that, as Henry Laycock put it, 'a phenomenon cannot have effects at *all* unless it actually exists'.[41] Cohen's response was that his purposes were modest – to make a case for a functional explanation as the best bet for historical materialism. After all, Darwin, who was much admired by Marx, postulated his theory of evolution before the mutation of genes was understood. Thus, so too can historical materialism make claims about causation without yet knowing the mechanism behind it; its claim to being scientific is not thereby undermined.[42]

For some Marxists, such as Richard Miller, Cohen's aim of drawing a sharp analytical distinction between the economic and the social misreads Marx's project. Productive forces should not be assigned an exclusive causal role, unsullied by social factors; modes of production are much more complex combinations of the material and cultural.[43] As Cohen's former graduate student Jonathan Wolff summarizes the complaint, Cohen's method here betrays a 'stultifying neo-positivist conception of rigour' that forces an unhelpful aspiration to 'conceptual hygiene' unrealized even by the sciences.[44] On the other hand, Vrousalis notes, admitting of a more complex, variegated story such as that proposed by Miller risks sacrificing Cohen's much prized analytical clarity. Better, perhaps, to abandon hope of a systematic theory of history and concentrate on the critique of capitalism instead.[45]

The most passionate critics, unsurprisingly, were those on the Left broadly suspicious of the 'analytical turn' proposed by Cohen and his colleagues. Although they were more critical of the new methodological individualist forms of contemporary Marxism such as that of Elster,[46] they nonetheless criticized Cohen for sharing a theoretical orientation too indebted to 'bourgeois social science'[47] and the 'analytic, formalistic model of academic political philosophy',[48] to be properly called Marxist. Thus the question of Cohen's fidelity to Marxist ideals and themes was particularly prominent among many critics. Some bemoaned the diminished role of key ideas like class struggle, and so in that sense shared Elster's concern that structures without agents were doing all the work.

Ellen Meiksins Wood, for example, much as she abhorred Elster's 'atomistic' alternative, took issue with what she argued was the 'ahistorical' nature of Cohen's argument that relied on a technological determinism without scope for collective agency.[49] Callinicos, for all his praise, worried about whether Cohen's contribution represented 'a development of, or an exit from, the revolutionary socialist tradition'.[50] The complaint made by one critic, that Cohen and his colleagues had simply given up a commitment to any fundamental philosophical or methodological difference between Marxism and mainstream social thought, was in fact precisely the avowed purpose of Cohen in his Marx book and his no-bullshit colleagues who joined him.[51]

More recent Marxist scholarship has sought to correct Cohen's technological reading, claiming that Marx's silence on political action was due not to the belief in the inevitability of capitalism's demise, but to a commitment to the working class's 'self-emancipation' which should not be prejudged theoretically.[52] Others have called for a return to understanding Marx in his historical context and in light of the class relations of his time.[53] But though Cohen did not say much about class conflict, the idea is not inconsistent with his view. Taylor observed that the role of human agency in Cohen's picture is somewhat murky, but that this could be said of much social theory that seeks to explain supra-individual phenomena.[54] Moreover, human agency can play a role in the grand narrative of historical materialism since, as Vrousalis avers: 'it is precisely *because* of what historically situated agents (individuals, groups or classes) do, not *despite* what they do, that certain economic and social forms are historically bound to occur'.[55] Nonetheless, the account did not make much room for the relevance of social relations, a point made by fellow Analytical Marxist Joshua Cohen.[56]

A quite different critique related to this matter of social relations came from Paula Casal, who targets the masculinist reading of history provided by Marx and accepted without argument by Cohen. For Casal, Marx's understanding of the productive capacity of a society omits the contributions of women, and its economic determinism cannot adequately account for sexist ideology.[57]

Cohen's Marxism: Political more than Analytical?

Not bullshit but ...

Cohen was said to have inaugurated the school of Analytical Marxism when he published his book on Marx in 1978.[58] As noted in chapter 1, Analytical Marxists sought to introduce a demanding discipline to radical thought. The school initially consisted of the philosopher Cohen, the political scientist Jon Elster, and the economist John Roemer, to be joined by a number of leading figures in philosophy and the social sciences who shared a 'commitment without reverence' to Marxism. The group met annually from 1981 onwards and called themselves 'the September group' in virtue of the time of year of their meetings. Another, more provocative self-ascription, on Cohen's suggestion, was 'No-Bullshit Marxists', to signal how they 'had come to abhor the obscurity that had come to infest Marxism'.[59] In particular, the school's exponents all rejected the claim that 'Marxism possesses valuable intellectual methods of its own', calling for the appropriation of sound methodologies external to it.[60]

However, it has been noted that the school contained a 'sometimes bewildering diversity of outlooks' (consider Cohen v. Elster on functional explanations). Moreover, for those looking to Marxism for social change, the school offered 'few if any tactical prescriptions'.[61] In later work Cohen described Analytical Marxism as analytical in virtue of being opposed to both dialectical and holistic thinking. However, functionalist explanation, in contrast to methodological individualism, certainly seems a holistic approach on Cohen's understanding of holism.[62] In 1986 he penned a couple of pages entitled 'Consequence explanation in historical materialism finally bites the dust'.[63] Yet for some years after the Marx book, Cohen still saw himself working within the Marxist tradition, concerned about the questions of what form socialist society should take, what is right about socialism and wrong about capitalism, and how socialism might be achieved.[64]

Was Cohen in fact an Analytical Marxist, in the sense of exposing Marxism to thorough-going critical scrutiny? The paradox that Cohen deployed so-called 'bourgeois' methodology for radical ends[65] is undercut by another, that arguably the founder of the school of Analytical Marxism fell short in his commitment to the analytical. Indeed, as we saw in the last chapter, that resistance to full analytical engagement may have accounted for the departure of two key figures some years later.

At issue here is how the Marx book was the fruit of a complex intellectual project that paid homage to the radical legacy of Cohen's family. It might seem his strategy was one of immanent critique, where the analysis adopts an internal perspective, assuming the premises of the object of inquiry in order to show its goals or conclusions are unrealized. Yet arguably Cohen brought analytical precision to his interrogation of Marxist ideas not to test them or determine whether they were true, but rather to provide the best possible reading of them.[66] Cohen's book did not entertain the possibility that Marxist ideas should simply be abandoned in light of the limitations of the most plausible, sympathetic analytical reading he could muster. The book was thus not wholly in line with Elster's emphasis on the school's devotion to 'insistent criticism' of all the tenets of classical Marxism and was not, strictly speaking, wholly analytical.[67] A commentator's remark that Cohen's book combined 'insight and ardour'[68] suggests the book was not a dispassionate critique. Thus, the emphasis on truth in his discussions of bullshit seems not quite to describe his aims here, even if Cohen was no bullshitter.

Cohen's description of the foibles of the 'honest dogmatist' who 'responds to criticism best he can, and who might even admit he has no good response to a particular criticism, while nevertheless sticking to his dogmatically held view'[69] seems not that far off from the argument and design of his defence of Marx. Cohen even criticized Elster for being 'too insistently analytical' in his rejection of functional explanation, with the rationale that a discipline can be understood to have reached a limited understanding at a certain point in time that might come to be revised or rejected.[70] And indeed, having written the book, as noted in the last chapter, Cohen referred to himself as having discharged his familial obligation, liberated to pursue other questions of political philosophy without constraint. Nonetheless, the core of Analytical Marxism – the scrupulous inquiry into the grounds for radical political convictions – continued to animate Cohen's work and, moreover, left a legacy among philosophers more widely.[71]

Cohen's Marx and Berlin's

Cohen's relationship with Berlin helps illuminate his philosophical attitude to Marx in the 1978 book. It was Berlin who offered guidance in the face of the thickets of analytical philosophy that frightened young Jerry upon his arrival in Oxford, and they shared, besides their Jewishness, an interest in Karl Marx (if on opposite sides regarding the question of Marx's merits). Moreover, Berlin, despite his anti-communism, supported Cohen's candidacy for the Chichele professorship.[72] Cohen discussed the Marx book with Berlin and they disagreed 'profoundly' about historical materialism. Yet they did not pursue the issue 'with vigour' in order to 'avoid predictable grooves'. Cohen recalls that to the 'scriptural premise' he defended, Berlin would often 'offer me a wry smile which said that in my heart I could not accept it either'.[73] It is interesting that in offering this anecdote, Cohen does not repudiate Berlin's attitude.

In a highly influential essay published shortly after the Marx book, Cohen took aim at Marx's labour theory of value. Not only is the concept incoherent, since the claim that the creation of value by proletarian labour is the precondition for exploitation thereby bizarrely renders feudalism devoid of exploitation. But also, for Cohen, the labour theory of value locates the normative critique of capitalism in the wrong place. Exploitation comes from private control of the means of production, and the unequal power that entails.[74]

Only five years after the publication of *Karl Marx's Theory of History*, Cohen went on to confess, 'I do not now believe that historical materialism is false, but I am not sure how to tell whether or not it is true'. He was quick to add that his 'belated reservations' did not weaken his belief in the socialist project's political goals, that it is 'both desirable and possible to extinguish capitalist social relations and to reorganize society on a just and humane basis'.[75]

Interestingly, however, what followed that disclosure was not an analytical dissection of the weaknesses of functional explanation, but rather some quite sweeping ideas about, contra economic determinism, the importance of culture, religion and nationality in a person's self-definition, the 'human need' to identify with others on the basis of non-material criteria.[76] The upshot, Cohen went on to say, was a 'restricted' historical materialism that limited what it had to say about non-material phenomena, for example religion.[77]

Particularly arresting is Cohen's insistence that, on the correct understanding of historical materialism, there is no place for Marx's philosophical anthropology, that is, the understanding of our capacity to labour as what makes us uniquely human. Cohen concludes: 'once an independent human interest in creativity has been acknowledged, there seems to be no reason to expect the activity which it generates to be pervasively dominated ... by material and economic conditions'.[78] Although such a claim was in keeping with Cohen's revisionist views about the restricted scope of historical materialism, it also seemed a loss. Eliminating from Marx's theory the importance of free, creative, productive activity, what distinguishes 'the worst architect from the best of bees',[79] sheds a distinctive element of Marxism's vision of emancipation. More recent scholarship has stressed that ideas about human flourishing are essential to Marx's contribution.[80]

Marxism, Post-Marxism and Dogmatism

The need for normative argument

The collapse of the Soviet Union in the early 1990s had a profound impact on Cohen and he evocatively captured his complex feelings of loss, as we saw in the previous chapter, with the idea of a boy who 'pummels his father's chest' but would not be 'glad if the old man collapses'.[81] Although Cohen had been under no illusions about the merits of 'actually existing socialism', as the Soviet model was then called, like many on the Left Cohen nonetheless had continued to hope that one day it might offer a genuine alternative to capitalism. That hope was now gone. Whereas one Analytical Marxist colleague said of the fall of the USSR, 'we're partying',[82] Cohen's reaction was much more complicated. As he put it, 'we can no longer say about the Soviet Union that "what is in preparation there is unfinished".'

The loss of the USSR for those, like Cohen, who had wished that it would come to realize the socialist ideal, meant that the ideal risked being abandoned altogether. The Left was susceptible to the problem of assuming, as Frederic Jamieson put it, that a 'wholesale obsolescence' had befallen the idea of utopia. The post-Soviet era emboldened defenders of the status quo, who now insisted that 'the system (now grasped as the free market) is part of human nature; that any attempt to change it will be accompanied by violence; and that efforts to maintain the changes (against human nature) will require dictatorship'.[83]

As mentioned in the last chapter, Cohen countered that, though a natural response to disappointment, disillusion with political ideals should nonetheless be rejected in the long term. To abandon the belief in socialism was irrational, a species of 'adaptive preference formation' in which one touts an inferior option because the superior is unavailable.[84] Moreover, given that socialists and anti-socialists were agreed that the Soviet Union had 'utterly failed to achieve a classless, or even a decent, society', Cohen came to agree that the fact it was no longer in the Left's orbit should be regarded as an opportunity. Socialist ideals could be couched in a new way, without the model of a disappointing socialist experiment.[85] Thus, Cohen went so far as to say that the loss of the USSR was 'a boon', enabling 'freer and more imaginative' thinking about socialism without its 'stigmatizing' example.[86] The conclusion to draw was not that the ideal of a classless society was not good, but rather that socialists should try differently and more cautiously to formulate and promote that ideal, in a spirit of 'chastened dedication'.[87] Much of Cohen's subsequent work should be understood as carrying out this aim.

Socialism without Marxism

Although Cohen continued to call himself a socialist for the rest of his life, he ultimately disavowed Marxism altogether. This disavowal was not principally the result of an analytical interrogation of Marxism, but rather the falling away of certain beliefs in light of historical events. Not only did Cohen call into question Marx's materialist philosophical anthropology, as noted above, but he also rejected orthodox Marxist views about social change: first, the inevitability of socialism; second, the 'world-historical' mission of the Soviet Union; and third, the revolutionary role of the working class.

To take them in turn, first, Cohen targeted the Marxist theory of history for being seriously impaired by what he dubbed the 'obstetric' view of the inevitable birth of communism from capitalist preconditions. Marxism is unique in aspiring to be, not just a normative theory about the injustice of capitalism and the superiority of communism, but also a predictive theory which forecasts the demise of one social order and its replacement by a superior alternative. Cohen added his essay 'Marxism After the Collapse of the USSR' to the 2000 edition of the Marx book, where he contended that the 'the restoration of capitalism' in Russia vindicated historical materialism's emphasis on the need for the appropriate forces of production to be in place for social change to occur. Thus, contra the second point about the special role of the USSR, the Russian revolution was an example of what Marx called a premature revolution, taking place in a society which was still largely rural, characterized by the 'incomplete development of productive forces', which find success only if it unleashed a global working-class revolt that could find a footing in more favourable, highly developed conditions.[88] In other words, the theory of historical materialism could not be assumed to have been disproved by the events of 1989; indeed, quite the contrary.

Yet elsewhere Cohen concluded that the collapse of the Soviet Union had shown that the predictive aspect of Marxism is 'patently false'.[89] Furthermore, in the spirit of a corrective to his functionalist account, Cohen lamented that the inevitability view exemplifies the tendencies of Marxism to resist real standards of confirmation since the Marxist can keep altering the temporal measure in order to salvage its predictive claims.[90]

This points to the third bit of orthodoxy Cohen came to abandon, that is, the idea of the proletariat or working class as an inherently revolutionary agent.[91] In his 1990s essay 'Back to Socialist Basics', Cohen gloomily declared that the broad movement that had underpinned the British Labour Party 'no longer exists and will never be re-created' because 'technological change means that the class base of that movement is gone, forever', an insight that nonetheless invokes, in a classical Marxist vein, the causal power of material forces.[92]

Furthermore, Cohen took the view that Marx's optimism that socialist relations of production would generate unceasing abundance that could be harnessed by proletarian revolution should be abandoned given the lessons of environmentalists about the fragility of nature's resources. The ecological crisis had demonstrated that the earth's stores were not 'lavish enough' to solve the problem of scarcity. Decades before governments proclaimed a climate emergency, Cohen captured what was at stake with the evocative statement, 'the planet earth rebels'.[93]

Marxism and justice

Cohen was concerned that, particularly in the wake of the collapse of the USSR, the stress on historical inevitability had moral costs. Marxists tended to assume the content of the socialist ideal would be determined by the historical conditions that obtain when socialism is 'born'. But Cohen insisted that questions of socialist design be considered to understand how power should be wielded, but also to attract people to the socialist camp.

A prominent debate among socialist philosophers at the time centred on whether Marx's historical materialism rules out the possibility of assessing a social order with the criteria of justice. Allen Wood, for example, stressed the complex way in which Marx's condemnation of capitalism was not couched in moral terms. For all the talk of workers' servitude, he argued, Marx's critique was not an ethical one, but rather rested on an account of the system's irrationality that would spell its own demise.[94] According to the 'Tucker-Wood thesis', Marx's historical materialism ruled out assessing a social order with reference to normative criteria. In short, it made no sense to say that Marx thought capitalism unjust.[95] Cohen was critical of Marxism for its 'venerable, deep, and disastrously illuded self-conception' on this matter, and was ultimately highly impatient with such scholastic preoccupations among critics. He offered by way of explanation that Marxism in fact deemed socialism both inevitable and morally right. Thus, 'while Marx believed that capitalism was unjust, and that communism was just, he did not always realize that he had those beliefs'.[96] Cohen did not pursue these issues at length, but he argued that exploitation, where the worker is 'robbed' of his product, must be understood as a species of injustice for Marx.[97] Indeed, what else could be at issue in the dispute between Marxists and defenders of capitalism, if not justice?

Analytical dogmatism?

Throughout his career, Cohen prided himself on his 'scientific' approach to social theory, enjoying the irony of using a term of art from Marx and Engels in order to part company with their methods.[98] Cohen notes Engels's tribute to Marx as the founder of 'scientific socialism' which, like Cohen and his colleagues, used 'the most advanced resources of social science ... within the frame of a socialist commitment', and which 'exploited ... what was best in the bourgeois social science of his day'.[99] Indeed, Cohen laments that if Analytical Marxism had been called instead 'scientific socialism', then left-wing critics would not have been disposed to ask the 'unproductive question' of whether Analytical Marxism was really Marxist. Thus, in later writings, although no less confident in the power of analytical philosophy, Cohen disparages the Marxist confidence in the scientific predictive power of historical materialism, and indeed calls into question the very dichotomy between utopian and scientific.[100]

Among the ingredients of a scientific approach, according to Cohen, was an anti-pluralism about philosophical method, and Analytical Marxists should have no truck with rival schools. This position contrasts sharply with the value pluralism Cohen avowed in his later work on justice, and it also seems dissonant with the openness of Cohen to non-Marxist political philosophies. As we will see in subsequent chapters, Cohen was certainly prepared to find merit in liberal, even libertarian, argument. However, likely the analytical nature of liberal views was a key reason why Cohen found their influence salutary.

According to Cohen, before Analytical Marxism, there may have been non-analytical Marxist theories that were intellectually respectable. However, once these theories encounter Analytical Marxism, they 'must either become analytical or bullshit'. The Analytical Marxist should deem his Marxism as 'uniquely legitimate'.[101] Here we see an affinity with a feature of the thought of Marx and Engels that is not wholly attractive. Consider the Communist Manifesto's scathing dismissal of other socialist views: 'In proportion as the modern class struggle develops and takes definite shape, this fantastic standing apart from the contest, these fantastic attacks on it, lose all practical value and all theoretical justification'.[102]

Even if philosophers are persuaded by Cohen's ruthless decimation of bullshit and are keen to avoid it in their own philosophical work, to reject all methods but one's own seems counter to the search for truth that Cohen insists should animate philosophical inquiry, and which, after all, in his own case involved entertaining new perspectives. Different approaches may shed light on different aspects of the socialist ideal, and to be open to them seems part and parcel of an imaginative preparedness for alternative futures. The 'admonition against surrender to the pull of conventional thinking' which Cohen saluted in Engels's rousing remarks on the death of Marx was perhaps not sufficiently heeded by Cohen himself.[103] After all, more discursive analyses might be illuminating of some questions not considered by Analytical Marxists.

Beyond the analytical

A fascinating and rare example of Cohen's capacity to be both analytically astute about and appreciative of creative philosophical approaches outside of Oxford philosophy lies in his little-known 1969 essay on the critical theorist Herbert Marcuse. There Cohen extols Marcuse's radical critique of capitalist society, bourgeois ideology and consumerism, though he also faults Marcuse for lack of nuance and precision.[104] Cohen's Marx book picks up on the consumerist theme, connecting it to capitalism's imperative to foster 'a desire for goods which necessarily outruns the capacity of the average person to satisfy it' and noting how workers are induced to work longer hours in order to pay for leisure goods that they lack the time to enjoy. Cohen also alludes to the 'Marcusean' reply to the problem of lack of radical consciousness among workers, though noting that 'workers are not so benighted as to be helpless dupes of bourgeois ideology' and that weight should be given to 'the costs and difficulties of carrying through a socialist transformation'.[105]

Cohen certainly made forays into the discursive in his many personal anecdotes about his background, his references to protest songs, or his literary quotes, that pepper and enliven his writings. And Cohen, a lifelong lover of poetry, does note in his discussion of bullshit that sometimes writing that is unclear, such as a poem, is nonetheless valuable because it is 'suggestive'. As such, 'it can stimulate thought' and it is thus worthwhile seeking to interpret such texts in 'a spirit which tolerates multiplicity of interpretations' and therefore 'denies that it means some one thing'.[106]

Cohen's confidence that one can tidy up the issue by stipulating that, unlike poetry, the lack of clarity in bullshit 'lacks this virtue of suggestiveness' seems unconvincing. After all, Cohen had an impressive grasp of, and admiration for, the philosophy of Hegel (which he pastiched brilliantly, as only a sympathetic reader can do, in a video posted on YouTube), and he was careful to exempt Hegel from the accusation of bullshit.[107] Hegel was no Analytical Marxist, yet for the uninitiated, Hegel certainly seems like a candidate for 'unclarifiable unclarity'.

It might appear Cohen had loosened up his analytical strictures when he advised his students to entertain seemingly foggy notions as they philosophize: 'One should aspire to clarity, but one should not avoid possible insight for the sake of avoiding unclarity'. However, this tip was intended not to confirm the value of alternative ways of doing philosophy but rather to acknowledge the halting steps one must take in the vital analytical project of aiming for clarity.[108] Thus, for Cohen, if one eschews relativism and seeks truth, a diversity of intellectual positions indicates confusion, not greater insight. True, the Analytical Marxists did not always agree, as we saw in Cohen and Elster's dispute on the question of functional explanation; Cohen's position suggests they were united and immoveable, however, on the question of what method is best placed to reveal the defects of an argument.

Cohen's eschewal of the interpretive in political philosophy seems especially austere, if one considers, in stark contrast, the distinction drawn between the natural and social sciences by his Chichele predecessor, Taylor, who insisted that human beings intersubjectively understand their own theoretical practices.[109] Murdoch, a critic of the philosophy of Cohen's supervisor Ryle, as well as a trenchant analyst of postwar social democratic politics, called for a 'living morality' which can give us 'the power to imagine what we know' to inform the Left.[110] In our post-Soviet era, the insistence on one path to philosophical enlightenment indicates a severity about doctrine, a holdover of the dogmatism of old-style orthodox Marxism that Cohen devoted his career to critically interrogating. Moreover, such dogmatism, if not producing the kinds of illiberal political consequences that Cohen abhorred, is itself a species of illiberalism, contrary to John Stuart Mill's view that society should make room for diverse 'experiments in living'.[111]

Conclusion

In sum, Cohen was the central figure in an invigorating philosophical school that sought to marry the pursuit of socialist ideals with philosophical tough-mindedness. Cohen's defence of Marx's historical materialism was an outstanding achievement, signalling a 'remarkable turnabout' where Marx scholarship came to hold a prominent place in English-speaking political philosophy[112] by means of a powerful case for the validity of Marx's central claims. However, Cohen's role in the forswearing of bullshit was ambiguous. The idea that analytical tools should be marshalled to ascertain the validity of Marxism is not in fact how Cohen's philosophical engagement proceeded. Cohen began as an analytical philosopher who worked outside of normative theory and his first efforts at political philosophy involved a cautious appropriation of analytical tools to shore up his Marxist beliefs, albeit to an exacting standard of clarity and rigour.

Yet in his increasing enthusiasm for the analytical, Cohen came to betray perhaps a new kind of dogmatism that in some ways cut against his own intellectual strictures. Nonetheless, though philosophers can be notoriously dismissive when it comes to thinkers they deem inferior, Cohen, in contrast, was always humane in his dealings with those less analytically minded, and his 'uncompromising intellectual honesty'[113] was truly inspiring. Perhaps the humanity that one found in the socialist bedrock of his beliefs, which as I have argued made the analytical story somewhat more complex, gave one the reassurance that analytical criticism wasn't everything, that progressive ideals always matter, even if one is not certain how they may best be pursued.[114] In the next chapter we will see how Cohen defended socialist principles against the arguments of an influential right-wing political theory.

3

Rescuing Freedom from Nozick

Cohen made his first foray into mainstream political philosophy in the mid-1970s. The area of inquiry that most urgently spoke to his political convictions was libertarianism, a view on the right end of the political spectrum. Libertarianism avows the overriding importance of freedom to own and dispose of private property, a creed so abhorred by most progressives as to be deemed not worthy of attention. For many admirers of Cohen's work on Marx, therefore, this was a surprising development. Cohen had made his reputation for what had become a canonical work on the Marxist doctrine of historical materialism, a far cry from engaging with arguments for a laissez-faire economy. Thus we can see a paradox in Cohen's interest in libertarianism.

However, this change of direction was in some ways not such a surprising step for Cohen. As we saw in the last chapter, after completing his book on Marx, Cohen had concluded that the predictive aspect of Marx's historical materialism was 'patently false'. This meant rejecting what he dubbed the 'obstetric' view, that communism would inevitably be born from capitalist preconditions. If historical materialism could not make any socialist guarantees and history would not inevitably deliver a more just and equal society, socialists were forced to engage in ethical reflection about their ideals and the case that could be made for them. Thus, Cohen followed his project on Marx with an inquiry as to what exactly should replace the relations of the market, and why. Cohen believed that the woolly thinking that beset Marxist thought was also evident in the lack of specification of the nature of socialism, particularly its relations of justice. And thus, just as Cohen considered analytical philosophy crucial to clarify Marxist method, its tools were no less necessary to critically assess its prescriptions and ideals.

It was in 1972 that word reached Cohen about the writings of Robert Nozick. Fuelled, as he put it, by 'a mixture of irritation and anxiety' by this encounter, Cohen 'vigorously engaged' with the libertarian creed in order to critically examine the concept of freedom and its relation to property and labour.[1] Cohen was once again bucking intellectual and political trends, and his creative and ingenious approach produced some highly influential, stimulating scholarship focused on the ideas of both Marxism and Marxism's harshest right-wing critics. Cohen's aim of illuminating and resolving the surprising commonalities between the two ends of the political spectrum drew him into a challenging, potentially insurmountable task.

Libertarianism and Inequality

Right-wing anarchism

Libertarianism is a school of thought founded on the principle that of all values it is freedom that is of overriding importance, particularly freedom from interference by the state. Jan Narveson goes so far as to say that for libertarians, 'the only relevant consideration in political matters is liberty'.[2] Canonical libertarians deem state intervention in individuals' affairs as inherently illegitimate. They propose an ideal society would be without government, leaving individuals alone to live as they choose. This is a familiar position, dating back at least to the heyday of anarchism in the nineteenth and early twentieth centuries. However, earlier anarchists took the view that individual freedom was fettered by the institutions of property, and that the coercive power of the state existed to protect private concentrations of wealth; for left-wing anarchists, eliminate economic inequality and private ownership, and you eliminate unfreedom. Thus, Emma Goldman wrote in 1910 that the anarchist movement had demonstrated 'the insatiable, devouring, devastating nature of property', its 'power to subdue, to crush, to exploit', and thus the time had come to 'strike the monster dead', along with the tyranny of government that is in league with the owners of property and protects their interests.[3]

By the late twentieth century, however, state institutions in western liberal societies, though they continued to protect private property owners' assets as lamented by the radical anarchists, had also been marshalled to mitigate the inequalities of property. Governments in many capitalist societies intervened in the economy through progressive taxation regimes to provide social welfare, healthcare, public education, pensions and so forth. This new 'welfare state' stimulated a right-wing libertarian revolt which centred on the conviction that individuals should not find their freedom to dispose of their property curtailed by state taxation. As Jason Brennan put it, 'we do not have to get society's permission to go about our lives'.[4]

The libertarian creed in its purest form retained the anarchist insistence on personal freedom in all domains – for example, that sexuality, drug use and so forth should be unrestricted – stressing the concern that state power should not be exercised against the individual whatever the policy.[5] Thus Narveson emphasizes that libertarianism is a species of liberalism, not conservatism, and other commentators have stressed libertarianism's lineage to the classical liberalism of John Locke and the idea of fundamental political and civil liberties.[6] Libertarianism thus had an uneasy relation to the New Right real-world politics of western leaders like Margaret Thatcher and Ronald Reagan, which married private enterprise economics with social conservatism on issues such as homosexuality and abortion.[7]

Nozick's defence of private property

In 1974 Robert Nozick produced a sustained philosophical defence of right-wing libertarianism. His book *Anarchy, State and Utopia* was a powerful demonstration, according to one of his critics, that 'it is no longer acceptable to criticize capitalism by platitude'.[8] Nozick's argument for most readers was bold, preposterous even, but also brilliantly marshalled, and charmingly told, with such memorable phrases as the state ought not to 'forbid capitalist acts between consenting adults'.[9] Thus, although Nozick offered an extremist creed with a minority of adherents, it proved to be highly influential.

Whereas pure libertarians advocated the elimination of the state altogether, Nozick contended that a 'minimal state' was required to protect citizens' life, liberty and property. In this, his argument draws on the natural rights tradition of Locke, although also modifying Locke's argument in significant ways. There are three core elements to Nozick's theory of property rights: first, a principle of acquisition, whereby the legitimacy of individuals' property holdings requires only that they were obtained without force or fraud (in contrast to Locke's idea of 'mixing labour' with nature); second, a principle of transfer, whereby voluntary transactions on the part of rightful owners are deemed just; and third, a principle of rectification, whereby distributions of holdings that violate the first two principles should be corrected.[10]

The current distribution of property in capitalist societies could hardly be said to satisfy the first two principles, which raises interesting questions about how rectification ought to be realized, particularly given the libertarian precept that government refrain from interfering in people's lives.[11] Nozick argues that individuals' rights dictate a state whose sole role is to protect individuals from force or fraud. Any other activities, from a postal service to roads, to public education or pensions – are illegitimate intrusions on individuals' rights. Nozick dubs his approach 'historical', insofar as it is concerned only that the path to current property arrangements is legitimate, devoid of rights violations. Alternative political arrangements which seek to distribute wealth in accord with criteria such as need or human interest, merit or desert, or even the promotion of freedom, involve 'patterning' and as such are unjust, indeed tyrannical.[12]

The Wilt Chamberlain example

Perhaps the most beguiling aspect of Nozick's position is his famous Wilt Chamberlain thought experiment, which centres on the entitlement of a sports hero to his wealth. In the Chamberlain parable Nozick supposes that in a socialist society of equal holdings (Distribution 1 or D1), an outstanding basketball player (as Chamberlain was back in the 1970s), much sought after by teams and fans, signs a contract where he receives twenty-five cents from each spectator for every game. People willingly buy tickets and are gratified by Chamberlain's performance, with the result that after one season, Chamberlain is $250,000 richer. Nozick argues that the resulting new distribution of income (Distribution 2 or D2) is unobjectionable, since those who are poorer willingly parted with their money, and everyone else is unaffected. Of course, Nozick teasingly notes, the fans could have spent their money on 'going to the movies, or on candy bars, or on copies of Dissent Magazine or Monthly Review' (the latter being influential left-wing periodicals). Those choices would have demanded respect too. Any effort to intervene and correct for the income inequality, or as Nozick puts it, to impose a pattern that overrides voluntary transfers, would be unjust.[13]

Property Rights contra Freedom

Cohen encounters Nozick

Cohen recalled that his first reaction to Nozick's argument was the hope that it 'depended on a sleight of hand' but also a 'looming fear that maybe it did not'.[14] This was not, of course, Cohen's first encounter with a defence of private property.[15] However, Nozick's argument about how the state coercively extracts the labour power of the taxpayer looked particularly dismaying from a Marxist point of view. Marx's critique of capitalism is distinctive for targeting, not just inequality, the usual preoccupation of progressive argument about markets, but also unfreedom. Contra many popular depictions, Cohen was convinced that the socialist ideal does not involve a trade-off of liberty for equality but rather fully realizes both.[16] Yet he was concerned that this position was too often assumed rather than argued for. He thus resolved to engage critically with Nozick's contention that efforts to achieve equality by means of the distribution of wealth compromise individual freedom. Cohen ended up writing several essays on ideas of self-ownership, freedom and property, and he credited the encounter with Nozick's libertarianism for rousing him from his 'dogmatic socialist slumber'.[17]

In all his encounters with Nozick, Cohen takes seriously the libertarian preoccupation with the relationship between property and freedom, scrupulously avoiding the temptations of what he termed, as we saw in the last chapter, 'bullshit'. This meant a careful delineation of various concepts in political philosophy. To make the case that state intervention in the economy to ameliorate inequality does not, contra Nozick, promote unfreedom, it was necessary to establish what is meant by freedom and what counts as its diminution.

Wealth and power

First, Cohen disputes Nozick's contention that 'whatever arises from a just situation by just steps is itself just'. For Nozick, the test of justice is voluntariness, or as Cohen paraphrases it, liberty always preserves justice. But Cohen notes that individuals can make decisions freely without full knowledge of the consequences which can turn out to create injustice. In the Chamberlain case, one such consequence may be that the basketball player now holds an unacceptable amount of power over others, not just basketball fans, but also third parties. This does not mean that individual basketball fans were irrational to buy their tickets, or that the parties could have anticipated the results, but rather indicates the complexity of individual acts with social consequences, something Cohen explores in subsequent work.[18] Nozick's representation of the example as simply providing pleasure to basketball fans glosses over how these transactions have the result that a society of equality loses 'its essential character' and is set upon a path of class division.[19]

Second, Cohen notes that the move from D1 to D2 (and thereby to D3, D4, etc.) means the diminution of liberty, if, for example, children become undernourished because of free market transactions and thereby have fewer options as to what they can do. Nozick argues that rights to liberty should be understood as 'side constraints', whereby considerations of liberty can only ward off interference; liberty is not something that can be maximized.[20] Any act that restricts liberty is forbidden; we cannot slightly diminish the liberty of millionaires to significantly improve the effective liberty of undernourished children.

Cohen argues that Nozick's understanding of freedom as the 'inviolability of persons' entails a blanket prohibition on efforts to attend to the lack of freedom of the disadvantaged.[21] Moreover, Cohen notes in another essay, the vocabulary of 'intervention', that is accepted by libertarians and egalitarian liberals alike, dissembles the fact that all state rules, including those that enforce private property arrangements, 'intervene on' individuals' actions.[22] The central question is whether or which such interventions are justified, in light of the claims of all individuals to effective freedom.

Third, Cohen notes that the argument gives short shrift to the interests of third parties (including the unborn) in the Chamberlain transactions. This consideration draws on the insight above of how children's freedom might be diminished. After all, they, and other third parties, do not voluntarily participate in the exchange. Yet, as Nozick admits, the exchange may reduce their options, for example, if D2 means that assets are unequally owned so that some must work for others. Nonetheless, Nozick contends that so long as all the choices and actions that led to D2 were voluntary, then even the most disadvantaged person in D2 cannot claim to be subject to coercion.[23] Cohen rejects this conclusion, noting that barriers to choice by definition reduce people's freedom, however those barriers were produced, and whether they are just or unjust.

The focus on freedom

Cohen stresses how Nozick slips between a 'moralized' account of freedom, as that freedom people have which he supposes is given by right, and an empirical understanding, as that freedom which people happen to have, whether lawful or not.[24] In so doing, Nozick seeks to dissemble the fact that capitalism significantly reduces the freedom of those without capital. Libertarians famously say that the unfettered capitalist market respects the liberal principle that individuals are the 'ultimate authorities on their own values'.[25] However, as Cohen's former graduate student Nicholas Vrousalis puts the matter, if, as Nozick claims, self-ownership is thwarted under collective forms of ownership, it is hard to say that the self-ownership of the poor isn't similarly thwarted under capitalist ownership.[26]

Cohen demonstrates that people's ability to control their lives is severely hampered under conditions of capitalist inequality; that is, the poor are in an important sense, unfree. Cohen thus exposes the 'conceptual chicanery'[27] at work in libertarian thought where the commitment to private property takes precedence over the ideal of the person as a free, self-determining being. Ultimately, libertarian capitalism 'sacrifices liberty to capitalism'.[28] Or in other words, 'capitalist acts between consenting adults', to use Nozick's humorous phrase noted earlier, produce unfreedom. Though he applauds Cohen's position, Jeremy Waldron contends that Cohen's rejection of a 'moralized' conception of freedom, albeit a key strategy against Nozick, was not without costs. Shouldn't freedom be understood in a morally rich way? Moreover, Waldron avers, Cohen fails to take account of the ethical value in the idea of possession.[29]

For his part, left-libertarian and Cohen's former graduate student Michael Otsuka points out that Cohen's exposure of the shortcomings in Nozick's view of rights as side-constraints does not amount to a positive case for another understanding of rights, such as the utilitarianism of rights implied in Cohen's critique.[30] Cohen entertained the possibility that private property need not be abolished but rather dispersed more widely; however, he did not pursue the matter further.[31] Nonetheless, for Cohen, the upshot is clear: a Marxist approach recognizes how property relations can constrain a person's opportunities and powers, so that a defence of freedom must tackle private property. Marxism thus emerges as the philosophy with the more principled stance on liberty.

Proletarian Unfreedom

Are workers forced to sell their labour power?

It seems fitting that, in his work on property and freedom after his book on Marx, Cohen took up, not just a critique of Nozick, but a defence of Marx. In his Deutscher lecture, Cohen made an eloquent case with broad appeal for how capitalism undermines freedom.[32] In an inventive essay, 'The Structure of Proletarian Unfreedom', Cohen focuses this critique and considers Marx's claim that the worker is 'forced' to sell his labour power. Cohen analyses this statement systematically. After all, he says, defenders of capitalism will say that the worker is free to choose an employer, and some may say workers are free even to choose not to work – to go on the dole, beg, take their chances or even starve. But Cohen insists that freedom must pertain to the quality of choices, not just the existence of some choice or other. When Marx says the worker is unfree, he must mean that there is no 'acceptable alternative' to working for a capitalist.[33]

Cohen also rejects, as we saw earlier, the view that the worker is not unfree because, on the libertarian view, no unjust actions in the capitalist economy explains the absence of an acceptable alternative. Such moralized accounts have the absurd upshot that the justly convicted criminal in prison is deemed not unfree.[34] Cohen stresses that 'forced' and therefore being unfree is a matter of fact, pertaining to a social relationship that obtains with the standard exercises of the powers constituting relations of production. To the critic who says there is no force without a forcing agent, the Marxist replies that the agent is the relations of production, which are after all peopled with human beings who maintain those relations.[35]

Perhaps the most common and powerful argument in favour of the view that workers enjoy freedom under capitalism involves the idea of social mobility, that individuals are not necessarily condemned to the class position of their parents but can ascend to the bourgeoisie. Indeed, Cohen quotes Marx as saying that 'an exceedingly clever and shrewd fellow, and gifted with bourgeois instincts and favoured by an exceptional fortune' can convert himself from one of the exploited to one of the exploiters.[36] It is commonly supposed that with hard work, talent and opportunity, workers can escape the proletariat and become members of the bourgeoisie.

Thinkers on the Left tend to dismiss such claims on behalf of capitalism as ideological fiction, designed to win workers' compliance to an unjust social order.[37] Cohen is similarly disposed, but he takes the class escape claim seriously, and carefully elaborates how it might be defeated. First, he notes that unfreedom cannot be demonstrated by building it into the definition of worker, in other words, that workers, in virtue of being workers, are necessarily forced to sell their labour power. The claim of unfreedom must involve some kind of time frame in which workers are forced to remain workers. As Cohen puts it, 'one is forced at time t to *continue* to sell his labour-power, throughout a period from t to $t + n$, for some considerable n'.[38] If there is an escape route in some elapse of time less than n, we can say that the worker can escape and is free after all. Nonetheless, though 'rags to riches' stories, which legitimize the system, are real, they are uncommon – any particular proletarian faces poor chances of escape from the proletariat and mass escape is not possible. Thus, it appears that workers are both free and unfree under capitalism.

Cohen's thought experiment

To solve this puzzle, Cohen draws an analogy or thought experiment, a time-honoured device in analytical philosophy that, as we saw, Nozick deployed to good effect with the Chamberlain example. Imagine, Cohen says, ten workers locked in a room with a heavy and cumbersome key on the floor before them that, if used with great effort to open the door, will only permit the escape of one worker. In all likelihood, no one leaves but no one is forced to remain. Nevertheless, whatever happens, at least nine workers will remain in the room.

It may be that no one even attempts to escape. Perhaps they are accustomed to the room, and don't want to leave it; or the room is unpleasant, but they are too lazy to attempt to leave; or no one fancies their chances, assuming erroneously that others will beat them to it. Long occupancy, what Marx terms 'the dull compulsion of economic relations', passed from parents to children, fosters a view that one's class position is inevitable and natural. Like the myth of easy escape, fatalistic acceptance of one's class position serves the stability of the system. In sum, it is true of each person that they are not forced to remain in the room, even though nine must remain, and as it usually turns out, all do.[39]

The upshot of the locked room thought experiment, Cohen says, is that 'even though necessarily most proletarians will remain proletarians, and will sell their labour-power, perhaps none, and at most a minority, are forced to do so'.[40] Workers' disinclinations to escape must be in place for any one person to be free, since as Cohen says, 'each is free only on condition that the others do not exercise their similarly conditional freedom'. Cohen concludes that there is 'a great deal of unfreedom' in the room; though the worker is individually free (though conditionally unfree insofar as they opt not to take the key), the worker suffers from 'collective unfreedom'.[41]

Cohen's conclusion finds more freedom for proletarians than in the standard Marxist view, which is that workers enjoy no freedom under capitalism. However, still central to the analysis is the Marxist emphasis on the exigencies of social class, whereby workers' political interest in emancipation can only be realized if joined by their fellows. The goal of collective freedom inspires comradeship to seek liberation from class society rather than individual flights from the working class. This would mean getting rid of the locked room altogether by abolishing capitalism, private property, the division of labour and class distinctions. Class solidarity makes manifest collective unfreedom, the fact that the proletariat is an 'imprisoned class'.[42] Cohen points out, too, that proletarian unfreedom involves a particularly lamentable condition – workers are 'forced to subordinate themselves to others who thereby gain control over their productive existence'.[43]

Significance of workers' collective unfreedom

Cohen adduces some further considerations. First, that we cannot identify a particular person responsible for collective unfreedom does not affect the veracity of the claim that workers experience a shortfall of liberty, just as they would be unequivocally free if the doors were faulty and opened without human intervention. Second, it might be thought that collective unfreedom is irrelevant so long as individuals are free, but Cohen stresses that collective freedom consists in the mutual conditionality of individual freedom. Insofar as the worker enjoys individual freedom it is on condition of collective unfreedom. Third, lack of freedom is unaffected by whether it is resented or at odds with people's wants – 'thwarted desire throws unfreedom into relief' but that one is disinclined to reach for the key (the consequence to some degree of the conditions of one's class position) does not affect the fact of collective unfreedom.[44]

Finally, given that Cohen's argument focuses on class as a social identity that limits one's options, it might be thought that the capitalist, too, is unfree, 'forced' to invest capital. Certainly, Marx contended that the capitalist experiences a certain compulsion. However, capitalists are relevantly different – they can cease to be capitalists by consuming their capital, or by joining the working class. It is revealing that whereas the worker might happily trade places with the capitalist, the opposite is not true; moreover, capitalists are also free to 'yield their wealth to society at large' and thereby escape their class position and bring about emancipation for all.[45]

Cohen's right-wing critics contended that he supposed an archaic, nineteenth-century capitalism, in which there is a fixed number of opportunities for social mobility, at odds with the reality of contemporary capitalism with its abundance of options to better oneself. Moreover, wouldn't a socialist scheme of guaranteed income also rely on the collective unfreedom of a class of people so that all could avail themselves of it?[46]

At the same time, the modest conclusions of this essay disappointed some critics on the Left, who found the distinction between individual and collective unfreedom obscure. Cohen entertains the more radical claim that where the individual proletarian is trapped in the proletariat because of personal failings – lack of talent, or get-up-and-go – it may indicate a lack of freedom. However, this is only the case if such incapacities are a standard result of class membership (workers are deprived of educational opportunities, or in the terms of the thought experiment, are so malnourished that they are too weak to lift the heavy key).[47] Cohen is sceptical that this is true to any sufficient degree, a somewhat surprising conclusion given the realities of capitalist inequality, even assuming the welfare state's mitigating measures.

In sum, Cohen reaches his conclusion about collective unfreedom with a significant concession to the idea that the proletarian is free to leave the proletariat via the ladder of success, even if he also wants to debunk the myth of the ease of the American dream. Cohen eschewed what he took to be murky ideas of positive freedom, so despised by his mentor Isaiah Berlin, that is, that freedom refers to self-determination or self-mastery, democratic participation or living by a moral law.[48] But having zeroed in on the classical liberal understanding of freedom as the sphere of unimpeded action enjoyed by an individual, Cohen's conclusions seemed sparse. In the end, the only unfreedom that obtains for the worker under capitalism does not pertain to individuals per se, but is a collective phenomenon, experienced by members of a class. This certainly diluted the moral force of the traditional critique. Moreover, the collective freedom idea entails that no proletarian is forced to work, so long as an exit from their class is available. 'For all its sophistication', as Vrousalis puts it, Cohen's argument goes 'against the grain of traditional Marxist commitment'.[49]

Self-Ownership: For and Against

Exploitation of workers and owners

Cohen notes that his 1980s work on freedom and capitalism did not betray his principal source of discomfort with Nozick's argument. His gravest misgivings became evident in a 1990 paper which had the subtitle, 'Why Nozick Exercises some Marxists more than he does any Egalitarian Liberals'. Here Cohen communicated the irony that thinkers at some distance from libertarians on the political spectrum had more in common than do their politically more proximate, liberal, bedfellows.[50]

Non-Marxist, liberal critics certainly took issue with Nozick's case for a laissez-faire economy, decrying Nozickian self-ownership as conflicting 'with even the most minimal requirements of humanity'.[51] Liberal critics stressed the extent to which Nozick's scheme entailed great losses of liberty for those without property, with no sense that such losses are 'worse than that which is involved in the alternative systems which he deplores'.[52] Thomas Nagel noted that Nozick's argument seems to produce the bizarre conclusion that 'a benefit to one or more persons can never outweigh a cost borne by someone else',[53] a point also made by Judith Jarvis Thomson, who though sympathetic to Nozick's hostility to the pursuit of equality, nonetheless contended that property rights might be overridden in cases of human need.[54] Moreover, Nagel argues, Nozick's assumption that private acts of charity will take up the slack left by the destruction of the welfare state overlooks the benefit to individual interests of a system of compulsory taxation to assist the disadvantaged rather than having to consult one's moral conscience about when to provide voluntary aid.[55]

Nonetheless, for Cohen, Marxists are not only unhappy with the inegalitarian effects of the market, and the unfreedom that lack of resources entails. They also share with Nozickian libertarians a commitment to the idea of 'self-ownership', that is, that individuals are entitled to command their bodies and powers. They too conclude that any effort on the part of a third party to interfere with an individual's agency is unjust and illegitimate.[56] Marx's argument that capitalists exploit workers when they extract value from their labour, Cohen thought, is analogous to Nozick's argument that the state exploits property owners when it taxes them to fund policies to mitigate inequality. Egalitarian liberals, worried about income inequality due to arbitrary factors like talent, are unfettered by the self-ownership thesis.[57] Paradoxically, then, it is the more moderate critics of the market who can endorse distributive policies such as progressive taxation to fund social welfare institutions without any sense of dissonance with their other commitments.

Enough and as good for others

Given its apparent Marxist pedigree, at first Cohen was reluctant to challenge the plausibility of the self-ownership thesis itself. Instead, he set about to counter Nozick's contention that egalitarian policy requires the violation of rights to self-ownership and therefore necessarily involves injustice.[58] Here Cohen zeroed in on Nozick's assumption, which Nozick shared with the classical liberal theorist of private property, John Locke, that individuals may legitimately appropriate the external world in any way they choose.

For all their emphasis on the sanctity of rights to private property, both Locke and Nozick conceded that rights had to meet modest consequentialist criteria.[59] Yet, Cohen points out that whereas Locke insisted that private appropriators 'leave enough and as good' for others, Nozick offers a 'bizarrely lax' proviso. For Nozick, private appropriation is just so long as no one has any reason to prefer it remaining in general use, or in the case of anyone who does have such a preference, they get something in the new situation that they couldn't get before.[60] Cohen notes that Nozick narrows the class of alternatives with which to compare any appropriation,[61] and thereby fails adequately to take account of how private appropriation unjustly worsens the situation of others.

Cohen counters that there are various alternative scenarios worth considering: the dispossessed certainly would have been better off if they got to the land first and appropriated it for themselves; the dispossessed might also have been better off if title was acquired by a more able appropriator, whose resource-extraction efforts would have yielded greater benefits than the person who actually got first dibs; furthermore, the dispossessed would have been better off prior to others' appropriation insofar as the new regime of private property means they are now under the command of new owners, for whom they must work.[62]

It is curious, Cohen contends, that Nozick disallows taxes to fund public health care, deeming them a paternalistic violation of people's property rights, yet allows A to appropriate against B's will, with the paternalistic rationale that B in fact benefits from the transaction. Nozick claims to be motivated by a desire to protect freedom, but what he really means is a very narrow understanding of freedom: 'the freedom of property owners to do as they wish with their property'.[63]

Joint ownership

Finally, Cohen points out that Nozick fails to consider the possibility that prior to any appropriation, rather than being 'unowned', the earth might have been held in common by means of 'joint ownership'. Indeed, other commentators have complained that, for all the talk of history, Nozick offers little 'in the way of a positive account' as to the processes by which individuals acquire entitlements to wealth.[64] Joint ownership entails that everyone must be consulted before anyone apportions a share, with the result that all parties are in a position to bargain over what kind of property arrangement will be adopted, a scenario which certainly would have meant most people would be better off than in Nozick's alternative.[65] In Cohen's engaging thought experiment of 'Able' and 'Infirm', the two inhabitants of a jointly owned society, the superior capacities of Able do not yield extra reward under self-ownership where there is also joint-ownership, given the necessity of bargaining over any distributive arrangement.[66]

However, Cohen came to realize that although capitalism means individuals are constantly subject to others' will, insofar as the propertyless 'lack real control over their lives',[67] joint ownership fails by this criterion too. Any system of collective ownership violates self-ownership, since it would mean individuals could find any of their proposed actions subject to the veto of others. The tendency of self-ownership to produce inequality can only be nullified by a rigid regime over external resources which rules out independent rights over oneself, an 'unacceptable sacrifice of autonomy' which the self-ownership principle disallows.[68] Ultimately, in the egalitarian picture, the tension between collective and individual renders self-ownership a problematic principle.

Communist Justice

Self-ownership and inequality

For all the power of Cohen's critique of Nozick, therefore, the upshot ultimately rendered the Marxist position problematic. After all, for Marx, capitalist production is exploitative because the owners of the means of production engage in theft of the worker's labour time to produce profit. Cohen contends that the idea of self-ownership is central to Marx's critique, since if the capitalist 'steals' from the worker, then the worker must be understood as the owner of the body and powers that produce the wealth that the capitalist unjustly appropriates.[69]

Thus it is not just that, in the hands of defenders of private property like Nozick (but also Locke with his view – indefensible, as Cohen argues – that labour is the source of all value), self-ownership is deployed to serve 'inegalitarian ends'.[70] Worse, it means that the communist alternative also cannot require workers to contribute to efforts at egalitarian distribution. Communism (and for that matter, the welfare state, which also requires that the able contribute to help the less able), is unjust by the criterion of the Marxist theory of exploitation. This is because distributive policy 'does to tax-paying workers exactly what, in the Marxist complaint, capitalists do to workers: it forcibly extracts product from them'.[71]

Thus Marx's first principle of justice regarding exploitation is at odds with his second, which animates the ideal social relations of communism, captured in the famous credo of 'from each according to his ability, to each according to his needs'.[72] Marx did not lay out in any detail how this principle was to be realized, but the ethic it presupposes is clear: wealth should be produced and shared in a collectivist project which ensures the needs of all are met through individual contributions, albeit socially organized, to the community. Accordingly, as Cohen reflected in an interview near the end of his life, it came to be thought by many of the Analytical Marxists that 'exploitation, while a very important concept, was essentially secondary, normatively speaking, to the concept of equality'.[73]

Communism as a jazz band

In his writings in the 1990s, Cohen affirms that Marx was able to evade the indissoluble tension between self-ownership and socialism with a theory of history in which a socialist future harnesses capitalist abundance to enable the satisfaction of all needs. In such a society, self-ownership need not be abolished because it ceases to be necessary. The 'elbows-up' posture of the exploited proletarian (like that of Nozick's aggrieved capitalist) becomes redundant in a society where wealth flows without limit.

On this picture, people's control of their powers seems easily to generate a communist order. Cohen submits that self-sacrifice and the suppression of individuality are not central to the utopian ideal, likening communism to a jazz band of self-directing individual musicians who nonetheless produce wonderful music together. The ideal society would be like a 'concert of mutually supporting self-fulfilments, in which no one takes the fulfilment of others as any kind of obligation'. Each is 'guided by his self-regarding goal, yet there is no inequality in the picture to exercise an egalitarian'.[74]

Thus, with scarcity abolished, there is no tension between self-ownership and the communist principle of distribution based on need. As Cohen put it in his inimitable pithy way: 'Since competition is necessary as long as it is possible, it follows that, as long as it is possible *not* to have communism, communism is impossible'.[75] If scarcity (and thus potentially, competition) persists, the communist principles of distribution are in tension with the Marxist critique of exploitation.

As we saw in the last chapter, however, Cohen came to conclude that this 'technological fix' was no longer plausible; human societies' environmental destruction renders scarcity inevitable.[76] The problem of distributing resources under conditions of scarcity requires a substantive, progressive solution and thus the radical Left must attend to principles of distributive justice, rather than supposing that in an ideal society such principles would be, because so easily realized, superfluous.

Need and labour

There was also the Marxist conviction of the inevitability of communism given certain views about the nature of the working class, another theme from chapter 2. In this case 'two claims to recompense, *need* and *entitlement through labour* are fused' because the exploited producers were deemed one and the same as those in need, be it of the benefits of the welfare state, or the fully egalitarian arrangements of communism. However, once the needy and the exploited producers cease to coincide, the revolutionary mission of the proletariat falls away.[77] This was the story in western capitalist societies in the late twentieth century, where the employed working class figures as a relatively privileged sector of society, something that the 'welfare bum' rhetoric of the political parties of the New Right was able to exploit. Claiming a commitment to fairness for working people, populist right-wing parties, movements and eventually governments (for example, Thatcher in the UK and Reagan in the US) called for reducing the distributive ambit of the welfare state.

Cohen illustrates the problem with what he terms the 'cleanly generated capitalist relationship'. If we suppose a society of initial equal capital endowment which permits everyone to appropriate according to their diverse talents, industry and frugality, it is inevitable that equality gives way to a capitalist stage where a class of labourers end up working for a class of owners. Such a society would be unequal, but, asks Cohen, on what basis could the Marxist, set on the injustice of exploitation, complain?[78] Stuck with their commitment to the theory of exploitation, Marxists get 'hoist by their own petard' when it comes to tackling the unequal consequences of self-ownership.

Thus, according to Cohen, Marxists must make the painful choice of giving up the 'traditional idea of exploitation' as premised on self-ownership, but in so doing they will be able to 'reach a deeper characterization of their own conception of justice' to advance the more important argument of distributive equality.[79] Systematic theorizing about justice was needed to fill the gap left by the Marxian concept of exploitation which, though it continued to motivate Cohen's political outlook, receded in his philosophical writings about justice.[80]

Left libertarianism

Cohen's conclusions meant that he parted company with left-libertarians, too (though it's been noted that he could not refute his paternity of this school).[81] Left-libertarians close to Cohen, such as Otsuka and fellow September Group member, Hillel Steiner, proposed to marry Lockean rights to life and liberty with an equal distribution of resources, rather than the 'first come, first served' scramble for acquisitions envisaged by Nozick.[82] Moreover, Steiner proposed that self-ownership was compatible with conscription in order to help others at risk of having their rights violated, so long as the conscripted are compensated.[83]

Cohen was attracted to their confidence in an alternative view that retains self-ownership without an unacceptable loss in freedom or equality. Nonetheless, he believed left-libertarianism to be unable to yield the 'equality of condition prized by socialists'.[84] Thus Cohen concluded that if Marxists are committed both to equality and autonomy, then they must reject self-ownership. Only then can equality be reconciled with 'a freedom more worthy of the name', that is, 'autonomy, the circumstance of genuine control over one's life'.[85]

Exploitation without Self-ownership

A place for liberty

Cohen concludes that the Marxist critique of exploitation must be abandoned insofar as it relies on the idea of self-ownership, with all its inegalitarian implications. True, he left open the possibility that exploitation could be theorized differently, centring on the fact that workers lack access to the means of production, and more fundamentally, that they must work for those who do have access and thus have their product forcibly extracted.[86] Capitalism is unjust because the effect of its 'unequal distribution of the means of production' is to 'force some to produce for others'.[87]

Beyond this idea of an 'unjust flow', however, Cohen did not elaborate on the justice of workers parting with their products to the capitalist. The abandonment of self-ownership made it difficult for Cohen to tackle the matter of the unfreedom of the worker in the production process itself.

Yet in his critique of Nozick, Cohen had in fact distinguished the concept of self-ownership from fundamental liberty-based ideals, insisting that one does not need self-ownership to reject slavery, or to value autonomy, or to refrain from treating people as means.[88] After all, Cohen's critique of Nozick demonstrates that libertarian self-ownership threatens the autonomy of the wage labourer and allows people to be used for others' ends. Contra Nozick, one should be obligated to forfeit title over property in order to allow others to reach a supply of water, or to provide a service to a needy person (one's mother, Cohen suggests, or a fellow citizen).[89] These finite, specified contributions to others' welfare do not constitute enslavement. If the Nozickian counters that nonetheless the obligated individual is deprived of self-ownership for those periods of time, Cohen can respond that Nozick himself requires individuals to labour for the state insofar as they must contribute to the maintenance of law-and-order services.

Moreover, although not exercised by Nozick, deontological left-liberals provided an account of why we should reject the consequentialist forfeiture of individual liberty for egalitarian ends. Ronald Dworkin and John Rawls, who were also writing at this time, were more comfortable with first principles that gave liberty priority, with such ideas as 'rights as trumps' in the case of Dworkin, or 'the priority of liberty' in the case of Rawls.[90] Such views can take a hard line on the inadmissibility of sacrificing body parts, for example, without subscribing to self-ownership.[91]

Several of Cohen's left-wing critics argued that the concept of exploitation is vital to the Marxist critique of capitalism and that it need not rely on the idea of self-ownership. John Roemer's work centred on the unjust distributive arrangements of private property relations.[92] Moreover, others noted that exploitation involved a violation of principles of contribution,[93] reciprocity[94] or, something akin to self-ownership without its problematic features, an 'ideal of equal individual sovereignty'.[95] According to Vrousalis, exploitation involves domination, the 'self-enriching instrumentalization of another's vulnerability'; it is a 'dividend of servitude' inherent in the relations of capitalism.[96] We can express the idea of liberation from exploitation and affirm the ideal of individual freedom without recourse to self-ownership. Moreover, the idea of self-ownership was not central to all libertarian theories, and arguably even Nozick's case for inviolable rights could be understood in terms of historical entitlement, rather than persons owning themselves (indeed Nozick did not actually talk about self-ownership per se).

As we saw in the last chapter, shortly after publishing his Marx book, Cohen argued that Marx's labour theory of value was not a suitable basis for the charge of exploitation against capitalism. The simple fact that capitalists control the means of production is where the 'theft' inherent in exploitative class relations resides; that is, Cohen contended, injustice is inherent in some controlling the means of production and having power over others.[97] A few years after, before he aired his disquiet about self-ownership, Cohen penned another essay in which he similarly argued that workers who take hazardous jobs are victims of the injustice of private ownership of the means of production.[98]

The place of alienation

Thus, it seems curious that Cohen was so exercised by self-ownership. Marx did not deploy the term, and indeed was at pains to affirm the social character of labour – the technology employed by the worker is a social product, and the worker labours in concert with others. Thus, far from lamenting the loss of self-ownership, Marx decries how exploitation leads to estrangement and alienation, not just from the worker's labouring process and the product of labour, but also in the worker's connections with others: 'the proposition that man's species nature is estranged from him means that one man is estranged from the other, as each of them is from man's essential nature'.[99]

Indeed, the idea of self-ownership, far from being an analytical tool to explain the character of exploitation, could be characterized as a manifestation of exploitation itself, where the worker's self-understanding is as a piece of property to be exchanged, in isolation from and at odds with other self-owners. Workers' capacity to labour is so distorted in the buying and selling of labour time that they understand their situation in bourgeois terms, as Locke equated property with personhood in his claim that 'every man has a property in his own person'.[100] Thus, far from a moral norm to be realized with the abolition of wage labour, the very idea of self-ownership is a species of alienation which should be overcome under communism.

Alienation is a key idea in Marx's critique of the exploitation of capitalism. For Marx, workers under capitalism find that labour, what should be a source of fulfilment, is so distorted by the oppressive conditions of capitalist production that workers feel estranged from their capacities, nature, fellow workers and the products that they help create. Cohen, however, for all his focus on self-ownership, labour and exploitation, says little about alienation in this discussion.

Cohen addressed the concept of alienation at length elsewhere. His unpublished papers include extensive lecture notes on alienation dated 1965, when Cohen was a young lecturer at University College London.[101] A quote from Marx's 1844 Manuscripts about alienation is the epigraph for Cohen's first publication, although the paper does not pursue the theme. However, in 1968 he published a nuanced and incisive essay on the different respects in which workers and capitalists are alienated.[102] The Marx book includes a few pages on alienation and provides an excellent exposition of the idea of commodity fetishism, a manifestation of people's alienated relationship to the products of human labour. Capitalist exchange makes a fetish of commodities, endowing them with mysterious and magical properties; these illusions about the artefacts of human creation can only be dispelled with the overthrow of capitalism. But Cohen's discussion there makes no reference to Marx's *Economic and Philosophic Manuscripts*, arguably the most important work of Marx on alienation.

In his exploration of proletarian unfreedom, Cohen alludes to the psychological reasons why workers might not pursue opportunities to escape their class position,[103] but such considerations play no real role in his argument. Moreover, Cohen never returned to the theme of alienation thereafter, preferring to address his socialist concerns within the context of familiar liberal normative ideas such as liberty and equality. In contrast, Cohen's 'no-bullshit' colleague, Jon Elster, in his highly influential 1985 book *Making Sense of Marx*, rejected the plausibility of historical materialism and instead made a case for the most important and enduring contributions of Marx to lie in the critique of capitalism in terms of alienation and exploitation, class struggle, politics and ideology.[104]

The fact that the concept of alienation plays a modest role in Cohen's thought after the 1970s is revealing. Perhaps he considered it too amorphous a notion, too Hegelian, too phenomenological, to be worthy of analytical elaboration. For all his disparagement of Althusser,[105] Cohen joins his company in seeming to reject, or at least overlook, ideas often attributed to the 'early' Marx, contrasted with the later, more 'scientific' Marx. Here Cohen's commitment to the analytical, the parsimonious approach to critique inspired by his Oxford education, seems a shortcoming, if it means he is deprived of a helpful tool to capture the crucial difference between the worker's relationship to the capitalist and the capitalist's relationship to the tax-collecting welfare state.

This point has been put well in another context, in Arthur Ripstein's commentary on the disbenefits of a rational choice approach to social theory. Marx's critique of the political economy of his day targeted its explanatory failures, but also its explanatory successes. That is, the accuracy of classical political economy's analysis 'reveals the failings of its object of study', where capitalist relations mean that our human activities are abstract and alienated. Under such conditions, we do approach our personhood as owners of property, but this is to generalize human nature from a 'domain of estrangement', to accept the limitations set by an unjust and oppressive set of social conditions, and to 'ignore the possibility of a better life'.[106]

Self-ownership and 'unselfing'

It is intriguing, therefore, that Cohen was in the grip of the idea of self-ownership, even if he eventually abandoned it. The concept suggests that there is something called a 'self', to which one stands in a relationship of possession. The idea of owning oneself thus looks like a weird vestige of the dualism of early modern thought, where there is a body on the one hand, a mind on the other, and where the human being's fundamental challenge is for one's mind to wrest control over oneself. But one just *is* oneself. Cohen disputed that self-ownership was anything more than a simple reflexive relation, not 'some deeply inner thing'. He contended that the concept did not suffer from incoherence or indeterminacy: 'the principle of self-ownership unambiguously confers' a right not to be forced 'to supply product or service to anyone'. The clarity of the concept is thus what renders it so problematic for those who endorse 'other-assisting' distributive policies.[107]

However, Cohen's confidence that the problems with self-ownership lie only in its implications for egalitarian institutions seems dissonant with the focus on relations of community in his later work. Jan Kandiyali proposes that Marx's critique of alienated labour should be understood as involving an ideal of mutual self-realization, where producing for others is key to personal fulfilment, a counter to the individualism inherent in self-ownership.[108] Here we could take the lead of Iris Murdoch, who countered the Oxford philosophical establishment led by Cohen's supervisor, Gilbert Ryle, in the 1960s. Murdoch argues that we eschew the philosophical obsession with a private entity, an alleged inner thing in the self.[109] The task of being a person is not to burrow within, but to orient oneself to the world outside, as Murdoch puts it, to 'direct attention' to others, to love.[110] Mary Midgley, Murdoch's Oxford contemporary and good friend, stressed that our need for each other is not a weakness, but a strength, 'it is our lifeline, our essential passport to the real world'.[111] Thus Murdoch's term, 'unselfing'[112] captures both a moral imperative and a way of expressing a more plausible philosophical anthropology, a nice counter to talk of 'self-ownership'.

Conclusion

Cohen's penetrating work on libertarianism accomplished a great deal. First, he provided a compelling argument for how libertarians give priority to property, not liberty, manifest in Nozick's case for allowing individuals to amass unlimited amounts of wealth, subject to extremely modest conditions. Second, he demonstrated the power of analytical tools for the radical Left to probe the faults in the argument of their political foes, as well as to reveal the problematic assumptions and claims of their own camp. And finally, Cohen made a pioneering contribution to Marxist scholarship in illuminating the tension between the critique of exploitation and the communist ideal, a tension that, if unresolved, could mean that the argument for a just distribution of wealth must be forfeited to liberal egalitarians.

Yet Cohen's preoccupation with self-ownership, however insightful, arguably hampered his Marxist philosophy. It is worth noting a methodological point here, picking up on the themes of the previous chapter, that is, the role of immanent critique for Cohen. The term means a critical inquiry that accepts the premises of its object, to show that the argument under scrutiny doesn't live up to its own criterion of success. Immanent critique can produce a particularly devastating refutation, but it can also limit the scope of inquiry. Cohen's commitment to take seriously politically challenging positions, which yielded such incisive work on libertarianism, therefore seems not to be without costs. The analysis of self-ownership ends up in some sense cowed by libertarianism, however much both were decisively rejected. In the next chapter we will consider the extent to which Cohen's encounter with more progressive liberal philosophies enabled him to make a case for the radical ideals of the socialist tradition.

4

Rescuing Justice from Rawls

Cohen's chief focus in contemporary political philosophy came to be a critical engagement with liberal egalitarianism. For Cohen, the most important arguments for egalitarian justice were coming from liberals such as John Rawls.[1] However, Cohen thought Rawls's doctrine was fraught with problems. Premised on the arbitrariness and injustice of inequality, Rawlsian justice nevertheless conceded that the productivity necessary to attend to the have-nots might require that the wealthy retain some measure of economic advantage. Cohen contended that the limited scope of liberal egalitarianism raised a larger question about the extent to which theories of justice should be construed as regulative policies tailored to real-world circumstances, or fundamental principles that transcended matters of fact.

Published in 2008, Cohen's masterful *Rescuing Justice and Equality* brought together in a revised and systematic form several writings on the political philosophy of John Rawls. What follows is an examination of the book's most important themes: the role of 'justificatory community' in egalitarianism and the critique of incentives; Cohen's pluralist approach to political philosophy, whereby justice is one value among many; the principle that justice should extend beyond the 'basic structure' of society; and that there are ultimate, 'fact-independent principles' in political philosophy. Cohen's proposals that justice pertains to personal relationships, not just institutions, and indeed that justice transcends empirical considerations, suggest another set of paradoxes. Such claims are radical in import, but they fly in the face of what many would take to be a canonical left-wing premiss: that political theory should be rooted in an understanding of material forces, productive capacity, political institutions and the opportunities available in a particular mode of production. This chapter will shed light on these paradoxes.

Cohen and Rawls could be said to share an 'egalitarian impulse', despite their differences on how it was best construed.[2] Indeed, it is often stated that there are claims in Rawls's writings that commit him to positions at no great distance from those Cohen favours, for all their apparent disagreement.[3] I will suggest, however, that it is doubtful that Cohen would have agreed that the differences between him and Rawls have little significance, and, moreover, that there are grounds for resisting such suggestions. Cohen took the view that we may need to settle for Rawlsian precepts in the imperfect institutions of justice within which we find ourselves, but this is a long way from the ideal of justice. This marked an important and decisive break with the terms of his liberal interlocutors.

A Theory of Justice

The thought experiment of the original position

Rawls's 1971 work *A Theory of Justice* is arguably the most important work in political philosophy of the past century. Cohen contended that the 'greatness' of Rawls lay in how he 'grasped his age in thought', and that Rawls's book ranked with Plato's *Republic* and Hobbes's *Leviathan* as the greatest books in western political philosophy.[4] It is often remarked that before Rawls, political philosophy was largely stagnant. Chapter 2 explored how Anglo-American political philosophy had lived in the shadow of positivist views that dominated philosophy after the Second World War and thus that the subject was enfeebled when Cohen arrived in Oxford in the 1960s. Although moral philosophy became a meta-discipline concerned with understanding everyday moral concepts, the intrinsically controversial nature of political prescriptions meant that such a metamorphosis was not available for political theory. Rawls changed all that with his systematic argument for an understanding of justice as requiring the amelioration of inequality.

Rawls invokes an engaging thought experiment to consider the requirements of justice: the idea of individuals reasoning in an 'original position'. Here all parties find themselves behind a 'veil of ignorance' where they do not know key features about themselves – their race, gender, social class or family background, even what their plans of life or personal values might be. Thus, just as classical political philosophers such as Hobbes, Locke or Rousseau reasoned about how best to order the affairs of their societies by reference to a pre-political agreement, Rawls rejuvenates the social contract tradition with his idea that justice would issue from a hypothetical decision procedure.

Rawls's thought experiment is fanciful since, as many critics point out, we could not be reasoning creatures if we were cut off from our personal background, traits and commitments. Nonetheless, Rawls bases his political prescriptions on claims of a quasi-empirical kind about human reasoning and motivation. Although individuals are capable of cooperation, we should work from the assumption that we are self-interested, and thus would reason about justice concerned about what would be our lot once the 'veil' is lifted. Here, too, Rawls has more in common, perhaps, with the classical liberal tradition of Hobbes[5] and Locke and their assumptions about human interests than he cares to admit, although Rawls ingeniously deploys self-interest to devise principles that commit us to aid our fellows.

Public justification and reflective equilibrium

For Rawls, if individuals deliberate about principles of justice without knowing who they are to be in the society they are designing, they would be concerned that society refrain from using political means to endorse one way of living over another. The parties to the original position would, however, commit to a set of institutions which guarantee basic liberties along with a distributive scheme. Thus, distributive justice is produced by means of procedural justice, which is designed to ensure that outcomes are just.[6]

Moreover, Rawls adduces other considerations on behalf of his political prescriptions. He maintains that we should think of society as a well-ordered system of social cooperation, and that citizens are free and equal persons with two moral powers, one, a capacity for a conception of the good, or what we think is of value in life, the other, a capacity for a sense of justice. The latter means that we are capable of understanding and honouring principles of fairness.

That capacity means that we can appreciate the pull of public justification, which signals the arbitrariness of some of us being more talented than others.[7] Rawls also ventures another, highly influential, consideration, that is, the idea of 'reflective equilibrium', where judgements about justice must meet the test of reasonableness or acceptability after due consideration of the alternatives.[8] That is, our philosophizing should not land us with far-fetched conclusions (such as Nozick's minimal state, perhaps) at odds with our careful weighing of what justice requires.

Rawls's two principles

The procedure of 'justice as fairness' results in two principles of justice.[9] The first, the priority of liberty principle, states that everyone should have equal basic rights and liberties, such as freedom of conscience and association, freedom of speech, democratic rights such as to vote or hold public office, and the assurances of the rule of law. The priority of liberty principle implies social welfare institutions insofar as it stresses the *'fair value' of political liberties*. Citizens should be formally but also substantively equal so that they may have equal opportunities to hold office or influence elections, no matter what their income.

This idea of genuine equality of opportunity is made explicit in the second most famous principle. It has two parts. The first stipulates that offices and positions are to be open to all on the basis of equality of opportunity, a concept which Rawls understands in a robust sense, not just lack of discrimination in the competition for positions, but also a levelling of the playing field by means of such things as public education. The second, and most significant part of the principle, is that inequalities are justified only if they are to the advantage of the worst-off in society. The latter, described as the 'difference principle', is premised on the claim that individuals are not entitled to more wealth in virtue of their talents. Indeed, even the ability to work hard or be thrifty are aspects of the 'natural lottery', contingent from a moral point of view and therefore not the basis for demanding greater rewards.[10] Inequality's only justification is the role it would play in ameliorating disadvantage, a position which suggests radical implications for the degree to which disparities of wealth would be tolerated.

Justice and Incentives

Permissible inequality

However, Rawls's approach to remedying disadvantage has limitations. Rawls contended that if it turned out that incentives are needed to induce the talented to produce extra resources to mitigate the position of the worst off, then they should be permitted.[11] Rawlsian justice was premised on the arbitrariness and injustice of inequality, and yet Rawls conceded that achieving sufficient productivity might require that the talented retain, to some extent, their economic advantage. Rawls states this almost in passing, as though there is no controversy at stake.[12]

Cohen zeroes in on this dimension of Rawlsian justice, arguing that it is in tension with the ideals of the difference principle.[13] He illustrates his concern by drawing on the political context in which he started thinking about these issues: the 1980s debate about the Thatcher Conservative government policy of cutting taxes for the wealthiest, from 60 to 40 per cent, which was justified as an incentive to boost productivity. 'We were ceaselessly told that movement contrary to that policy, in a socialist egalitarian direction, would be bad for badly off people by advocates of a regime that seems itself to have brought about the very effect against which its apologists insistently warned.'[14]

Highfliers and kidnappers

Cohen begins his volume's first chapter with a quote from a libertarian, not Nozick this time, but Jan Narveson, who mocked Rawls with a dialogue between 'Well-off' and 'Worst-off' where the permissibility of incentives is feebly defended by the wealthy interlocutor.[15] That talented people might claim they cannot be productive without greater income, Cohen says, is akin to the behaviour of the person who kidnaps a child and then faults reluctance to pay the ransom as betraying a lack of regard for the child's fate. What makes the kidnapper's posture 'morally vile' is that the fact to which the kidnapper appeals – that you will only get your child back if you pay – is one that the kidnapper deliberately causes to be true.[16] The complaint of the pioneering egalitarian thinker, R.H. Tawney, about 'the dictatorship of the capitalist' seems apposite here.[17]

The moral defects in these cases, Cohen says, are evident when uttered in the first person by kidnappers to distressed parents, or 'highfliers' who try to justify the retention of their greater wealth to those who are made worse off. Cohen contended that any policy which reduces the funds available to ameliorate disadvantage could not be justified to those who would bear the brunt of that reduction. Such an 'interpersonal test' reveals how a self-serving choice would appear to a less advantaged person.[18] The 'I-thou' character of such an exchange helps one understand and prevent situations where one might be tempted to shirk one's moral responsibilities.[19] Cohen's idea of mutual justification has similarities to the ideas of other liberal thinkers who propose that what we 'owe to each other', a 'second-person standpoint', or the idea of 'reasonable demands' figure as a measure of justice.[20]

Cohen elaborates this point further with his idea of a 'strict' versus 'lax' interpretation of the difference principle: on the former, inequalities are necessary apart from people's chosen intentions, but on the latter, 'intention-relative necessities' dictate inequality. In other words, it comes down to 'can't or won't'.[21] For Cohen, what made Rawls's thought experiment so innovative, to arrive at a radical distributive principle via self-interested reasoning behind a veil of ignorance, ends up setting meagre distributive terms for market actors after the veil is lifted. Aware of their talents and prospects, self-interested market actors can now press for diminished egalitarian policies. Rawls's citizens profess a principle of justice that they then cannot summon the will to practise, made legitimate by the concession to incentives, but at odds with the principle of public justification and public reason foundational to Rawls's theory. As Cohen complains, 'the flesh may be weak, but one should not make a principle of that'.[22]

Mutual justification

Cohen deploys immanent critique, the strategy which we encountered in his argument with Nozick, to contend that Rawls's conception of justice fails by Rawls's own lights, which depends on the idea of 'justificatory community' to override the logic of the market. Theories of justice that permit constraining egalitarian distribution for reasons of psychological motivation betray their own principles. If all members of the community are committed to the principle of equality, the talented among them cannot turn around and demand higher pay. To do so is to put them, as Cohen says, 'outside the community'.

Cohen's invocation of community here is not, he says wittily, 'some soggy mega-*Gemeinschaftlichkeit*'[23] which assumes a 'standing disposition of warm mutual identification', but rather a way of elaborating Rawls's own views about the duties of citizens to engage with reciprocity and fairness.[24] It is a rigorous test of mutual justification, where we consider how our self-regarding actions might appear to others. Thus, if it happens that we arrive at equal distribution, for example due to a Protestant creed that dictates asceticism on the part of the productive, this would be a case of a society that is accidentally, rather than constitutively, just.[25] Indeed, Cohen comes to the conclusion that justice is to be 'rescued', not just from incentives and the basic structure, but from the difference principle itself, since the permissibility of inequality seems essentially at odds with Rawls's 'maximin' aim of doing the best possible for the worst off.[26]

Rawls explicitly disavows the word 'community' to describe a democratic society, given the fact of 'reasonable pluralism' where our varied interests render such unity of purpose impossible. Instead, parties to the principles of justice find agreement through an 'overlapping consensus', derived from their diverse positions.[27] However, Rawls's ideas of the well-ordered society as a fair system of cooperation, involving public justification, reciprocity, indeed civic friendship, fraternity and a concern for the dignity of others, could be argued to play a role similar to that of Cohen's idea of justificatory community. Indeed, it has been suggested that, in this light, solidarity might be added to the primary goods that we seek to afford individuals when reasoning about justice behind the veil of ignorance.[28]

Cohen's value pluralism

For Cohen, there are many worthy distinctive political values in a society, be they community, efficiency, freedom, justice or equality. He accordingly commends a pluralist approach to the complexity of moral and political discourse, where the variety of values are not reducible to each other and are often in conflict. One value takes precedence in one context, another value in another, depending on the factors at stake, and sometimes we confront a single situation where more than one value has weight. This 'metapolitical' pluralist view about concepts follows from Cohen's insistence on a demanding understanding of what the principle of justice requires. Facts about implementation or rival considerations may necessitate legitimate trade-offs when it comes to putting the principle into practice.[29]

Our understanding of human behaviour, for example, may give us pragmatic grounds for departing from full equality, perhaps allowing for incentives.[30] Cohen insists, however, that such considerations should have no part in the principle itself; Rawls misidentifies the question of justice as a matter of how to adapt our principles to regulate our affairs.[31] After all, Cohen argues, soundly based rules for social living 'will reflect both values other than justice and practical constraints that restrict the extent to which justice can be applied'.[32] Perhaps, as Kyle Johannsen suggests, we can even come up with a decision procedure with which to make fair judgements about when such compromises are merited.[33]

Cohen nonetheless insists that we remain aware of what's at stake when 'justice is unattainable, and we do well to settle for something else'.[34] These are occasions of 'justifiable injustice', where other considerations do, and should, take priority and justice cannot be fully realized.[35] Here we can see Cohen's 'no bullshit' approach at work. Analytical clarity necessitates that we distinguish when our principles must be compromised given pressing rival considerations, rather than glossing over the difficulty and dubbing those considerations principles of justice. Cohen contends that the incentives argument not only licenses an insufficiently egalitarian position, but also fails to appreciate what's at stake: reneging on the project of a theory of justice. Ultimately Rawls proffers, not principles of justice, but mere 'rules of regulation'.[36] It may be sensible, Cohen says, in order to make the worse off better off, 'to bribe the better-off people unconsciousably to produce the much needed bigger pie', but it is unfair.[37]

The radical implications of Rawls's theory of justice

It should be emphasized that despite the concession to incentives, Rawls envisaged that his principles of justice would yield a society significantly more equal than the welfare state capitalism of his day. For all Cohen's criticism, *A Theory of Justice* had clear progressive distributive purposes, and this is apparent not just in the difference principle. Martin O'Neill contends that the fair equality of opportunity principle is 'hardly a minimalist commitment', amounting to 'nothing less than the idea of the abolition of social class, at least when seen as a feature that structures life chances from one generation to the next'.[38] Moreover, even freedom is given a progressive cast in *A Theory of Justice*, insofar as Rawls is concerned that citizens enjoy the genuine 'worth' or 'fair value' of equal political liberties.[39]

The radical impact of these principles was emphasized in Rawls's lectures in the 1980s, which were revised and published in 2001 as *Justice as Fairness: A Restatement*. In that work, Rawls was at pains to emphasize that the 'capitalist welfare state' failed to realize his principles of justice.[40] Moreover, Rawls took the view that both liberal democratic socialism and what he called a 'property-owning democracy' were candidates for realizing his principles of justice. Articulating this as the effort to find an 'alternative to capitalism',[41] Rawls was picking up on the claim in his political philosophy lectures that Marx's idea of 'freely associated producers' involves a 'democratic economic plan'.[42]

Indeed, one commentator refers to Rawls as a 'reticent socialist' whose principles ultimately amounted to a doctrine of 'liberal socialism'. Rawls demurred from saying as much, it is argued, for fear the socialist label would prove divisive, taking his commended 'overlapping consensus' approach to heart.[43] Such considerations indicate that Cohen and Rawls may not have been that far apart when it comes to the impact of their views on distributive justice, even if Rawls's incentives argument was anathema to Cohen's socialist principles.

Political liberalism

Cohen does not say much about the ideas in Rawls's later work, *Political Liberalism*.[44] Yet arguably, in one sense at least, this book was even more vulnerable to Cohen's radical critique. Political liberalism is presented as a distinctive constitutional doctrine, reflecting Rawls's increased preoccupation with procedural issues and the scope of government policy when it comes to influencing how people should live. Rawls contends that 'the basic institutions and public policies of justice' should be understood as 'neutral with respect to comprehensive doctrines and their associated conceptions of the good'.[45] Rawls's 'neutrality of aim',[46] dubbed by Joseph Raz an 'epistemic withdrawal from the fray',[47] dictates that the scope of the political be constrained by formal procedures to keep government's reach in check. The decision process of the original position from *A Theory of Justice* is thus amplified with an emphasis on the tenets of public reason and the need to exclude considerations about the good life.

Rawls's proceduralist ethic so dominated this later work that there was little mention of the remedy of economic disadvantage, a development which attracted much critical comment.[48] Cohen might have complained about the short shrift given questions of distributive justice here. Furthermore, he could have taken the view that the concern for legal impartiality and proper procedures should not be allowed to have imperialistic designs on all political questions, so that the community forfeits its responsibility to foster equal human wellbeing.[49] After all, as we will see in the next chapter, Cohen's preferred egalitarian metric involves considerations about living well. Nonetheless, given Cohen's meticulous approach in an already long (430 pages) book, if he discerned such issues, he doubtless decided that they would have to be postponed for another day, or more likely, another philosopher.

Another later work by Rawls is his book, *The Law of Peoples*, which claims that rich countries have only limited duties to worse-off countries. Rawls's position generated considerable controversy and one might have expected that Cohen the radical egalitarian would have targeted Rawls on this issue too.[50] However, Cohen was candid about his philosophical approach involving choices about what to focus on and what to leave to other philosophers to consider. Global justice was a striking example of the latter. Although in an interview Cohen declared himself a 'knee-jerk cosmopolitan', adamant that the state is 'unsuited to be what determines the boundaries of justice', he did not tackle such questions in his philosophical writings.[51] Again Cohen's painstaking approach to philosophical argument meant that there were some questions he felt he must leave aside even if he had strong views about them.

Justice and the Basic Structure

The focus on institutions

Cohen's argument about incentives and principles led to another area of disagreement with Rawls. For Cohen, principles of justice entailed a broader scope of applicability than that envisaged by *A*

Theory of Justice. The concession to incentives reflected what Rawls considered the appropriate subject for justice, the 'basic structure' – public institutions governed by law. Self-seeking behaviour such as the pursuit of financial incentives, therefore, was allowed so long as such behaviour wasn't unlawful. Rawls holds that the basic structure is the appropriate locus for justice for two reasons: first, it issues from the decision procedure of justice as fairness; and second, because its effects are 'so profound and present from the start'.[52] Cohen professes that the latter rationale is especially questionable, given the profundity of many factors that do not issue from state institutions that nonetheless can have unjust effects.

Rawls's argument had attracted a powerful feminist complaint that his argument hardly considers the matter of the justice of the family. Rawls accordingly added gender to the list of characteristics hidden in the original position. He also came to include 'the monogamous family' in the basic structure, acknowledging its role in socializing children in the principles of justice (although he stressed that such principles do not apply to 'the internal life of the family' beyond the dictates of family law).[53] However, such amendments seemed like an afterthought, ripe for criticism from acute sexual egalitarians like Susan Moller Okin, who noted his assumption that 'heads of families' would be the parties to the original position, as though no questions of justice, power and inequality pertained to the intimate domain of reproduction, care and domestic labour.[54] For Okin, Rawls's theory was nonetheless full of feminist potential, particularly the idea of designing a society from behind a veil of ignorance with an eye to the position of the worst off.

Cohen claimed, however, that a fully egalitarian resolution wasn't available to Rawls, for whom the divide between public and private was inviolable, and personal behaviour beyond the purview of justice. Economists evocatively put this idea in terms of the citizen having a split personality, acting selfishly in the marketplace and altruistically at the ballot box.[55]

Cohen avers, however, that people should not 'shun' justice in their daily lives; the exclusion of the activities of incentive-takers or tyrannical spouses from the domain of justice is arbitrary and indefensible.[56] Institutional design should be supplemented by 'some self-restraint in everyday life', so that, for example, people will forgo the opportunities for self-enrichment that law cannot fully eliminate. The state needs help from its citizenry to fully realize its egalitarian ideals. Cohen's critique of incentives thus generates the view that justice requires individuals to devote themselves to the remedy of inequality in their personal choices more generally, rather than leaving the pursuit of egalitarian distributive principles solely to state institutions.[57]

Justice outside the state, though still economic

Cohen was inspired by the famous feminist slogan, 'the personal is political', coined to illuminate the unjust power relations, and particularly the oppression of women, within the intimate domain. Such injustice was also in need of resolution by reference to political principles of justice, equality and freedom. Cohen believed these ideas are instructive for socialist equality too, which needs more than public institutions to achieve its goals. Rawls, who vacillated on the matter of whether the family was a subject of justice, admits that coercion need not attend an institution of justice, thus making it possible to consider a range of decisions, activities and behaviours as relevant for the pursuit of equality.[58]

Indeed, Cohen finds the form of the feminist critique instructive precisely because it finds that choices not regulated by the law fall within the primary purview of justice,[59] or as he puts it, the: 'personal choices to which the writ of law is indifferent are fateful for social justice'.[60] Examples of just personal choices include, not only, as we have seen, highfliers forbearing from demanding high salaries or low taxes,[61] but also talented people pursuing socially useful occupations,[62] or affluent parents forswearing private schooling for their children.[63] Indeed, Cohen proposed that a commitment to egalitarianism should mean, if one is well off, drawing on one's income to help those in need. As Cohen argues, 'how can one deny, without ado, that one is obligated to forgo the benefits one enjoys as a result of what one regards as injustice, when one can forgo them in a fashion that benefits sufferers of that injustice?'[64] Just as Peter Singer called upon the duty of a passer-by to save a drowning child,[65] Cohen declares that many of us have the opportunity to supplement state policy by means of our own efforts.

It is worth noting that Cohen's concern for the persistence of injustice outside of state institutions remained focused on economic matters. He did not delve into what's been called the 'politics of difference'[66] in any sustained way in his philosophical writings. For all his admiration for Okin's feminist intervention, Cohen did not consider gender, race or ethnicity in his analysis of inequality or disadvantage.[67] It was not that Cohen did not find these issues worth considering – as related in chapter 1, he supported causes like anti-racism and feminism all his life. Yet, despite his increasing distance from Marx's historical materialism, Cohen's conception of justice remained resolutely materialist. Perhaps it was a question of strategy; given that much of the writing on issues of race and gender was at the time highly influenced by poststructuralism, Cohen might have deemed it prudent to avoid what could have turned out to be a harsh analytical interrogation of his fellow progressives. Moreover, as we noted earlier, Cohen took the view that there must be a division of labour among philosophers. Better to do justice, as it were, to his own patch and live up to his disciplined standards of inquiry than to attempt to address a myriad of issues, however relevant, beyond.

Responses to Cohen's basic structure objection

The 'basic structure objection', as it came to be known, prompted many philosophers to come to Rawls's defence, insisting that justice is uniquely the property of institutions that have the force of law. These thinkers counter that Cohen misconstrues Rawls's purpose, since justice as fairness refers not just to matters of regulation but also the way in which we should arrive at mutually acceptable regulative principles consistent with our conceptions of justice. According to Samuel Scheffler, the focus on the basic structure, and its operational principles of reciprocity, cooperation and public justification, would not result in the accommodation of the untrammelled pursuit of selfish interests or a paltry measure of egalitarian distribution.[68] Cohen's friend Thomas Scanlon also defends the focus on the basic structure, arguing that a theory which concerns institutions does an enormous service for the understanding and realization of justice, even if it is not an understanding of justice Cohen shares with Rawls.[69]

Cohen's former graduate student, Seana Shiffrin, though inspired by Cohen's critique of Rawls, proposes that voluntary behaviour be distinguished from compliance with coercive institutions by considering the justification for Rawlsian principles. As she puts it, 'the principles governing the Basic Structure may not directly apply to individuals and vice versa, but they may nonetheless exert mutual influence on one another'.[70] Indeed, perhaps we can, following Ian Carter, distinguish the duties of individuals from those of political institutions.[71] Cohen's former doctoral student, Serena Olsaretti, also suggested that Rawls's idea of a basic structure is compatible with expecting individuals to reinforce its principles through their personal choices.[72] In other words, there might be a Rawlsian 'social ethos', to borrow a term which, as we shall see, is central to Cohen's critique.[73]

Jonathan Quong argues that, rather than a pristine ideal separate from other values, justice is best understood as a complex value, possessing a variety of features that reflect the different considerations at stake.[74] Pablo Gilabert makes a similar argument, contending that rather than a value that might lose out to rival values, justice should be understood as supremely important, but involving a plurality of considerations, all of which must be taken into account in deciding what justice commands.[75] Others sought to resolve the divide between Cohen and Rawls by proposing that although the two thinkers are at odds over the concept and conception of justice, what's most important is that they converge over the more practical matter of regulative principles.[76]

The burdens of personal responsibility

In thinking about our ethical duties, as citizens and as persons, we often insist that we should 'think global, act local', emphasizing the ways in which individuals should step up and alter their behaviour to effect social change, for example, in matters of racism or climate change. How exactly we are to act on that principle is hard to specify, and it is probably especially difficult when it comes to elaborating individuals' personal responsibility to facilitate a just distribution of wealth. Paying our taxes and acting on our democratic rights to support progressive political parties are relatively straightforward matters. Less obvious, however, is how to figure out and act on the responsibility to further justice outside the scope of what is legally required.[77]

Thus, it is alleged that principles of justice are above all action-guiding and so must satisfy a publicity requirement which is enabled by restricting justice to the basic structure. Applied to the economic context, Cohen's alternative understanding of justice, Andrew Williams contends, is too complex and confusing and thus fails to enable citizens to follow its dictates. Moreover, unjust results would ensue, since the take-up of citizens would vary, some doing more than their share, others doing less.[78]

An effective rebuttal is made by Cohen's former graduate student, Paula Casal, who observes that Cohen's discussion of gender in the context of Rawls contrasts with Cohen's inattention to the sexist assumptions of Marxian historical materialism and its focus on the productive activity of largely male workers.[79] She applauds Cohen's feminist awakening in his philosophical writings as evidenced by his articulation of the basic structure objection and sides with Cohen against Williams. Williams's publicity requirement, Casal contends, is fatal also for gender justice; such a preoccupation, what she calls 'checkability', is unwarranted.[80] Jobs are unequally burdensome and time-consuming, and people unequally able and resilient. It is impossible to determine whether all individuals are meeting the demands of egalitarianism and doing their share on behalf of the good of all. But that is not a reason to abandon the idea of a personal obligation to do one's share as best as one can.

Highfliers and husbands

To return to the gender case, sometimes it is hard to detect when husbands are shirking domestic responsibilities; indeed, relations of intimacy in families are likely to obscure principles of fairness. However, it seems irrelevant to the demands of domestic justice that it be public whether others are living up to feminist norms: 'gender inequality is unjust, and the fact that it cannot be made to disappear with simple, clear, easily checkable rules does not make it less so'. Gender inequality in one household can hardly be defended by reference to the fact that we do not know whether it may be found in other households too.[81] This point can be evoked with the image of a police officer banging on the doors of family homes to determine whether selfish and lazy husbands dwell within; certainly, such action violates important norms of freedom and privacy. But the fact that we cannot legitimately use the resources of the coercive state to check on slothful partners does not render an unequal division of domestic labour any more just.

In the case of the workplace, Rawls would be right to think that laws might be more effective in coordinating people's actions. But this doesn't rule out supplementary, self-directed measures that seek to guide workplace and market behaviour. We may need to settle for Rawlsian regulation in the imperfect institutions of justice within which we find ourselves, but as Cohen stresses, that is a long way from the ideal of justice itself.[82] This becomes especially evident in two further themes to which we now turn: the idea of a social ethos and the relationship between facts and norms.

Social Justice and Social Ethos

The socialist camping trip

Cohen appreciates the difficulty of individuals working out how to contribute to the promotion of justice outside of the strictures of explicit, mandatory rules. An ideal socialist community, he contends, should find ways to promote voluntary egalitarian behaviour; a fully just society thus needs 'a social ethos which inspires uncoerced equality-supporting choice'.[83] In the absence of such an ethos, it would be unfair to blame and shame individuals who pursue legally permitted, self-oriented goals. We might hope that people 'choose against the grain of nurture, habit, social pressure and self-interest' but it is unreasonable to expect them to do so.[84]

Cohen's social ethos is captured in his example of a camping trip in one of his final works, *Why Not Socialism?*, where all participants pool their resources, be it equipment, skill or knowhow, in order to enjoy their time together.[85] In this context, 'share and share alike' is the operative principle: the person who forgot to bring a necessary tool is given a helping hand, and the person who knows the best fishing spot is happy to share that knowledge with others. In response to critics who contend that a camping trip involving a small group of friends is a poor model for large-scale social organization, Cohen adduces real-life cases in times of crisis where an ethos was initiated by the state but pervaded civil society, for example, during the Second World War when the British stepped up and made personal sacrifices to do their part to help fight the Nazis.[86]

It might be objected that British behaviour during the Blitz is, like the camping trip, an exceptional situation. However, it is worth considering how classical liberal thinkers such as Hobbes and Hume, for different reasons, supposed that states of war or extreme scarcity would fail to provide the bare minimum 'circumstances of justice', leaving injustice to run rampant. The fact that a kind of 'super-justice' obtained in such situations gives one hope that under the right conditions we could be motivated by an extra-legal ethos in peacetime too. Moreover, in fact, public spiritedness continued after the war in Britain, in an 'ethos of reconstruction' a sense of a 'common project, that restrained desire for personal gain'.[87]

Doing your bit

Cohen also adopts the useful vocabulary of 'moral pioneers' who subscribe to a progressive social ethos and in so doing help shape the behaviour of others. Husbands who in the early days of feminism took on their share of domestic labour without the strictures of law or even convention to prod them are one example. These were individuals who not only lived by but also initiated an ethos which raised the bar of social justice. Another example, Cohen says, is the 'rise in ecological consciousness' where 'at first only people who appear to be freaky' take on a personal obligation to reuse and recycle, but their example becomes a catalyst for wider social change.[88]

Efforts to 'do your bit' among patriotic Britons were distinctive, too, for their voluntary character, which Cohen claims, is an integral part of the ethos in action.[89] The ethos would have failed if it needed to be coercively applied. Individuals should show initiative to fill the gaps left by institutions, and relations of community cannot be achieved if people act only out of fear of punishment rather than genuine feelings of fellowship.

Moreover, the application of the ethos requires discretion in light of the particular circumstances of the agent: 'it is sometimes right not to force people to do what they are obliged, as a matter of justice, freely to choose to do'.[90] This is because people should be given scope to exercise a 'personal prerogative', not in order to shirk their responsibility to contribute as we might suspect the incentive-seeking market actor is wont to do, but because people are best placed to know the 'total situation' of their lives. As Cohen puts it, 'one person's easy bit is another person's hard bit and figuring out what's hard for whom is an unmanageable task'.[91]

The value of community

The ethos of a genuine egalitarian community would therefore have a 'live and let live' component which accepts diversity in contributions given people's various circumstances, just as Marx proclaimed with the slogan 'from each according to his ability, to each according to his need'.[92] Though institutions might be envisaged that would reinforce the social ethos, the social ethos can be sensitive to variations in people's lives in ways that coercive law cannot.[93] Thus a social ethos 'encourages citizens to internalize and act upon a sense of justice' rather than calling upon coercive state power to distinguish between worthy and unworthy recipients of the community's aid.⁹⁴ Not only does an approach where people 'unreflectively live by an egalitarian ethos'⁹⁵ facilitate the equal distribution of society's resources, it might also be said to equalize what really matters, human wellbeing, by taking stock of diverse needs, interests and our shared conviction that we should accord each other autonomous decision-making in a spirit of fellowship and goodwill.⁹⁶

Cohen's conception of ethos is thus perhaps an example of precisely that 'soggy *Gemeinschaftlichkeit*' which he put aside in his argument against incentives. These communitarian elements, as we will discuss in the next chapter, may turn out to be in tension with some of Cohen's other commitments about justice. For now, it should be noted that Cohen's ambitious ethos of fellow feeling and connection prompts him to describe socialism as: 'collective property and planned mutual giving', where 'community and justice' are extended 'to the whole of our economic life'.⁹⁷

Debating the ethos

Cohen's proposal that personal choices be guided by a social ethos that furthers social justice prompted considerable debate. Cohen's Analytical Marxist colleague Joshua Cohen argues that to 'take people as they are' need not mean conceding to the greediest of impulses. Rawls may have expected his prescribed system would ward off excessive self-seeking, not by tackling people's motivations directly, but by a progressive policy agenda that would effect a change in behaviour.⁹⁸ Indeed, Joshua Cohen proffers that institutional changes, such as more consensus-based decision-making or changes to labour market institutions, could have considerable potential to promote more egalitarian distributions, particularly if we are prepared to countenance some measure of self-regarding behaviour.⁹⁹

Cohen's former graduate student Jonathan Wolff defended the idea of a social ethos, defining it as a social group's 'underlying values, principles and practices' which are internalized to encourage behaviour that furthers the group's goals. For Wolff, these values are not merely instrumental: there is 'more to a society of equals than a just scheme of distribution of material goods'. Some goods are non-material and 'depend on the attitude people have toward each other'.[100] Wolff joined other philosophers, such as Elizabeth Anderson, in elaborating a 'respect egalitarianism' that centred on these issues of social standing. Indeed, for some 'respect egalitarians', distributive justice was a mere means to the more fundamental goal of relational equality.[101] We will return to these ideas in the next chapter.

Like Wolff, Cohen finds a social ethos is not just instrumentally valuable for securing egalitarian justice; it also has a substantive role as a constituent of community, social bonds and fellowship. Markets are to be abandoned because they breed injustice – but also because they tend against the value of community. Cohen is particularly critical of the attitudes of 'greed and fear' that he contends are the deliverance of a market ethos of self-interested behaviour.[102] It matters to Cohen what are the motivations and attitudes of members of the egalitarian community. As Nicholas Vrousalis puts it, justice judges distribution; but community judges motivation.[103]

Making the Machinery Run

The role of solidarity

Solidaristic relations are not an alternative to legal institutions but, for Cohen, play a crucial role in maintaining these institutions in order that they may fully achieve their social justice goals. Nonetheless, relations of solidarity, even if encapsulated in a social ethos, might seem obscure for the purposes of giving guidance to individuals as to how to plan their lives and act according to the norms of egalitarian justice. This is especially so given that, as noted above, Cohen concedes the particularistic character of the social ethos's application, whereby individuals make reasonable judgements in their own cases about where their duties lie (allowing for such considerations as 'Max has a bad back' or 'Sally has a difficult child').[104]

A typical challenge to the socialist ideal is that human beings will not have the motivation required, but as we saw, Cohen thought such challenges could be overcome. The avarice instilled and fostered by market society is not essential to human nature; people can live by an ideal of social unity required for the full realization of an egalitarian community. The Left economist and fellow Analytical Marxist John Roemer discusses Cohen's ideal and provides heartening anecdotal evidence that, in the Soviet Union, doctors earned less than steel workers and spent more time on their education, yet there was no doctor shortage.[105]

Cohen concluded, therefore, that the big difficulty facing socialism is figuring out 'how to design the machinery to make it run'. It is a 'design problem' – the lack of 'a suitable organizational technology'.[106] Human societies came up with the ingenious though fatally flawed idea of the market to organize our productive activities; similarly, economists should invent 'clever ways of harnessing and organizing our capacity for generosity to others'. It is possible for us to inculcate a social ethos imbued by a 'reciprocating attitude' or 'general social friendship' – the real challenge remains how to ensure the social ethos can be harnessed to organize a functional fully egalitarian society.[107]

Roemer argued that Cohen was right to identify the need for a robust social ethos, though he countered that market mechanisms, in their capacity to coordinate economic decisions, can function in a socialist community without engendering negative attitudes.[108] Even if people are no longer concerned with getting rich or ensuring survival, 'most of us want to feel useful and respected by our co-workers and seek to develop our capacities and fulfil our potential, to get out of the house and feel part of society'.[109] Roemer puts it to Cohen that non-material incentives to become trained and to innovate would persist and would be important, valuable features of society.

Self-interest and altruism

Cohen's ethos of community should not be understood to mean that individuals' interests would be indistinguishable from the interests of others. In an earlier essay, Cohen scorned the view of the Bolshevik jurist Evgeny Pashukanis that under communism the individual 'submerges his ego in the collective and finds the greatest satisfaction and meaning of life in this act', that individuals' concerns are supplanted with those of the whole.[110] For Pashukanis, the disappearance of class conflict and bourgeois egoism with the overthrow of capitalism would be such that selfishness would disappear altogether; there would no longer be social conditions that necessitate mediation by law and government.

Cohen proposes instead that we understand how we should check and regulate, to a reasonable degree, our self-regarding interests to consider the interests of others. Pashukanis, he argued, showed 'an infantile unwillingness to countenance a measure of self-denial as a way of dealing with the inevitable difficulties of social existence'.[111] Cohen here seems to agree with Marx's remark that communism would not be 'the love-imbued opposite of selfishness';[112] people's discrete interests and concerns do not disappear with the full realization of socialism.

The idea that socialism need not require the exclusion of self-directed interests can draw on the influential moral philosophy of Bernard Williams, Cohen's colleague at All Souls. Williams maintains that altruism be construed, not as 'a strenuous and unsolicited benevolent interference' but as a general disposition to regard others' interests as having a claim such that one's own projects may be limited.[113] Self-regarding behaviour is compatible with, indeed a precondition for, fellow feeling. Altruistic behaviour would be impossible in a society where all define their interests to be to further those of others – there would be no one who would confess to having self-regarding interests that others could try to fulfil as their own. Thomas Nagel argues in his essay on altruism that 'altruistic reasons are parasitic upon self-interested ones'. Taking account of others' circumstances is facilitated by our realization that these are 'circumstances which those others already have reason to consider from a self-interested point of view'.[114] Successful altruistic acts result when the altruist empathetically imagines what they would value were they the person for whom they are acting.

For Cohen, a socialist society of equals requires a richer understanding of the moral capacities of the individual than simplistic ideas of self-aggrandisement or self-sacrifice. The interests of the individual and the community should coincide not because individuals want whatever the community wants, but because individuals see that by joining forces with the community, they will better achieve their own wants, whatever they may be (although of course Cohen the socialist also takes the view that among our wants are likely to be living in community and the flourishing of others). As Marx and Engels put it, 'the free development of each is the condition for the free development of all'.[115]

Socialism and justice

Law and justice need not be tethered to private property and the sentiments of avarice that attend it, but the 'happy harmony' of individuals' interests would not be so thorough-going that there would no longer be disagreement and dispute. Hume invoked the 'circumstances of justice', where the need for justice arises because resources are not so abundant that anyone can have an infinite supply of whatever they want, but also because individuals possess the virtue of justice. For Hume, moderate scarcity and limited generosity together dictate the institutions of justice; if we were all a 'Second-self to another' and made 'no division betwixt our interests' there would be no need of justice.[116] If, as Cohen says, according to the social ethos, individuals endeavour to engage in 'voluntarily just behaviour' that supplements the legal institutions of a fully egalitarian society, they would nonetheless look to those institutions for guidance.

Cohen's discussion of Pashukanis was sparked by a 1980s debate about the plausibility of socialist justice, often considered with reference to the theories and practice of Soviet law. It might seem obvious that ideas of justice underlie the socialist ideal of a society where human needs are met under non-alienated conditions of fellowship and community. But as we have seen in chapter 2, with the conviction that 'history is on our side', Marxists were traditionally resistant to grounding communism in distinctively moral arguments, a perspective Cohen was at pains to reject. Cohen's salutary intervention made it possible to argue that a socialist approach to law was possible, and that Marxian ideas could be a fruitful source for legal theory.[117]

Socialist basics and market socialism

Cohen's position on the ideals of socialist community emerged in a 1990s public debate about a perceived move to the right on the part of the British Labour Party.[118] His paper 'Back to Socialist Basics' was published in *Equality*, a collection of responses to the policy documents of the UK Commission for Social Justice. Cohen argued that we need 'fundamental socialist values which point to a form of society a hundred miles from the horizon of present possibility', both 'to defend every half-mile of territory gained' and 'to mount an attempt to regain each bit that has been lost'. It is important, therefore, 'to think the values afresh in a spirit of loyalty to them' to discern 'what new modes of advocacy of them are possible'.[119]

In 'Forward to Basics', Cohen's Oxford colleague Bernard Williams countered that calling for a recovery of the traditional values of the Left amounted to a 'trip down Memory Lane' instead of a 'firmly unsentimental picture of what made people act'. It is an irony, Williams said, that 'the beliefs of Marxists as opposed to the Utopian socialists they tended to despise' are to be found, not in Cohen's critique, but in the ideas of the Social Justice Commission, insofar as the latter are seeking to rethink principles in light of historical circumstance.[120] Williams parted company with Cohen on substantive issues too, noting the repressive elements of community and the value of mutual advantage as a motivating principle.

The implications of this debate can be seen in the question of market socialism. In the 1980s and 1990s it was increasingly argued that a socialist society could remain true to its principles yet avail itself of market mechanisms.[121] Market socialism would involve worker or state-owned firms that are run democratically so that workers may benefit from the firm's success, but where the firm nonetheless behaves as a profit-seeking enterprise. Cohen's Oxford colleague, David Miller, contended that market socialism offers an efficient capitalist tool of resource allocation based on principles of justice understood along the lines of desert.[122]

Cohen was unconvinced. Given its inegalitarian consequences, desert seems an improbable socialist principle of justice. In any case, under capitalism market success is due largely to the contingencies of demand, opportunity and arbitrary talent – desert-related considerations like effort have limited relevance.[123] Although desert features as a dimension of the Marxist claim that the worker is 'robbed' of his product, as we saw in the last chapter, Cohen came to abandon this quasi-libertarian view.

Joseph Carens proposes that a socialist market system could be devised where desirable jobs are highly paid and talented people gravitate towards them, but inequality of reward is eliminated by means of a radical taxation system so everyone ends up with equal income.[124] Cohen admires Carens's innovation but relegates it to the best of a bad set of options. For Cohen, 'every market, even a socialist market is a system of predation'; the advantage-seeking behaviour of market actors could not be fully mitigated by distributive policies, no matter how radical.[125] Carens's proposal might be the best way of incorporating market principles, but it remains a compromise, at odds with the socialist ideal of community and fellow-feeling.

Facts and Principles

A venture into metaethics

Cohen's concerns about 'realpolitik' concessions prompted him to venture into metaethics, that is, not what is moral, but what morality is. Earlier in this chapter we saw that Cohen insisted that principles of justice should hold even if circumstances are inhospitable to their application. 'Facts may constrain possibilities of implementation and determine defensible trade-offs (at the level of implementation) among principles', but the principles themselves are unaffected by such considerations. 'Failure to distinguish between rules of regulation and the principles that justify them leads to confusion of different questions' – in particular, questions about decisions and action as opposed to those about norms and ideals.[126] With this conviction, Cohen went on to elaborate a view about the status of morality, whereby normative principles should be understood as ultimately fact independent. For Cohen, any moral or political principle that seems to be grounded in considerations about facts can be traced to a more ultimate, fact-independent principle.[127]

There is considerable critical literature about the extent to which Cohen's position advances our understanding of the nature of inferences about morality.[128] Of particular interest for political philosophers is how Cohen's conception of the fact-independence of normative claims is related to politically salient questions about value, objectivity and the socialist ideal. Here we encounter another striking paradox about Cohen. Again, his view drew the ire of some left-wing critics, who contended that isolating principles from facts, divorcing theory from action, was at odds with fundamental socialist convictions. Cohen's argument for a theory of justice that eschews the domain of facts seemed to undermine his claims to providing, like Marx, a scientific approach to radical politics.

Critical responses

Lea Ypi's essay draws on Plato's dialogue *Parmenides* to suggest that infinite regress threatens Cohen's search for ultimate fact-independent principles. The accusation of Platonism, a preoccupation with ideals that in some sense by their very definition cannot be realized, was also made by others, such as Thomas Pogge, who argued, contra Cohen, that it is by reference to the failures of justice in the world of facts that we should revise and improve our principles.[129] Ypi warns that 'in the case of Marx, any attempt to isolate principles from the world of facts, any theoretical stance which is also not a political one, cultivates a doctrinaire spirit'.[130] Yet Cohen was explicit that he agreed with Plato that 'justice is the self-same thing across, and independently of, history'. He explained, 'Plato thinks, and I agree, that you need to have a view of what justice *itself* is to recognize that justice dictates P when F is true. That is how justice transcends the facts of the world.'[131]

Kai Nielsen also complained that such metaethical accounts, even if they are right, have little to do with the project of socialism. Finding a 'Marxist in Platonic robes' disconcerting, he worried about the use of such a fact-independent political philosophy, retorting that 'some consideration' of how theories 'bear on the facts of the human condition' is essential for their justification for a socialist alternative.[132] Likely Cohen would bristle at the relevance of objections that he is insufficiently faithful to the Marxian canon. We should heed his counsel: what matters is not whether Marx would agree with Cohen, but whether Cohen's case is sound; if Marx is thereby refuted, so much the worse for Marx.

The relevance of feasibility

Nonetheless, Cohen's critics raise an important issue for radical politics regarding the relation between ideals and real-world considerations. Miller rejected Cohen's effort to rescue justice from facts, arguing that a political philosophy 'for earthlings' must be thoroughly action-guiding. We should 'allow the unavoidable limitations of the earthly city to shape our understandings of justice' in order to 'mark out a road down which we might travel'.[133] Otherwise we are left, Miller says, with 'political philosophy as lamentation' which 'places justice so far out of the reach of human beings that nothing we can practically achieve will bring us significantly closer to the cherished goal'.[134] Though Cohen warns against concessions that compromise our ideals, Miller finds radicals risk resignation, their ambitious ideals finding no purchase in a real world that is hopelessly 'contaminated'.[135]

Certainly, if political philosophers are alive to questions of feasibility, their analyses should perform what Adam Swift calls 'a crucial practical-evaluative role'.[136] In this, though political philosophers may not, as Ingrid Roebyns argues, scorn issues of application,[137] Cohen makes the valuable point that they should nonetheless strive to understand when the exigencies of application call for a sacrifice of ideals, in the knowledge that the ideals are worth struggling for. David Estlund concurs: whether principles of justice can be put into practice does not settle the matter of their truth.[138] Cohen's position reminds us, contra Miller, that it is also a kind of resignation to rein in the ambit of one's political ideals, to insist that the feasible rule the roost.

Conclusion

Political philosophy is distinctive among the diverse fields in philosophy in that it asks the abstract, normative question of how we should live together according to principles of justice, but within a context of an empirical reality in which we are acutely conscious of problems of scarcity, the constraints of human nature, or the dynamics of social change. Cohen's value pluralism meant that he recognized the relevance of both these dimensions, but he worried that our understanding of the former, the normative, risked being compromised by the latter, the feasible. This had happened, he argued, with Rawls's ground-breaking political theory, which tailored its principles of justice to accommodate the potential for self-seeking behaviour.

Cohen's esoteric view about fact-independent principles emerged from a lifelong concern that socialist ideals should not be diluted in the face of the disappointments of the real world. When it comes to implementation, our principles might need to be trimmed to accommodate facts about human frailty and the dynamics of power. Indeed, our principles are all too likely to be at odds with the world as we find it, but that should not stop us from aspiring to realize them, continuing to be guided by their highest ideals of human progress and social improvement. Thus, Cohen the 'scientific' (analytical) Marxist was also a utopian socialist,[139] who feared that if justice and equality were not 'rescued' from 'facts', the result would be a diminished ambition for normative political theory. In the next chapter we look at Cohen's ideas about responsibility and equality which suggest a dissonance with his radical political encounter with Rawls, and an ambitious conception of socialism that is, in some respects perhaps, not so ambitious after all.

5

Taking Responsibility for Egalitarianism

Equality stands out as the most important of all the political values we associate with the legacy of G. A. Cohen. From his early work on Marx, to his engagement with Nozick and Rawls, Cohen's commitment to the ideal of rendering people more equal in their wealth, prospects and wellbeing underlies his concerns and arguments. Cohen himself said that the belief in equality guided him all his life: 'a powerful current bears me back to it ceaselessly, no matter where I might otherwise try to row'.[1] As we saw in the previous chapter, Cohen's concern for equality was such that he stressed our obligation to further it in our personal lives. Yet, likely because of his ambitious understanding of what equality requires, Cohen the egalitarian is also a value pluralist, prepared to admit there may be circumstances where equality may be outweighed by other values or considerations.

This chapter will look at the picture of egalitarianism that emerges in Cohen's thought: his ideas about what it is that a society should equalize, centring on the concept of 'access to advantage', an amalgam of resources and welfare; the 'expensive tastes' debate, in which Cohen's Marxist ideas about need inflect his view about what inequalities should be mitigated; Cohen's conviction that egalitarians should distinguish between brute luck and option luck and thus that some inequalities are not unjust; and, in contrast to this, a theme we encountered in the last chapter, the extensive obligations of egalitarians to remedy inequalities, even in their personal choices; and finally, his socialist ideal, in which property and goods are shared, and the principles of society radically overhauled. The theme of responsibility emerges as a running thread: individuals have significant responsibilities to contribute to the amelioration of others' disadvantage, and they are expected to take responsibility for choices which may contribute to their own disadvantage.

The question of our responsibilities for equality is the centrepiece of Cohen's later work and, as we saw in the last chapter, his work on Rawls in particular. 'If You're an Egalitarian, How Come You're So Rich?' is the humorous title that Cohen formulated to pinpoint his misgivings about how little Rawlsian justice can demand of people's personal commitments. The slogan is irresistible, prompting grins among students at its very mention, and inspiring several imitations.[2] Interestingly, Cohen does not supply a definitive answer to the question, pointing to further questions about the ambition of our commitment to equality. Cohen's ideas about equality are complex, multi-faceted, insightful and compelling in many ways, but also arguably in tension with each other. Thus, I suggest we can identify a fourth paradox that bears on the whole of Cohen's thought, which centres on his egalitarianism: the tension between his preoccupation with individual responsibility and his ideal of a socialist community.

Equality of What?

Equality and sufficiency

Cohen did not produce an egalitarian theory per se, and indeed, as we saw in chapter 1, he expressed considerable humility about his contribution being largely responsive to the work of others. The route by which Cohen engaged in debates about equality – largely in discourses with prominent liberal egalitarians – made for a somewhat piecemeal approach. However, what emerges is a powerful picture of the egalitarian ideal. At issue here is not just Rawls, but also that of Cohen's friend, colleague and rival, Ronald Dworkin, whose liberal egalitarianism was the first to come under critical scrutiny in Cohen's work. Another influential figure is the economist and philosopher Amartya Sen, whose time at All Souls briefly overlapped with that of Cohen, and whose capability approach garnered Cohen's enthusiastic, though also qualified, endorsement.

Remedying disadvantage is not the same as seeking equality, and some theorists of distributive justice commend a reorientation from equal shares to sufficient ones. 'Sufficientarians' contend that a focus on equality per se can generate a 'levelling down' problem where equal poverty is always preferred to inequality, even in cases where an unequal distribution would bring the worst off above the poverty line.³ People's relative shares is beside the point, according to this doctrine. The aim should be ensuring that everyone has enough, rather than everyone being equal in their wealth.⁴

Back in 1931 the egalitarian R.H. Tawney proclaimed that the matter of whether one earns more or less than another are 'details of the counting house' that may be ignored, so long as education, power and culture are equally enjoyed.⁵ Some socialist interpreters of Cohen are sympathetic to this view. Jeff Noonan insists that Cohen's socialism was not essentially an egalitarian doctrine, given the 'bourgeois perspective of invidious interpersonal comparisons' that underlies the 'abstract metric of equality'.⁶ For his part, Pablo Gilabert argues that the communist credo of 'to each according to his needs' is indeed a sufficientarian view.⁷ Yet Cohen did not stray from the conviction that equality should be the animating principle of distributive justice. His response to the levelling down problem was to invoke the distinction between principles and policy. Cohen declares that one should not be a 'justice fetishist'; good policy avoids levelling down. Nonetheless, insofar as good policy produces an inegalitarian distribution, it marks a departure from principles of justice, and should be recognized as such.⁸

The egalitarian plateau

Amartya Sen helpfully frames the diverse views about equality among political philosophers in terms of a metric, or what he called 'equality of what'. Sen argues that there is an egalitarian plateau in political philosophy, where virtually all thinkers endorse the idea that people be treated as equals, differing only on what ought to be equalized. Thus, even libertarians favour equality, albeit equality of rights to life, liberty and property, which is compatible with profound social and economic inequalities.⁹ Certainly it seems fair to say that there are no respectable positions in contemporary political philosophy that urge political institutions be designed to reflect a 'natural' hierarchy based on class, caste, race or gender.

The answer to the question of what is to be equalized among contemporary egalitarians can be grouped into two main categories: first, goods, resources or income (what Rawls calls 'all-purpose means' to people's goals), and second, welfare, that is, satisfaction, or the realization of preferences. Welfare is usually identified with utilitarianism and consequentialism more generally, where the criterion for right or moral action is the outcome of an action, its effect on human beings. Welfare also has affinities with Sen's 'capabilities' approach, which stresses that we should be interested not in the distribution of goods per se, but in how goods enable people to realize functions like nutrition or health, being housed or educated.[10] Human flourishing is another metric that attends to how people live, the constituents of living well including material resources as well as access to culture and nature.[11]

Dworkin's equality of resources and liberal 'goods fetishism'

Dworkin provided a distinctive answer to what should be equalized. He argued that rather than welfare, resources should be the distributive metric. Like Rawls's primary goods, resources can be directed to whatever ends one prefers; whether they produce welfare is up to the individual who receives their share of resources. Dworkin illustrated his argument with a thought experiment that evoked market transactions: an auction on a desert island, where parties bid with their equal shares of clamshells on different bundles of goods. A distribution is just once everyone's preferences are met, verified by an 'envy test' where no one envies another's bundle. In order to mitigate unjust inequalities that might arise thereafter due to unchosen circumstances, Dworkin calls for an elaborate insurance system to address unchosen disadvantages such as disabilities or shortfalls in talent, modelling the welfare state's social insurance policies.[12]

With his capabilities approach, in contrast, Sen sought to avoid what he called the 'goods fetishism' of Rawls's primary goods (and by implication Dworkin's resources), stressing instead what goods 'do to human beings', their impact on people's functionings. In stressing the impact of goods, Sen did not deem equality a mere matter of satisfaction or happiness. As Sen argues, 'the extent of a person's deprivation' will not necessarily 'show up in the metric of desire-fulfilment, even though he or she may fail to be adequately nourished, decently clothed, minimally educated and properly sheltered'.[13] One can become accustomed to, indeed satisfied with, disadvantage, just as one can take privilege for granted and be discontented. Indeed, if one puts all the onus on satisfaction, a distributive scheme risks being hijacked entirely by the miserable though rich person at the expense of the sunny but disadvantaged person.

Cohen joined Sen in this worry that welfare may not track deprivation. Cheery Tiny Tim in Charles Dickens's *A Christmas Carol*, for example, although physically disabled and impoverished, seems to have plenty of welfare even if the affluent, able-bodied but miserable Scrooge, an inefficient converter of goods into happiness, leaves Tim with few resources. It is a poor theory of equality that reinforces the effects of unequal distribution and concludes that the demands of equality are met simply because the poor are undemanding. As Cohen puts it: 'the fact that a person has learned to live with adversity, and to smile courageously in the face of it, should not nullify his claim to compensation'.[14]

Access to advantage

With the title 'Currency of Egalitarian Justice' for his seminal article, Cohen pokes fun at the market orientation of Dworkin's view. He proffers 'access to advantage', albeit somewhat tentatively, as his preferred metric for equality. Access to advantage draws on Sen's idea of functionings. According to Cohen, 'advantage' refers to 'a heterogeneous collection of desirable states of the person reducible neither to his resources bundle nor to his welfare bundle'.[15] Incorporating both goods and their impact, access to advantage can take account of the complex disadvantages of the person who, for example, both lacks mobility and experiences pain. By 'access', Cohen intends that one can have access to a good that one does not possess if one has both the opportunity and capacity to obtain it.

Cohen considers the combination of opportunity and capacity found in his idea of access to advantage to be much the same as Sen's capability, whereby external wherewithal is key.[16] He has, however, a modest reservation about what he dubs the 'athleticism' of Sen's focus on capacities. He agrees with Sen that we must look at people's nutrition level and not just, as Rawlsians do, at their food supply, or as welfarists do, at the utility they derive from eating food. But Cohen also maintains, contra the capabilities approach, that we must distinguish 'what the good does for the person from what he does with it'.[17] Thus a baby derives nutrition from food even if there is no exertion of a capability on the baby's part.

Cohen coins the term 'midfare' to capture what it is that should be equalized; functionings are really what is at stake when it comes to disadvantage, not opportunities or capabilities to function, which require active engagement.[18]

Cohen expressed regret that his position suffered from an 'unlovely heterogeneity'. His access to advantage view aims to capture a range of considerations: that people enjoy equal wellbeing whatever their favoured pursuits, be they photography or fishing; that pain and disability be mitigated; and that the unequal wellbeing caused by 'despondency' or 'gloominess' be taken into account.[19] However inelegant, the diverse dimensions of Cohen's access to advantage capture the complexity of what matters in human beings' lives better than simpler measures like resources, welfare or even capabilities to function.

Adonis, Shrek, Pollyanna and Eeyore

Cohen illustrated the importance of making room for welfare along with resources in the egalitarian *distribuendum* with the example of two families seeking housing. Though they may be identical in all other relevant respects, the Happy family and the Sad family differ in their attitudes: the former are serene, the latter in great distress. For Cohen, such considerations should play a role in selecting which family should be given accommodation, though welfare shouldn't simply override considerations of resources either. 'It is because welfare equality can lead to crazy resource results and resource equality can lead to crazy welfare results that I was led to float a pluralistic answer to the "Equality of what" question.'[20]

Disparities in human flourishing involve, after all, a range of factors, from nutrition levels, which can be measured in simple empirical terms, to more complex needs such as shelter, to questions of access to valuable or fulfilling pursuits, to matters of disposition, mental wellbeing, self-realization and self-fulfilment.[21] Cohen does not express his position in terms of equality of flourishing, but his motivations seem to indicate concerns along these lines. Diversity in, not just abilities, but also temperament, likeableness and so forth means that however radical our distributive policies, some of us may not flourish as much as others.

This suggests that we should take onboard the role that, for example, Tiny Tim's temperament makes to his lot in life, even if it is not decisive when considering his means and capacities. We may be a beautiful Adonis or a homely Shrek, a Pollyanna, constitutionally optimistic, or an Eeyore, the glum donkey in *Winnie-the-Pooh* who is unable to find joy in life.[22] Personal attributes, though elusive to address, have a powerful impact on people's lives. Our looks or disposition are obvious candidates, but so too are self-destructive tendencies which society could help us overcome. To pursue toxic relationships, or too easily give up on one's goals, can mean our lives go badly in ways that may cause regret.

As Cohen insightfully observes: 'cheerfulness is a marvellous thing' in part because it 'diminishes the sadness of failure', as well as contributing to a 'successful life' in itself.[23] Thus he concludes that considerations like whether people are happy or sad, in extreme situations and within limits, might have greater weight than whether they have a 'fair' share of resources.[24] Moreover, this focus on whether people are indeed doing well, rather than whether they can choose to do so, is consistent with Cohen's warning against 'athleticism' in the capability approach.

A role for wellbeing

Cohen did not elaborate on his idea of access to advantage beyond these early forays into egalitarian philosophy. His critique of Rawls, for example, tended to assume the primary goods metric in order to zero in on the difference principle. Nonetheless, in his discussion of the role of occupational choice, Cohen was critical of how 'Rawlsian justice is blind to the distribution of everything but social primary goods', that is, what Rawls deemed objectively measurable, all-purpose means that are neutral with respect to different plans of life. As a result, Cohen complained, the theory makes no room for the important consideration of 'quality of work experience'.[25] Cohen again expressed impatience with Rawls's metric in his remark that, in actual human cases, the focus is not the provision of primary goods but 'the facilitation of a fulfilling life'.[26]

Another mention in passing regarding the relevance of considerations other than goods is in Cohen's discussion of the person who would prefer to garden rather than doctor, notwithstanding the greater usefulness of the latter. It is relevant, he says, that an occupation is fulfilling, in the sense of 'psychological satisfaction and extent of realization and exercise of creative powers'.[27] These 'perfectionist' intimations suggest that valuable ways of living figure as a dimension in distributive justice. Perfectionism grounds moral and political theories in an account of a good human life,[28] something which alas Cohen does not explore more fully. Nevertheless, among the attractions of access to advantage is its scope for considerations such as whether people are living equally well.[29]

Expensive Tastes and Human Needs

Plovers' eggs and pre-phylloxera claret

In his argument for the metric of resources rather than welfare, Dworkin cited the unfairness of a society catering to people's tastes to ensure an equality of satisfaction. This move elaborates Rawls's contention that people should be responsible for cultivating their preferences. For Rawls, it was no objection to his metric of primary goods that such goods could not 'accommodate those with expensive tastes', who simply 'lack foresight or discipline' when it comes to choosing how to live.[30] Dworkin went on to say that among the problems with welfarist approaches that focused on disparities in satisfaction is that they risked being held hostage by those with expensive tastes, not just the chronically miserable, like Scrooge, but also the extravagant aesthete.

Dworkin offered the character of Louis, who requires rare plovers' eggs and fine wine ('pre-phylloxera claret') to have the same level of satisfaction as the ordinary person.[31] To elaborate Dworkin's point, think of how although Homer Simpson may be happy with doughnuts and beer, it would seem unfair that he therefore gets less income than Louis. The problem of expensive tastes was a point of contention between Dworkin and Cohen, and though the wording of the issue invited ridicule, Cohen made a cogent case against Dworkin for the egalitarian considerations at stake for those whose tastes were costly to satisfy. The case of Louis, where someone deliberately develops costly elitist tastes, was designed to provoke indignation, but Cohen alleges that the issues are more complicated.

Special burdens

Cohen's metric of advantage means that although, as we saw in the last chapter, incentive-based rewards are prohibited, additional compensation for onerous work looks like a different matter. Cohen refers to the problem of people working longer hours or doing more arduous work as cases of 'special burdens' which a just egalitarian scheme should ensure are compensated so that they may enjoy equal wellbeing with their fellows. His example is that of overworked surgeons, but lower-status, gruelling and less fulfilling jobs are perhaps better candidates for special-burden compensation; for example, oil rig workers, office cleaners or those who do shift work.

Arguably expensive tastes could also be described as involving 'special burdens'.[32] Some pursuits are more expensive because they are minority tastes that don't enjoy economies of scale or because they involve costly equipment. It seems an arbitrary and contingent unfairness that people who happen to have such interests are less able to fulfil them. Here again we see the influence of Marx's distributive credo, 'from each according to his ability, to each according to his needs'. Needs are diverse; instead of allocating equal income, treating people as equals may involve unequal shares to enjoy the same access to advantage.[33] As any Canadian 'hockey parent' shopping for (and hauling to a remote ice rink) an expensive bag of skates and equipment can attest, their children's pursuits are more costly than that of others' offspring who take up chess, even if the social class connotations of the latter are more privileged. What is needed is to determine whether expensive pursuits were pursued simply because they were expensive, that is, because of their prestige, as Dworkin intended with his Louis example.

Tastes and value

It might be thought one can track these matters by distinguishing between those tastes one cultivates and those one does not. But this is difficult to ascertain – it is unlikely, for example, that someone whose musical tastes are expensive to satisfy would want to give them up, even if they are frustrated by the obstacles to their pursuit.[34] The unrich rare music afficionado wishes their taste was not expensive, not that they didn't have that taste. The fact that they don't want to relinquish their interests seems an unreasonable ground for denying them their fulfilment. Cohen notes that Rawls discounts the entitlement of the more productive to the rewards of their efforts on the basis that their ability to make money is a morally arbitrary characteristic. It is odd therefore that Rawls is so harsh when it comes to taste formation and the diverse inclinations of people, a dissonance which is exploited by the libertarian Nozick.[35]

There is another dimension to the expensive tastes debate worth signalling. Dworkin portrays tastes for fine things as the frivolous pursuits of the few; his example of a penchant for rare wine and food is revealing. But what of tastes for a non-degraded natural environment, a culture of care and civility, the preservation of historic buildings, the visual and performative arts? Cohen flags the taste for 'countrysides with hedges' along with threatened societal cultures as expensive tastes, the satisfaction of which the minority may have a legitimate claim against the majority to provide.[36]

One could go further and say that such goods, though they may be costly, merit support so that they may be accessible to all because they are constituents of an objective, public good, a rich and diverse cultural environment that enables a plurality of genuinely valuable choices. Dworkin's argument portrays the individual as a consumer in an idealized marketplace, making unfettered choices in full knowledge of their effects. There is no mention of the deleterious effect that real markets have on human pursuits, where the loftiest goods are victims of market failure, economies of scale, the exploitation of resources, the commodification of culture. As noted earlier, Cohen does not explore these perfectionist issues about the role of the valuable in the egalitarian community. However, his idea of advantage, his critical posture towards the market, his appreciation for nature and architecture and, as we will see in the next chapter, his idea of conserving value, invite such reflections.

Just and Unjust Inequalities

Option luck and brute luck

Given Cohen's differences with Dworkin on the matter of expensive tastes, it is perhaps surprising that the two were agreed when it came to the broader question of how matters of responsibility should affect distributive shares. Indeed, Cohen came to adopt the 'equality of opportunity' talk he had earlier disparaged in critiques of Dworkin.

Recall that Rawls's project to mitigate the position of the worst off does not set any conditions for the amelioration of disadvantage. 'Worst off' is a general category, without differentiation in respect to the cause of disadvantage. Other egalitarians, however, interpreted Rawls's idea of a 'natural lottery' – that our capacity to generate wealth is largely beyond our control – to demand more attention as to how it is that some are worse off than others. This is not to say the talented deserve to be better off; Dworkin argues that a hierarchy of reward is unfair if it is the result of circumstances such as talent.[37] Disadvantage that is the result of brute bad luck merits amelioration; however, shortfalls in resources are justified if they are the outcome of freely chosen decisions or deliberate gambles.[38] The influence of Dworkin's argument is such that some version of 'luck egalitarianism' came to be endorsed by many contemporary egalitarians.[39]

'The most powerful idea in the arsenal of the anti-egalitarian right'

Cohen's former doctoral student Kasper Lippert-Rasmussen points out that it is the appreciation for the unfairness of contingency which put Cohen at odds with Dworkin on the question of expensive tastes but which also prompted him to endorse Dworkin's luck egalitarianism.[40] Yet as a result, whilst Cohen took what seems a generous approach in the debate about tastes, he took what might look like a hard line in the debate about responsibility for disadvantage.

Cohen affirms that egalitarian theory should distinguish between different kinds of disadvantage, those for which persons are responsible, and those for which they are not. Amelioration should zero in on 'accidental inequality' or how some come to be disadvantaged 'through no fault of their own'[41] rather than inequality that is the result of peoples' choices and decisions.[42] As Cohen puts it, 'brute luck is an enemy of just equality, and, since the effects of genuine choice contrast with brute luck, genuine choice excuses otherwise unacceptable inequalities'.[43]

Cohen agrees with the critique of Rawls's unconditional difference principle made by his former doctoral student Will Kymlicka: 'it is unjust if people are disadvantaged by inequalities of their circumstances, but it is equally unjust for me to demand that someone else pay for the costs of my choices'.[44] Cohen did not elaborate his luck egalitarianism in much detail, but throughout his career he affirmed the 'animating conviction' that 'an unequal distribution whose inequality cannot be vindicated by some choice or fault or desert on the part of (some of) the relevant affected agents is unfair, and therefore, *pro tanto*, unjust'.[45] Cohen went so far as to applaud the doctrine as a response to the right-wing critiques of the 'Nanny State': 'Dworkin has, in effect, performed for egalitarianism the considerable service of incorporating within it the most powerful idea in the arsenal of the anti-egalitarian right: the idea of choice and responsibility.'[46]

Cohen intended to show how a great deal of inequality was the result of unchosen circumstances and should be remedied. Nonetheless, there is a sense in which luck egalitarianism betrays a certain 'mean-spiritedness' in tension with Cohen's radical socialist ideal. This ideal emerged, as we saw in the last chapter, in Cohen's critique of Rawls's concession to incentives and what Cohen perceived as the restriction of the ambit of justice to society's institutions or 'the basic structure'. Moreover, contra luck egalitarianism, the rich egalitarian argument for parting with income to help others does not seem to find any relevance in the choices that led people to seek groceries at the food bank or ask for coins in a cap on a street corner.[47] The spirit of community that animates the socialist ideal seems threatened by the 'divisive claims about prudence and virtue' that attend luck egalitarian principles.[48] For some socialists, luck egalitarianism seems to hearken more to Stalin's dictum that 'those who do not work do not eat' than it does to Marx's original ideal of distribution on the basis of need.

Fatalism and free will

Certainly the luck egalitarian distinction between chosen and unchosen outcomes is hard to draw within the capitalist context. If economic condition affects choice-making capacity, bad choices may result from economic disadvantage, not the other way around. Indeed, who is to say what counts as a bad choice when conditions are unjust: poorly paid employment can engender a desire for gratification that is unavailable at work and pessimism about the prospects of prudent investment in the long term.[49] The familiar 'culture of poverty' acculturates people into fatalistic attitudes that can hinder them from improving their lot but which also can be counted as rational given people's circumstances. Tawney declared it a sad irony of capitalism that it endures, not just because the rich exploit the poor, but also because, 'in their hearts, too many of the poor admire the rich' and accept their lot.[50] The 'get-up-and-go' attitude commended to the disadvantaged is hard to cultivate in a class-divided society where the prospects for success look slim and the ranks of the 'precariat' beckon.[51]

Samuel Scheffler offers a metaphysical criticism of luck egalitarianism, that it relies on an implausible conception of free will and the capacity of the person to make choices independent of social influences.[52] The question of responsibility enters murky waters about free will, determinism and common-sense sociology about class divisions and social capital, family background or social class. Think how fortunate the young Jerry was to grow up in a family which, though of modest means, valued ideas, political engagement, community and debate.

If we look back on the events in our lives, it is difficult to isolate those that were the result of conscious decisions as opposed to factors beyond our control.[53] Moreover, it is one thing to freely choose to do x; it is another to be held responsible for the consequences, particularly if our social conditions incline us freely to choose badly.[54] Even bracketing the socioeconomic context, prudent decision-making skills, arguably even more than expensive tastes, seem akin to the results of Rawls's 'natural lottery', for which one cannot take credit or blame.[55] Our level of rationality or prudence, our optimism or pessimism about life chances, our imaginative capacities – the dispositions noted by Cohen in his access to advantage metric – can render some of us better choosers than others.[56]

Cohen on choice

Cohen's luck egalitarian writings did not invoke the tradition of socialist argument about poverty's social causes, how estrangement from one's agency often comes with a class position of low expectations that might account for the poor choices of disadvantaged people. This may be related to the modest role the concept of alienation plays in his thought in general, as noted in our discussion of libertarianism in chapter 3. Though well acquainted with the theme in Marx, Cohen's austere analytical method is perhaps ill-suited to such an amorphous idea, and so Cohen opted for a parsimonious account of capitalism's injustice which conceives of individuals as making choices for which they must take responsibility.

Yet in other contexts Cohen takes stock of the forces shaping choice. As noted in earlier chapters, Cohen addressed the problem of 'adaptive preferences', in which one's choices can be distorted by disappointment, pointing to the deleterious effect of this phenomenon for progressive politics in the immediate aftermath of the Soviet era.⁵⁷ As we saw in chapter 3, Cohen's story of the proletarians in a locked room who cannot collectively exit their class makes reference to the obstacles to self-improvement. Moreover, the metric of 'access to advantage' seeks a fine-grained conception of genuine interests that avoids dispositional distortions as, for example, in the case of deprived but sunny Tiny Tim. In fact, Cohen himself, perhaps in line with his view about the complexities of taste formation, pondered that if there is no such thing as genuine choice, then all inequalities would be unjust (an idea which he did not elaborate, nor pursue in connection with the possibility that imprudent characters may be borne of injustice).⁵⁸

Moreover, a person's choices can have an unequalizing impact on other people, as Cohen pointed out in his critique of Nozick's Wilt Chamberlain example. Cohen's former doctoral student Michael Otsuka raised the problem of the effect of others' actions. Indeed, for Cohen's Oxford colleague David Miller, such considerations rendered luck egalitarianism 'incoherent'.⁵⁹ Reflecting on the Chamberlain argument in his earlier work, Cohen came to agree that 'one man's choice is another man's luck', raising the possibility that choice and justice are fundamentally at odds. These ruminations appear at the end of a contribution to a Festschrift for his Analytical Marxist colleague and friend Hillel Steiner, published the year of Cohen's death.⁶⁰ Sadly, the paper's promise of 'back to the drawing board, later!' could not be kept.

Moral luck

We are accustomed to focusing on responsibility in other domains of justice. In criminal law, for example, responsibility is key in deciding culpability, and sentencing considers mitigating factors that diminish the responsibility of the convicted person. People stand to lose a great deal in such cases.⁶¹ Thomas Nagel developed the idea of 'moral luck', arguing that different forms of luck permeate our lives: constitutive luck, that determines our characters and talents; circumstantial luck, which pertains to the problems or situations we face; causal luck, whereby what we attempt to achieve can turn out differently; and consequential luck, in which the same behaviour, such as negligent driving, can have vastly different consequences depending on the context. These are all cases where one's actions are subject to praise or blame even though one cannot be said to be fully in control.⁶²

Scepticism about the role of luck for distributive justice was expressed by Cohen's All Souls colleague Susan Hurley. She pointed out a conflict between, on the one hand, Cohen's refusal to reward the prudent choices of the highfliers in his critique of incentives, and on the other, his insistence that considerations of prudence play a role in remedying disadvantage. Cohen's response was to bite the bullet and say, though incentives are impermissible, in principle a just distribution would assign weight to the choice to give additional effort.[63] Hurley also argues that responsibility judgements should not guide distribution because they cannot apply to counterfactual situations and, moreover, because interpersonal relations are not within their purview.[64] Interestingly, Hurley, known for her complex, technical methodology, came to conclude that 'what would best serve justice' was not 'fine-tuning the demands of ideal justice and of the distinction between poverty for which individuals are and are not responsible'; rather, egalitarians' goal should be simply 'reducing abject poverty'.[65]

Other philosophers come at this issue from the opposite direction, doubting the plausibility of 'a shelter against luck'.[66] George Sher argues that respect for autonomy often involves allowing people to shoulder the costs of life's contingencies that are difficult to separate into the categories of chosen and unchosen.[67] Cohen's Oxford colleague Bernard Williams, who as we saw in the last chapter was broadly supportive of egalitarianism, doubted that blame, responsibility, guilt and regret were only appropriate in cases of voluntary control.[68]

'Standing to blame' the imprudent

It is puzzling why Cohen is particularly stringent about determining the merits of the disadvantaged, rather than taking aim against the fortuitous situation of the advantaged. True, he noted that 'there are more reasons for objecting strongly to the corporate welfare bum than the able-bodied plain welfare bum who gets as much as the working stiff does', but this point was an aside in another context's discussion about how unjust inequality is more objectionable than unjust equality.[69] An interesting parallel perhaps is Cohen's controversial discussion of 'standing to blame', which was prompted by the Israeli state's condemnation of the bombings by radical Palestinian groups in the early 2000s. Cohen was critical of 'the oppressor' expressing moral admonitions, even where what is admonished is certainly wrong; 'a critic may be disabled from condemning' even if they would be speaking the truth.[70] Similarly, we saw in the last chapter that Cohen likens the highflier who criticizes the state for resisting incentives to the kidnapper who criticizes the reluctance of those from whom they demand ransom. The harshness of luck egalitarianism, where the better off require the worse off make prudent decisions, seems analogous; we might say that the rich, who enjoy a better position whether or not they have been prudent, have no standing to blame the imprudent poor.[71]

In Cohen's foray into luck egalitarianism, we seem a long way from the tough-minded assessment of lax policies that favour the well off. Why say unadulterated misfortune is a qualification for attending to the poor, whereas the unadulterated good fortune of the rich is, in this context at least, of no interest? Many people who are very well off owe their advantage to factors beyond their control; often those in the 'One Percent' are not the talented or productive, but rather people whose wealth is the result of inheritance, dividends, mere ownership of assets. In other words, corporate welfare bums are the beneficiaries of brute luck; they do not contribute to society and could be said to be undeserving of their wealth.

Cohen's former doctoral student Nicholas Vrousalis charges that luck egalitarianism is neither necessary nor sufficient for socialist distribution: not sufficient as it leaves some members of the impoverished classes without the means for their projects and goals, and not necessary because it is not required to settle the question of what counts as a need or a cultivated taste.[72] Indeed, the luck egalitarian view seems largely of polemical value to ward off right-wing challenges to the principle of just distribution, rather than a philosophical device to reduce the eligibility for amelioration of disadvantage. And yet, the luck egalitarian position tended to be deployed, not to extinguish hostility from the Right, but rather in debates among egalitarians, to delineate the choices for which disadvantaged people should take responsibility.[73]

Left-wing luck egalitarianism

It should be stressed that the luck egalitarian model assumes a background of substantive equality, where there are genuine opportunities for education and self-development, a far cry from the capitalist conditions in which the doctrine was penned. That was the understanding of both Cohen and Dworkin, especially Cohen who was of course to the left of Dworkin. Indeed, Cohen insisted that the market is 'at best a mere brute luck machine'.[74] A left-wing luck egalitarian therefore might insist that circumstances, not choice, account for most cases of disadvantage in market societies.[75] Thus responsibility would come to have real bite only upon the elimination of systemic obstacles such as class inequalities; only then can people be held to account for choices that may seem reckless or irresponsible.

Left-wing luck egalitarians might also insist that responsibility would not mean the imprudent go without food, shelter or healthcare. After all, even the most beleaguered systems of socialized medicine in capitalist democracies do not deploy considerations of prudence for the distribution or triaging of health care; doctors and nurses do not deny cancer treatment to the lifelong smoker, or knee surgery to the feckless extreme skier.

Aware of the relevance of social position for one's lot in life, Cohen's Analytical Marxist colleague and friend John Roemer, for example, produced a radical version of the luck egalitarian doctrine. Roemer modelled equality of opportunity to correct for different choice-making capacities based on demographic data to ensure that reward truly reflects effort.[76] He also charted the influence of circumstance on the course of childhood, concluding that children's prospects were so mired in circumstances beyond their control that they should not be held responsible for their choices before the age of consent.[77] Indeed, given how much a young person's experiences set them up for success or failure later, Roemer's findings suggest luck egalitarianism's choice–circumstance distinction is difficult to sustain throughout people's lives.

The Fortunes of Luck Egalitarianism

Nuances of circumstance and choice

Luck egalitarianism underwent significant refinement in response to the charge that it made for a callous form of distributive justice. The next generation of political philosophers, many of them Cohen's former students, made notable contributions. Particularly interesting is the argument of 'responsibility-sensitive egalitarians' that their position need not involve niggardly judgements about compensation.[78] Serena Olsaretti argues that rather than constraining the consequences of responsibility, we should flesh out its demands. She calls for a 'principle of stakes' account of what consequences follow in cases of responsibility, what those who bear responsibility bear responsibility for. Whereas as we will see community is deemed separate from justice in Cohen's account, Olsaretti submits that considerations of community would help specify the stakes for 'community-friendly' equal opportunities.[79]

Zofia Stemplowska advances that society should mitigate the impact of bad decisions in cases where the costs risk outweighing the benefits of free choice. The idea that one should 'trade freedom for security' is the rationale for unconditional socialized medicine, or compulsory car insurance, among other policies of the contemporary welfare state.[80] Treating people as moral equals requires a responsibility-sensitive principle so that the imprudent don't take advantage of the prudent, but it also requires principles that can limit the impact of choice, principally through robust systems of insurance.[81] Andrew Williams and Tom Parr go so far as to argue that the political community should 'mimic the operation of a fair and efficient insurance market', where the paramount principle is that there be individual choice as to the appropriate insurance package, premiums and liability.[82]

Share and share alike

In different ways, these views concede that luck egalitarianism is not a complete theory of distributive justice and requires a prior principle to tell us the limits of responsibility, after which considerations of fortune and choice may apply. Rather than justice dictating luck egalitarianism, with considerations of community then stepping in to mitigate its effects, community considerations are built into luck egalitarianism itself. Some, like Stemplowska, fleshed out this project in response to the objections of egalitarians who consider matters of distribution to be instrumental to more fundamental concerns about equal respect and social standing. As she puts it, 'accepting that the avoidability of an outcome may sometimes make a difference to people's entitlements does not entail accepting that it should make much or all the difference'.[83] For Stemplowska, proactive measures like social insurance are designed to protect equality of opportunity, and thus are an important contribution to the egalitarian toolkit, in all its diversity.

Such revisions from the next generation of egalitarians may well have been welcomed by Cohen. However, whether they would address the fundamental tensions at stake is unclear. Cohen's socialist ideal of 'share and share alike' still seems compromised under even the most finely tuned luck egalitarian view. The warnings of Cohen's friend and philosophical interlocutor Thomas Scanlon about overestimating the significance of voluntariness, that choice should have a limited role, seem apt. For Scanlon, the case for strict equality follows from the 'evil' of feelings of inferiority that come with differences of wealth, whatever their cause.[84]

Thus Marc Fleuerbaey proposes that feelings of 'mutual solidarity and respect' so central to an egalitarian society involve a more generous attitude to the 'serial squanderer' whose preferences for leisure and moderate help can be satisfied without too much difficulty.[85] A similar point was made by Cohen's Analytical Marxist friend Philippe Van Parijs in his work on the idea of a universal basic income, captured in the evocative essay title 'Why Surfers Should be Fed'.[86] The insurance model especially, which seeks to be guided by 'individuals' own values and attitudes to risk'[87] seems some distance from the spirit of solidarity that Cohen invokes against Rawls.

Egalitarians' Responsibilities

The demands of equality

Responsibility plays a role in Cohen's picture in a quite different sense, as we have seen in the last chapter's discussion of the problem of the rich egalitarian. This dimension is worth exploring further here. For Cohen, personal obligations to bolster equality are not just remedial measures necessitated by the flawed here and now. Even in the egalitarian utopia individuals would be expected to abide by obligations to top up, and enhance, public policy. To invoke an earlier example, in the case of someone who prefers gardening but would make a more valuable contribution to society as a physician, their career choice should reflect a personal obligation to do what they can for the equal society.[88]

Cohen acknowledges there should be scope for exemptions, 'personal prerogatives' to give priority to other considerations such as the wellbeing of one's nearest and dearest. Moreover, as we saw in the last chapter, individuals should make their own determinations about where their duties lie: 'it is sometimes right not to force people to do what they are obliged, as a matter of justice, freely to choose to do'. What is needed, Cohen says, are informal processes that engender 'a structure of response lodged in the motivations that inform everyday life', rather than rules which 'severely compromise liberty if people were required forever to consult such rules'.[89] Thus, although institutions might be envisaged that would reinforce the social ethos,[90] Cohen is convinced that it is up to individuals to interpret the social ethos rather than look wholly to coercive law.[91]

The value of occupational choice

Cohen's views about occupational choice attracted objections. Patrick Tomlin advanced that luck egalitarianism is at odds with the ethos enterprise: a distribution which reflects only choices and not luck can be achieved no matter how much people decide to work. Cohen's ambitious understanding of justice demands we make choices that are productive, not just ones for which we take responsibility.[92]

Jonathan Quong submits that though purporting not to be coercive, Cohen's ethos asks individuals to constrain their occupational choices in light of a set of ethical principles that are not easily put aside. Cohen maintains that justice can pertain to choices people make outside of the domain of coercive law. For Quong, however, the person who fulfils a Cohenite obligation, for example to forsake their preferred occupation of gardening for the more useful one of medicine, is deprived of their right of occupational choice, unless one makes 'utopian' assumptions about persons whereby their choices would always be socially maximizing. Cohen faces a trilemma of choice, equality and efficiency that, on his terms, is intractable.[93] The principles confronting the would-be gardener may be those of justice (to produce the best distributive arrangement) or efficiency (the duty to maximally contribute to the social product); either way, Cohen's claim that freedom of choice is preserved since one may have 'a right to do what is wrong to do'[94] is at odds with the idea that there is a duty of justice to those who would fare less well if one did not discharge it. There is thus a tension between the personal prerogative and the social ethos that Cohen cannot resolve.[95]

The obligation to contribute

However, perhaps the dilemma is not so stark. After all, even in our own flawed, unequal market societies, individuals reflect on their choice of occupation by considering moral criteria: whether their chosen path gives them happiness, whether they are making the best use of their talents, or whether they are contributing to the public good. This effort can be impeded by structural constraints such as disadvantages that result from family background or immigrant status that denies the legitimacy of foreign qualifications. Thinking of the moral obligation to develop one's abilities as a kind of Kantian categorical imperative is probably overly austere, but nonetheless, if we are able, most of us are attentive to a call not to waste our potential and to try to 'make a difference'. Even if unfettered by coercive law or the full-throttled ethos favoured by Cohen, we tend to regard not fulfilling our potential or contributing to society as regrettable, indeed sometimes tragic.

Moreover, though the law does not coerce us to do so, there are various sources of encouragement to contribute as best one can. Readers of this book, for example, have likely been pressed by family members as to whether the pursuit of philosophy is useful to society. The question may be annoying but that is in part because it alights upon something about which we tend to care; we worry about failing to live up to such expectations. Commentary on Cohen's idea of an ethos tends to assume unencumbered choice as the default position, but people's choices about how to live have numerous, often profound influences. As was noted in our discussion of luck and responsibility, we do not choose our occupations in a vacuum, but rather in light of a myriad of influences that come from friends, family and society, some consciously considered, others providing an unconscious cultural background to choice-making of any kind. And we often end up making compromises given various considerations about how to live, perhaps taking up gardening as a hobby rather than a job, if we ruefully conclude the more responsible choice is to contribute to society as a physician.

The egalitarian conscience

Thus, although Cohen has in mind an ambitious ethos, it is not the case that its constituents are utterly alien to the way we live now. As we saw in chapter 1, Cohen sought to live an ethical life, without being particularly saintly, and certainly not preachy or sanctimonious. He was uneasy about the title for the collection of essays in his honour, noting with his usual wit that the 'egalitarian conscience' might suggest that he is 'holier than I am. I am certainly not holier than I am; indeed, it's a good bet that I am not even holier than thou'. The idea of an egalitarian conscience, he feared, made him seem 'so grim, so inspecting, so admonishing, so unremittingly judging'.[96] Cohen was not a puritan about his socialism, expressing impatience with figures like George Orwell or Ludwig Wittgenstein who at times lived as though to be an egalitarian involved a kind of purity, a forswearing of earthly pleasures.[97] For his part, though raised an atheist, Cohen became agnostic, even finding inspiration in Christian theology for the idea of a personal obligation to live by a social ethos.[98] Thus although Cohen extolled analytical philosophy for its rigour, the plausibility of his position relies on important considerations outside the analytical toolbox about the human condition and the constituents of a flourishing life.

Nevertheless, even with these considerations in mind, Cohen's ethos may seem burdensome.[99] Its open-endedness respects individual freedom, but the ethos nonetheless risks needling individuals to do more for equality even when the best possible egalitarian institutions are in place. For the egalitarian who cares about equality, this prospect risks being oppressive, a danger which Cohen admits in his critique of the basic structure objection.[100] As Daniel Weinstock points out, individuals are 'truly conflicted' about social justice: 'they want to want to help, but they often find themselves wanting not to help'. Institutions perform a valuable service in ensuring people act 'on the basis of what they want to want', rather than leaving them to muster the will to do so voluntarily.[101]

Egalitarianism should aim to equalize without causing mental hardship for those who seek to help. Oscar Wilde remarked that the 'chief advantage' of socialism would be that people no longer 'spoil their lives' by 'very seriously and very sentimentally' devoting themselves to 'remedying the evils' of poverty, remedies that 'do not cure the disease' but in fact 'are part of' it.[102] Cohen acknowledges Wilde's point in his concern for a 'right to a private space', that would be difficult to enjoy if one must 'keep the demands of the poor before or at the back of one's mind'.[103]

In a famous argument against utilitarianism, Bernard Williams purports that the creed damages people's integrity, reducing them to vehicles for a social goal, a channel for maximum satisfaction of the aggregate aims of society. Utilitarianism ends up undermining the moral individualist principle which is its foundation, the idea that everyone's wellbeing matters.[104] Likewise, egalitarians should be wary of treating persons as equality maximizers, where the goal of equality presses us to give up our other personal commitments.[105]

Personal responsibility for justice and beyond justice

It may be that we cannot achieve a fully equal society with laws and institutions alone; perhaps Cohen is again biting the 'no-bullshit' bullet and delivering the sober news that the ideal socialist society cannot eliminate all dilemmas and conflicts. Yet one might wonder why, under rightly ordered conditions of justice, Cohen puts so much stress on individuals doing more than conform to egalitarian rules. If our institutions are well designed, the role of personal responsibility would likely be modest; recall that Cohen's original move against Rawls was with the example of tax cuts which can certainly be reversed by institutional means.

A possible explanation for the stress on egalitarian personal choices is that what Cohen calls 'socialist equality of opportunity' ends up being compatible with persisting, perhaps significant, inequality. Because luck egalitarianism excludes the remedy of inequalities that are the outcome of choices or gambles, relations of community must step in where principles of justice fail, enlisting individuals' uncoerced efforts guided by an ambitious social ethos. A burdensome load is thus placed on individuals to make up for the shortfall in institutions, pitting the value of egalitarian community against the wellbeing of egalitarians.

Such a solution seems precarious, as implicitly acknowledged by revisionist luck egalitarian views that seek to mitigate the potential for harsh outcomes. The social ethos of generosity sits uneasily with responsibility-driven principles of justice. People may not be disposed to attend to the needs of others if, as on Cohen's understanding of justice, inequalities that result from the choices of disadvantaged people are nonetheless just. Charitable gift giving is arguably much easier to motivate in cases of disadvantage accruing from brute bad luck (evident, for example, in the outpouring of philanthropy after the 2004 tsunami and other natural disasters) than it is in cases where people are badly off because of poor choices which, on the luck egalitarian view, do not meet the criteria for state amelioration.

Why Not Socialism?

Respect egalitarianism

Also at odds with the socialist ideal is the intrusive surveillance involved in discerning precisely which disadvantages merit amelioration and which do not. This might be thought to be an implementation problem. Indeed, Cohen countered criticisms of his luck egalitarianism with the argument that they pertained to rules of regulation but left untouched the fact-independent principles of justice that animated the emphasis on responsibility and choice.[106] However, arguably the matter of surveillance is one of principle regarding the social relations inherent in the egalitarian ideal. Critics such as Cohen's former graduate student Jonathan Wolff argue that the assumptions behind these measures of 'shameful revelation' seem to be derived from a libertarian suspicion of sharing with others, which ought not to belong in a society whose egalitarian ambitions are bound up with principles of mutual respect and social solidarity.[107]

Luck egalitarianism conjures up the well-known intrusions of the suspicious welfare state: policing the home life of welfare recipients, designating expenditures through a coupon system, insisting that people submit to training or report for work – such measures disrespect the privacy and self-determination of individuals. Thus, Vrousalis argued that the sparing approach to distribution dictated by luck egalitarianism contradicts Cohen's vision of socialism where all see themselves as full participants with duties of mutual aid.[108]

Whereas Cohen commended luck egalitarianism for heeding the suspicions of the political right, Elizabeth Anderson, one of the creed's harshest critics, retorted, 'if much recent academic work defending equality had been secretly penned by conservatives, could the results be any more embarrassing for egalitarians?'[109] Anderson's alternative, dubbed 'democratic', 'respect' or 'relational' egalitarianism, focuses on the social relationships of equal citizens whereby people live in conditions of mutual respect, free of domination or servility. One's material situation is relevant only insofar as it bears on one's status as a citizen. Anderson nonetheless shares with luck egalitarianism a 'strings attached' view of distributive justice and explicitly 'heads off the thought that in an egalitarian society everyone somehow could have a right to receive goods without anyone having an obligation to produce them'. For those capable of work, the material benefits of citizenship are 'conditional on participating in the productive system'.[110]

Cohen did not directly engage with this school of egalitarian thought,[111] but he certainly recognized constituents of wellbeing besides income with his idea of access to advantage and his concern for self-realization in his critique of Rawls. In his unfinished essay, 'Notes on Regarding People as Equals', Cohen was concerned to set out how people's relationships are characterized by mutual regard and respect.[112] The theme that material equality, though important, should be accompanied by equality of respect, was stressed by Bernard Williams back in 1962.[113] Yet for both Williams and Cohen, though respect matters, material conditions are more than instrumentally relevant. Moreover, Cohen would likely be unhappy with the significant inequalities that might remain if the egalitarian test is simply what suffices for equal citizenship.

Back to camping

This brings us back to Cohen's argument for socialism and his example of the socialist camping trip. In the last chapter we noted how Cohen commends a social ethos to enable individuals to make equality-supporting choices that further the egalitarian project.[114] Cohen asks 'why not socialism?' to show how such an ethos might be realized, deploying the example of a solidaristic camping trip where campers share equipment and knowhow.[115] As Roemer noted, the book was somewhat atypical for Cohen, not 'an iron-clad logical demonstration as was his wont', but the outline of an argument, and an exhortation that the means to achieving a fully egalitarian society be found.[116]

The principles of the camping trip are markedly at odds with the values of the capitalist market, according to Cohen. Anyone who is tempted to behave like a self-interested market actor, keeping the benefits of their good fortune, wise planning or superior skill to themselves, would be subverting the ethos of the friends' time together. Cohen hopes the obvious attractions of such a venture and the flourishing of all who participate demonstrate the appeal of the socialist ideal.

This engaging essay reveals some fault lines in Cohen's socialist principles. The importance of the social ethos for the achievement of egalitarian justice suggests that justice and community are not, as Cohen supposes, separate values. We saw that in his critique of Rawls, Cohen uses a restricted sense of community as 'interpersonal justification' to make a justice-based argument against incentives. In his portrait of socialism Cohen offers a more thorough-going understanding of community, proposing that the capitalist market is to be faulted not just for its inequality, but also because it engenders attitudes that undermine fellowship and solidarity.[117] 'Communal caring' means that we care about and care for one another and, moreover, care that we care, and thus inequality, whatever its source, is repugnant.[118] The unprepared and feckless camper who chose unwisely is not left outside the tent or denied a seat at the picnic table; rather, the venture involves meeting the needs of everyone, the irresponsible included.

Communal reciprocity

Critics complained that Cohen's camping scenario was of little assistance in assessing the relative merits of capitalism and socialism, that it unfairly compared idealized communism and real-world capitalism.[119] Yet arguably many of Cohen's critics themselves assumed a false contrast between idealized capitalism and Stalinist communism. Moreover, the power of Cohen's essay is that the camping trip is not a fantastic dream, but a familiar real-world example which exemplifies socialist ideals.[120] Recall from the previous chapter that Wolff zeroes in on those ideals, noting that 'the attitude people have toward each other' is relevant for the achievement of equality.[121] Vrousalis reassures us that socialism would not expect introverts to 'join hands and "kumbaya" with others, whether they like it or not'. Rather, the camping trip shows that members of a socialist community would need to cooperate – indeed forge a social plan for their common production – to achieve equality.[122]

And yet Cohen is candid that, notwithstanding the attractions of the camping trip model, his view of socialism which, underscoring its luck egalitarian constituents, he dubs 'socialist equality of opportunity', would permit inequalities that are the result of 'regrettable choices'. He admits such inequalities would be at odds with his proffered ethos of 'communal caring'. Perhaps he recognized, as Richard Miller put it, that luck egalitarians would be 'pains in the neck' on the socialist camping trip.[123] Justice understood as communal reciprocity dictates luck egalitarian principles, but Cohen proposes that 'in the name of community' inequalities that result from choice or deliberate gambles, though fully just, would be remedied. Cohen is not comfortable with this upshot, and remarks, without resolving the matter, that 'it would be a great pity if we had to conclude that community and justice were potentially incompatible moral ideals'.[124]

Community versus justice

Thus, Cohen's conversion to luck egalitarianism causes him to sever justice and community in a way that seems at odds with his broader socialist commitments.[125] Pablo Gilabert suggests that the principle of community might figure as a competing justice principle that can overrule socialist equality of opportunity.[126] Yet such a solution, not entertained by Cohen, continues to compartmentalize equality and justice. If justice refers to equality of wellbeing (drawing out Cohen's idea of access to advantage), and among the constituents of wellbeing are values such as companionship, friendship or belonging,[127] then community appears to be part and parcel of justice, not just an additional support or remedy for the parsimonious consequences of a narrow view of justice's principles. Cohen was adamant that need, not desert, should be a criterion for distribution, not only in *Why Not Socialism?*, but also in his blast against the Labour Party in the 1990s. Indeed, this theme can be found in *Rescuing Justice* too, even though in that text Cohen also stated the contrary, that responsibility for one's disadvantage counts against its remediation.[128]

In the 1980s, when he was making his assault against libertarianism, Cohen seemed largely untouched by the ideas of other influential, progressive critics of liberalism at the time, such as Michael Sandel and Charles Taylor, who called for a 'communitarian' focus in political philosophy and the understanding of persons as 'intersubjective' rather than 'atomistic' beings.[129] Perhaps Cohen agreed with Rawls, that a theory of justice should be 'political not metaphysical', or that this brand of communitarianism smacked of holism and was insufficiently analytical, or that it had intimations of, as Bernard Williams purported, a 'Right-Hegelian' political view. Cohen's lack of interest in alienation at this stage of his career is likely relevant too.[130] Yet ideas of fellowship, community and social unity are integral to so much of Cohen's philosophy. It is interesting that Cohen's Oxford colleague David Miller, more conservative perhaps in countering, as we saw in the last chapter, Cohen's utopianism and hostility to market socialism, took the opportunity to cast doubt on the communitarian credentials of luck egalitarianism.[131]

No-sucker socialism

There is another way of explaining the paradox of Cohen's endorsement of luck egalitarianism alongside a demanding socialist ideal of fraternity and equality. Cohen's methodological commitments forged early in his career could be key here. Committed to analytical, no-bullshit philosophy, Cohen took issue with his fellow leftists for 'wishing away' difficult problems by reference to vague radical ideals. Thus, it might be argued that the problem of the free rider, the person who although fully capable shirks the duty to contribute, is a real one for the socialist project. It's one thing to show up for the camping trip ignorant of what equipment to bring along; it's another to show up empty-handed as a deliberate strategy of expecting one's fellows to pick up the slack.

Indeed, Cohen speaks not just of communal caring but also communal reciprocity in the context of the camping trip. Furthermore, such a view is faithful to Marx's distributive principle insofar as it insists that each contribute according to their ability.[132] However much one gets satisfaction from serving others and does not regard serving as a mere means to being served, Cohen insists that 'my commitment to socialist community does not require me to be a sucker who serves you regardless of whether (if you are able to do so) you are going to serve me'. The socialist camper gives because you need or want and expect a 'comparable generosity'.[133] In his 'Notes on Regarding People as Equals', Cohen warned about the 'wild goose chase for defining characteristics' in determining whether to regard someone as an equal.[134] Though Cohen's counsel may indicate attending to others' needs without qualification, it could also involve holding others responsible for their duty to contribute; treating others as 'unconditional equals'[135] may entail forfeiting the requirement of responsibility, or demanding it.

Certainly, Cohen hoped that socialist equality of opportunity would guide the community in relations of reciprocity without the pathology of market attitudes. To be held to account for imprudent decisions, to attend to the cost of one's choices, may figure as a form of respect and care for others. On this view, far from being a way of simply blocking right-wing critics, Cohen's endorsement of luck egalitarianism was a matter of principle at the heart of a frank reckoning of the demands of the socialist project, particularly once the assumption of post-capitalist abundance has been abandoned.[136] In short, no-bullshit Marxism ultimately engendered a no-sucker socialism.

Downplaying desert

Yet it remains that Richard Arneson's counsel that socialists should 'downplay' desert and focus instead on the simple moral requirement of giving aid animates the camping example.[137] What might also be said, however, is that the trip's success involves the cultivation of an ethic of contribution and doing one's part; this too could be understood as a constituent of enjoying the common project of camping together. Those who fail to contribute are in some sense missing out on the enjoyment, even the purpose, of the enterprise. Instead of focusing on the responsibility of the disadvantaged as a distributive constraint, however mitigated by insurance, Cohen's picture of the camping community suggests that non-contribution is itself a form of disadvantage, a shortfall in wellbeing. On this view, desert would be marshalled, not to determine entitlement to access to advantage, but to improve it.

Indeed, feeling deserving of resources – which comes from being productive – is a significant constituent of wellbeing. Not being hungry, of course, is a more important source of wellbeing than feeling deserving of food.[138] Yet getting and feeling that one has earned what one is getting is better than just getting, and Cohen's interest in the many sources of advantage has the potential to be sensitive to such considerations. Being responsible is a crucial basis for self-respect and furthers human wellbeing. On this view, we should consider the matter of individuals' contributions, not to punish under-contributors, but to attend to their lack of advantage. No one would know better than the industrious Cohen how working gives structure and meaning to one's life, exposes one to different experiences and people, provides scope for cooperation and interaction with others, enables one to develop skills and earn respect for them, to become self-directed and ethical.[139]

Though John Stuart Mill contended that 'help perpetuates the state of things which renders help necessary',[140] recent studies suggest that guaranteed income may have no such effects.[141] Equality of access to advantage might therefore be best achieved, not by foisting good choices on people, nor by punishing them for making bad choices on grounds of desert, but by helping them to become 'good choosers' who choose responsibly.[142] As Kymlicka points out, trusting people to follow a social ethos by their own lights is a way of avoiding the disrespect that could come with a focus on responsibility. Indeed, as we saw in the last chapter, Kymlicka, who had helped inspire Cohen's luck egalitarian turn in the 1990s, came to propose that responsibility be a self-directed principle, among the just personal choices of the egalitarian, rather than a coercive rule of distributive justice.[143]

Conclusion

Although a value pluralist, equality was for Cohen the highest ideal. Yet his commitment to this ideal involved complex and ambivalent positions. Access to advantage suggested an ambitious and inclusive metric for equality. Although critical of the market's attitude of 'greed and fear', Cohen was also concerned that unchosen circumstance plays a gatekeeping role in the amelioration of disadvantage. In seeking to determine the extent to which a person is responsible for their socioeconomic position, Cohen sought to apply his toughminded philosophical approach to deeply controversial questions. For some, in practice this still meant a radically egalitarian view and, moreover, one that took a principled stand on irresponsible behaviour. For others, Cohen's position meant a disappointing step back from the ideal of community that animated so much of his critique of liberal egalitarianism elsewhere.

Like many on the Left in the 1980s, Cohen was preoccupied with the backlash against the welfare state, the rise of the New Right, and the decline of the labour movement. Committed to alleviating poverty where the predicament of becoming poor is bound up with decisions that play some causal role, or perhaps the optics of such cases, Cohen abridged his socialism. As an historian of liberal political thought remarks, this 'risky' strategy, wherein 'egalitarian principles incorporated conditionality into their universality' seemed a 'capitulation to the right' where 'ideas of responsibility were used not to attack the rich but criticize the behaviour of the poor'.[144]

One of the more serious (though still entertaining) Cohen videos on YouTube is from a UK Channel Four programme in 1986. Cohen makes a case for socialism by invoking an Al Capp comic in which an odd entity called a Shmoo willingly, and unstintingly, uses its body to provide for the satisfaction of human beings' needs and desires. So desperate are capitalists to ensure that people will continue to buy and sell in the market, that war is declared on the Shmoo. Cohen concludes that the Shmoo parable demonstrates the desirability of a socialist alternative to capitalism.[145] The fable conveys optimism about overcoming scarcity (an optimism which as we've seen Cohen came to reject), but it also inspires us with the ideal of community as integral to the equal society.

In the land of the Shmoo, there is no distinction between those who merit, and those who do not merit, the amelioration of their poverty. Responsibility emerges as a concept only in the sense of our collective responsibility to overcome inequality and to ward off those who would seek to impede us in this goal. Cohen's conversion to luck egalitarianism, with its very different focus on the problem of egalitarian obligations, seems to put that understanding of responsibility in peril. Otsuka called one volume of Cohen's posthumous essays *Finding Oneself in the Other*, a phrase that evokes the ideal of fellowship at the core of Cohen's socialist beliefs.[146] It is a quote from Cohen's essay on conservatism; it is to that essay, and all the paradoxes it poses, that we now turn.

6

Rescuing Existing Value – For or Against Socialism?

To the surprise of many, towards the end of his career Cohen published an essay that endorsed a form of conservatism, in the distinctive sense of 'conserving intrinsic value'. Cohen contended this 'conservative attitude' involved an appreciation for the fleeting, worthwhile things that are vulnerable to change and destruction. The essay argues for the importance of 'existing value' and calls for an appreciation of the conservative insight that change can mean loss.[1] Intriguingly, Cohen elected to entitle his essay 'Rescuing Conservatism'. The title indicates, most astonishingly of course, that like justice and equality, conservatism is a doctrine which Cohen believes should be defended. Yet the title also tells us that the doctrine deserves rescuing, disabused of misconceptions and misunderstandings, just as justice and equality merited rescuing from liberalism. Indeed, the essay's original title was 'Rescuing Conservatism from the Conservatives'. This raises interesting questions about precisely what needs rescuing, how, and to what purpose.

Cohen's ruminations on this theme are unexpected, but also insightful, even profound, shedding light on the finitude of the human condition and our relationship to the world and ourselves.[2] Cohen resisted thinking of his claims as having any right-wing political implications. However, it is uncertain whether his defence of conservative values can be squared with his egalitarian commitments and the spirit of social change, indeed revolution, that informs so much work in the socialist tradition. Thus, our final paradox is how Cohen, socialist critic of liberal theories of justice, might also be, in some sense, a conservative, and what is the significance of this for Cohen's political philosophy.

Conservatism – Context and Meaning

Conserving and rescuing

Conservatism is a puzzling creed. Some have doubted whether it is a creed at all; the literary critic Lionel Trilling sneered that conservatism was not a system of ideas, but rather, mere 'irritable mental gestures'.[3] Cohen's University College London colleague Ted Honderich scorns that if conservatism is at root a preference for the familiar, then it is a mystery how such an 'egregious idiocy' could be the basis for an entire political doctrine.[4] The word's etymological root dates to the fourteenth century and refers to 'tending to preserve or protect',[5] but that leaves open the matter of what is in peril and what are the values that merit preservation. As a doctrine, arguably conservatism comes on the scene only when there is radical change to oppose; conservatives offer a counter-ideology to movements seeking progress. In a book on the conservative figures of All Souls College, conservatism is commended as 'a form of grieving' for the losses that come with 'disruptive change'.[6] The European doctrine of the divine right of kings, for example, was a defence of absolute monarchism in the face of attack, devised in response to radical calls for greater parliamentary power.[7] Throughout history there have been conservative forces seeking to halt or reverse social change.

Conservatism is now a position we trace especially to Edmund Burke, and his canonical work, *Reflections on the Revolution in France*, which Cohen cites in his essay.[8] Burke's purpose was to provide a critique of the tumultuous events on the continent to warn against their replication in Britain. Burke also stressed the risk of undertaking far-reaching change based on abstract, untested ideas, articulating a 'precautionary principle' about the problem of uncertainty when it comes to political action.[9] It is not this prudential maxim, however, that appeals to Cohen. At issue is not wariness of the unforeseeable consequences of radical change, caution in the context of uncertainty, 'looking before leaping', as Cohen puts it. What is most important, for Cohen, is that existing value is conserved; we should not change things, even slowly, and even if we know what's coming next, simply because change involves destruction of the valuable.[10]

The contextualism of conservatism

As we will see, Burke's essay outlines some substantive conservative ideals, but it also renders conservatism highly contextual; if conservatism is an orientation to change, then much depends on the current situation and the changes that are afoot. Thus, in the Soviet era, western commentators often referred to 'conservatives' in the Communist Party, who would not give up their fidelity to statist communism and were opposed to market reforms. The status quo that is at risk of being lost may be left-wing policies or institutions in the western context too. Cohen humorously referred to 'palaeo-Marxists' who insisted on the veracity of Marx's texts in the face of evidence to the contrary in a changing world.[11] Yet we might also call conservative, 'old fashioned socialists' like Cohen who oppose the decline of the welfare state at the hands of radical but right-wing politicians such as Margaret Thatcher. Indeed, as we will see, Cohen stresses the progressive potential of anti-Thatcher conservatism in his essay.

There is also something conservative, therefore, about those socialists who decry the move to the right of their progressive political party, for example, the opposition of the radical Left to 'New Labour' in the British Labour Party (Cohen being a prime example of this position, as noted in earlier chapters). One of the epigraphs to the essay Cohen says he heard many times over the decades is the phrase, 'It's not like it was', attributed to his father, Morrie Cohen, who was disappointed in the changing trajectories in progressive politics but also the loss of familiar cultural forms and social practices.[12]

Old and new things

The conservative disposition endorsed by Cohen involves appreciating the value of existing things, seeking to conserve them, and lamenting their loss. Central is the idea that change is not always for the good. As George Sher postulates the conservative outlook: 'if something exists, then you need a reason to change it but you don't need a reason to keep it'. Certainly, one can be a conservative by temperament, finding change inherently disconcerting, without subscribing to any particular political doctrine. Yet, Sher worries, temperamental conservatism might therefore seem to have no rational basis.[13]

One can both lament the loss of one old thing and welcome the arrival of a new thing yet still be conservative in one's attitude to the old.[14] Even if good new things are arriving, it is still the case that good old things are disappearing.[15] In his disavowal of conservatism, the right-wing libertarian Jan Narveson jokes that a conservative is someone who thinks that 'things are going downhill, and wants to keep it that way'.[16] The remark is intended to show the absurdity of the conservative attitude, but there is some truth in the conservative idea that, as Cohen himself puts it, though in some ways today is worse than yesterday, in those same respects, it's better than tomorrow.

Small c and large C conservatism

In his critique of the French Revolution, Burke planted a flag for resistance to change, the importance of conserving existing things of value. In this, he also elaborated and defended substantive conservative ideals which he feared were in jeopardy: for example, respect for traditional institutions such as the church, the belief in natural hierarchy and the importance of people keeping to their appointed station, and the conviction that governance should be the prerogative of an experienced elite.

Cohen defends the status-quo bias articulated by Burke,[17] but he dissociates his view from a Burkean political philosophy, emphasizing the distinction between a 'small-c' conservative attitude from a conservative political position. The former focuses on the idea of holding on to valuable things that are at risk of being destroyed, as opposed to an endorsement of traditional institutions such as the patriarchal family. Cohen puts it simply: 'Conservatives like me want to conserve that which has intrinsic value, and injustice lacks intrinsic value – and has indeed, intrinsic disvalue', although he admits there are cases, such as the pyramids, which have an intrinsic value that can be distinguished from the extrinsic feature of being built by slaves.[18] This bears further discussion, as we shall see.

Existing Value: Particular and Personal

Value and attachment

Cohen outlines two kinds of existing value which should be conserved: first, personal value, the attachment one has to something in virtue of one's relationship to it; and second, particular value, a distinctive value an object has that cannot be replicated or substituted by something else. The two can come together, of course, in a valuable object which also has personal value for a person; something both valuable and valued. Indeed, the conservative emphasis on existing value means that those things one values personally would likely also have a case for being conserved for their particular value. Existing value, be it personal, particular, or both, can be great or small. Historic buildings, antiques, works of art are obvious cases of significant existing value.

Cohen also gives an example of modest existing value: his pencil eraser or rubber, which he had had since he began his career as a lecturer.[19] This object has value in virtue of his connection to it, its history for him; however modest, the eraser played a meaningful role in the fabric of his life. The eraser is not the best eraser in the world – it is grubby and worn – but it is not its function which matters. The criterion of function suggests that so long as an existing object's function can be replicated by another object, it is replaceable. The focus on existing value seeks to correct that orientation. (Cohen doesn't comment on the irony that in this case the object itself removes vestiges of the past, or that its function condemns it to diminution and disappearance.)

Against maximization

Related to this is the idea that objects with existing value are not construed merely as a means to an end, a vehicle for good results. The conservative attitude, Cohen says, is at odds with the maximizing consequentialist, whose measure is outcomes, net gains, oblivious to the costs of those gains except insofar as they enter the calculation of the overall result. Things with existing value are ends in themselves; they command a certain loyalty, as Cohen puts it.

What is at stake is not just the conservation of value, but the conservation of *what* has value. Cohen's target then is not just a maximizing attitude, but any approach that separates value from the things in which it is found. Cohen likens the conservative's view on existing value to that of love for another person; the person one loves is 'the' one, and substituting another person, even with near identical qualities, is out of the question. Indeed, the loved person should continue to be loved even if their qualities decline; Cohen invokes Shakespeare: 'I want love not to alter when it such alteration finds'.[20]

Some critics have doubted whether maximization-avoidance is achieved in Cohen's argument; after all, there are occasions when decisions must be made about choosing to preserve one thing rather than another.[21] Although Cohen's conservative attitude amounts to 'a goal to be respected rather than promoted',[22] Cohen admits in response to an objection from former graduate student Michael Otsuka that consequentialist conclusions may play a role. They are certainly easier to draw when it comes to making choices about destroying things, rather than persons.[23] However, Cohen claims we would still feel regret in cases where something is certain to be replaced; the conservative bias applies both to that which will no longer exist and that which will exist in the future.

Cohen's point, what's been dubbed the 'mere destruction view', where the concern is only avoiding destruction, is that regret always attends loss, whatever follows next. We might rejoice in the value of the new thing, but that does not mean being glad it replaces the old.[24] The badness of death, as noted by Frances Kamm, refers not just to the deprivation of additional goods, but that an existing life is now 'all over'.[25] Moreover, as Samuel Scheffler points out, the value of old things is distinctive: 'valuing involves attachment, attachment requires acquaintance, and one cannot be acquainted, in the relevant sense, with something that has never yet existed'.[26]

Value and the valuable

Thomas Scanlon, Cohen's friend and with whom he was in conversation about these ideas, gives a different account of value. For Scanlon, value is not an extra property that a thing has, that would be added to its functions and qualities. Rather 'to be good or valuable is to have other properties that constitute ... reasons' to respond to a thing in a certain way.[27] On this account, Cohen's consideration about something's existence might be added to the kinds of properties that Scanlon thinks give us reason to value. Scanlon thinks 'the valuable' as an objective assessment cannot be applied to contingent connections. Arguably we do not expect others to share our attitudes to what we might care most about, for example, our children, although of course our children have value the way everyone does, as persons.

Thus, on Scanlon's terms, the personal value which Cohen speaks of is not best captured by the idea of the valuable, which is inherently abstract and universal.[28] Nonetheless, Cohen's position may prove illuminating, since he can speak meaningfully not just of the personal value of one's children to one as a parent, but also their particular value as discrete, worthy entities that are irreplaceable. Kant's idea that one cannot use a person as a means, that each person has dignity as opposed to worth or a price which could find an equivalent, is important here, and arguably not at odds with Cohen's focus on personal connection.

Some philosophers stress how accounts of value need an emotional element, what is called a 'vulnerability' in one's relation to what one values, which gives us a special reason to single out a thing one values as 'being good or worthy or valuable'. Scheffler takes this view, but he emphasizes that vulnerability cannot be the only dimension in play. For example, Cohen's pencil eraser has personal value for only one person and is thus an exception that proves the rule, since the things to which we attribute value should be candidates, at least, for a broader consensus about their worth.[29]

Duties and Rights

Stewardship and property

Is there a duty to conserve existing things of value? If so, it is an interesting question to whom such duties might be owed. Duties in the deontological sense are commonly thought to be owed to persons; thus we cannot have a duty to the cathedral, as it is not a moral agent. Cohen argues, however, that the repudiation of maximizing criteria such as consequentialism does not entail a human-centred deontological alternative. After all, what is at issue for Cohen is the valuing of things with intrinsic value. We cannot say that the destruction of historic buildings, per se, involves the failure to perform a duty to a person, or a violation of a person's rights. We might want to talk of people's rights to valuable things like historic buildings, but for Cohen, the valuable thing itself is the object of ethical concern. Indeed, what is important for the deontologist, the rights of persons, could mean indifference about the relative merits of old things and new things; people's rights therefore do not capture what is at stake when it comes to conserving things with value.[30]

One might think the duty to persons plays out in terms of their rights as owners of existing things. But ownership usually means a title to dispose – and destroy – one's property as one wishes, at odds with Cohen's purpose. In any case, given his critique of property-based ethical theories such as that of Nozick as elaborated in chapter 3, Cohen would not be prone to regard human beings' ownership of society's resources as the basis of a moral entitlement. Yet although ownership claims cannot serve as a foundation for conservative ideas about value, our relationship with existing things can. Tenants who have lived a long time in an old house, who appreciate its character and history, like Cohen and his pencil eraser, have a relationship of personal value with their home which has weight against the landlord's property right.

Our relationship with existing things can be understood in terms of our history with them. As Erich Matthes puts it, we have a sense of 'belonging' with those things which have personal value for us, which can give rise to conflicts over heritage where there may be competing claims to connection.[31] For example, Cécile Fabre defends the claims of humankind's common heritage against the demands of the territorial state.[32] Cohen makes his conservative case 'not by appealing to rights or other deontological constraints', but by 'asking us to rethink our understanding of value itself'.[33] Here again we see intimations of Burke, who though he defended the institution of private property, also stressed the obligations we have as stewards of resources with duties of care. Burke invokes the metaphor of a house, where citizens are 'temporary possessors and life renters' who, if they 'commit waste on the inheritance', hazard 'to leave to those who come after them a ruin instead of an habitation'.[34]

Change and loss

Cohen notes that against the lament of the loss of valuable things, it might be objected that social change has brought many advances that benefit humankind. He replies that though we may be better off because of modernization, that doesn't mean we should not be sorry that the cost has been the loss of things of value. The Cohen-conservative is not opposed to new things, so long as the production of new things doesn't entail destroying the old. A new painting is not to be disparaged, so long as it is not understood in terms of replacing an old painting, even if the new painting is judged a better work of art.[35] On this perspective, one could applaud a new building and deem it better than what lay there before, or think a new culture would be superior to the current one, yet continue to resist the destruction of the old. Of course, puzzles abound, for example, new things that replace old things also become things with existing value, such that one comes not to regret their existence.[36]

Heritage activists often say 'it's not good because it's old, it's old because it's good', but there is a sense that both are true on the conservative outlook articulated by Cohen. Old things are good in virtue of existing; and our commitment to conserve old things is an acknowledgement that their existence endows them with goodness. These considerations cast light on the thorny issue of reversing regrettable change. Cohen maintains that it is metaphysically impossible that we might dial back the clock and retrieve valuable objects that were damaged or destroyed; however, it may be possible to restore or replicate them. Of course, reversing recent change means destroying what now exists, which itself has a claim to existing value. Yet Cohen contends that familiar things that have value for us, recently destroyed, when we are 'still oriented to a life that includes them', might be worth restoring or reproducing as replicas, in order to salvage personal value.[37] The conservative bias is defeasible, Cohen acknowledges. It may be that the object of existing value cannot be saved, such as a dying dog whose place is one day taken by a young puppy (though on Cohen's understanding of love, one dog cannot 'replace' another).[38]

Cohen does not give any guidance as to how to determine what has value in cases of conflict. On this point, his position seems more intransigently conservative than that conveyed by 'Chesterton's fence', the principle that reforms should not be made before inquiring into the reasons for an existing institution that risks replacement.[39]

Acceptance of the Given

Finding peace with the object

The conservative, Cohen claims, also has a cluster of other, interconnected attitudes that come with the appreciation for existing value: acceptance of the given, being congenial to variety and, related to this, being favourably disposed to the results of accidents. The subject finds peace with the object by accepting the given, Cohen avers, and that idea of finding peace also means welcoming the results of contingencies and the variety they produce. A certain humility about our role in mastering and manipulating our fates, perhaps what Iris Murdoch calls 'selfless respect for reality', is in play here.[40]

This view has implications for medical science, where interventions in the human body certainly are at odds with 'acceptance of the given'. Cohen provides a thought experiment of a man who replaces defective 'fleshly parts' of his body with 'perfect artificial substitutes', producing a largely 'plasticized' person. Cohen proclaims, perhaps against the current of a lot of contemporary thinking,[41] that this is 'surely a ghastly scenario'. To prevent it, the conservative impulse would seek to stall or halt the process of greater permissibility of 'plasticization'. Such moves are needed in anticipation of how otherwise our future selves would become so accustomed to this process of replacing the imperfect, so insensitive to its ethical implications, that they would therefore usher in evermore horrifying and irreversible social change that destroys what is valuable about the human condition.[42]

Indeed, the idea that existing things have value is bound up with features of our own existence. We live finite lives in the knowledge that others came before us and others will come after; a valuable life has temporal limits but also partakes of an ongoing enterprise. Some of these ideas are explored by Scheffler in his argument that our values are very much shaped by the knowledge both that we will die and that there will be future generations.[43]

Medical research, perfection and misfortune

Cohen goes further, confessing his unease with stem cell research, 'even as a means for curing a horrible disease', because of fear of a slippery slope. Since the current use of living things for research will open the door to a culture tolerant of ever more problematic forms of research, we have 'a strong reason to prevent that successor culture from supervening'. Cohen is quick to stress that his wariness about stem cell research means that he favours, not outright prohibition, but rather that we be aware of the moral costs of innovative medical procedures.[44] Cohen does not draw out further, non-medical implications; however, his insights could apply to other significant technology-driven cultural changes, such as social media and artificial intelligence, where even the writing of a philosophy essay can be done by a machine. Some social critics call for a pre-emptive pause to such innovations to take stock of potential negative ethical consequences.

Cohen gives as another example, genetic manipulation to eliminate people's undesirable features. Flawed human beings, he counters, are specific creatures of value whom we personally cherish. Furthermore, 'we court vertigo if we seek to place everything within our control'.[45] Michael Sandel articulates similar concerns in an argument 'against perfection', targeting a range of aspects of western culture, especially the drive to manipulate genetic traits. Genetic engineering, he says, introduced to cure disease, persists to 'tempt us' with the prospect of genetic enhancement as though we are 'masters of our nature', threatening 'to banish our appreciation of life as a gift', leaving us with 'nothing to affirm or behold outside our own will'.[46] It is our nature to be imperfect, mortal beings; to remove our flaws would do violence to who we are, to our existing natures.

Bioethicists have argued that Cohen's position does not rule out modest genetic enhancement. Pugh, Kahane and Savulescu point out that Cohen's luck egalitarianism provides grounds for enhancement that could reduce the impact of the 'genetic lottery' on people's life chances, eliminating inequalities that are the result of brute luck. Furthermore, 'moral enhancement' could mean we diminish a character trait that threatens marital happiness or boost a sensitivity among decision-makers hitherto impervious to the wrong of environmental destruction. Indeed, life-extending drugs could be understood as precisely a case of enabling us to conserve existing value, enabling us to live the kinds of lives we're living for longer.[47] Pugh, Kahane and Savulescu admit that such proposals nonetheless risk jeopardizing what Cohen's Oxford colleague Bernard Williams termed our 'ethical identity as a species', showing what Cohen might term 'disloyalty' to who we are.[48] Appropriately delineated and organic in their impact, however, perhaps such interventions would enable us to continue in the lives we currently inhabit. Modification would thus figure, paradoxically, as a kind of loyalty perhaps consistent with Cohen's conservative attitude.

Heritage and the Past

Partnership with the dead and the unborn

Acceptance of the given entails a deference to the past, an acquiescence to the world as we find it. Although Cohen rejects Michael Oakeshott's antidemocratic politics, he echoes Oakeshott's idea of 'the depth that defies articulation', that identity has a 'lived nature' rather than something we create, that our social existence involves elements that are 'unsayable'.[49] In accepting the given, we are engaged in what Oakeshott called a 'conversation with mankind', a link with generations before and after us, what Burke famously called a 'partnership not only between those who are living, but between those who are living, those who are dead, and those who are to be born'.[50]

This idea of obligations to the past is also put forcefully by G.K. Chesterton, who insisted that 'tradition is the democracy of the dead' which 'refuses to submit to the small and arrogant oligarchy of those who merely happen to be walking about'. Whereas 'democrats object to men being disqualified by the accident of birth; tradition objects to their being disqualified by the accident of death'.[51] Cohen echoes this point evocatively:

> We do not keep the cathedrals just because they are beautiful, but also because they are part of our past. We want the past to be present among us. We do not want to be cut off from it. We rejoice in the culture of *our* past.[52]

This theme was anticipated in the second edition of Cohen's treatise on Marx, where he revisited the epigraph he had chosen from his favourite childhood book, *The Little Boy and His House*. The story concerns a child without a home who travels the world to see all kinds of dwellings – a Romany tent, an igloo, a Chinese houseboat – but opts to build a red-brick bungalow upon his return home. Cohen had originally interpreted the story to confirm the Marxist story of the causal role of material circumstances, but he concludes here the importance of forms of life, traditions and customs: for people 'to be home' unlike 'to be housed' involves the 'potent force of familiarity' and 'traditions which tell them who they are'.[53]

Conservation and restoration

In his battles against nineteenth-century efforts to destroy ancient buildings, the art critic and professed conservative John Ruskin stressed the importance of our connection with the past. He referred to the 'sanctity in a good man's house' that cannot be renewed by any building that 'rises on its ruins'. The buildings of previous generations should be understood as a record of 'their honour, their gladness or their suffering' that 'sheltered and comforted' them; if their buildings are 'dragged down to the dust' it would show that all that had been 'treasured was despised'.[54] Indeed, Ruskin goes so far as to say of 'buildings of past times' that:

> We have no right whatever to touch them. They are not ours. They belong partly to those who built them, and partly to all the generations who are to follow us. The dead have still their right in them: that which they laboured for ... we have no right to obliterate.[55]

Debates in the domain of heritage conservation address these interesting claims. The pioneering figure in the study of heritage, Adophus Riegl, coined the phrase 'age value' – the perception of age in an object that communicates a sense of its life cycle, its meaning and significance. Reproductions and radical restoration, Riegl declared, risk disrupting our understanding of an artefact's context. We have an emotional connection to objects that are unmistakeably from the past, what Carolyn Korsmeyer calls 'real old things'.[56] The appeal is the experience with the tangible manifestation of another time, evoked by sight, touch, even odour, what Nietzsche mocked as a 'moldy smell' that (metaphorically at least) conservationists submit is inherent in our encounter with artefacts.[57]

Indeed, some maintain that restoration does violence to the integrity of heritage artefacts, which should be left in their ruined state to convey the value that comes from their history, rather than repaired so they are 'as good as new'. More recent art historians, however, have disputed Riegl's preoccupation with authenticity, contending what matters most is that the ordinary person encountering the artefact understands its 'pastness', not the authenticity of the artefact itself.[58] Contra Riegl and Cohen, such a concept does not refer to a property immanent in the artefact, but rather an object's context and ability to communicate with its audience.

Objects and people

Both Riegl's canonical view and revisionist approaches focus on artefacts' contribution to human culture. Cohen, however, seems to vacillate on the matter of the significance of human experience when it comes to existing value. His remarks about cathedrals, for example, stress the significance of valuable things for human beings, be it the relationship between a person and a particular object, or the role of objects as transmitters of culture and meaning for humankind. This is in line with his point about how an object recently destroyed has a claim to being restored or reproduced because of its role in our human experience and culture.

On the other hand, Cohen also downplays the relevance of the human connection to existing value. For one, the fact that a person happens to desire genetic manipulation of their body obviously does not carry much weight with him. But he goes further in the essay, saying 'I do not celebrate' the *experience* of valuable things; indeed, things can have value in a '*wholly* perceiverless and conceiverless world'. Blind people would appreciate, Cohen says, the fact that there are beautiful paintings in the world, even if they cannot view them.[59] Yet putting the matter in these terms still suggests that the human perspective cannot be wholly removed in the conservative bias. Intrinsic value, it seems, cannot do without those who do the valuing or who note the fact of value. As Cohen points out, such debates are not unique to the conservative argument; the case for any kind of intrinsic value runs up against the problem of the relevance of human experience.[60]

Socialist Implications

Revolution and destruction

In true Cohen fashion, the essay scrupulously entertains objections from critics, among them metaphysical puzzles such as whether an artist's unpainted sculpture has existing value that risks being lost if the artist, as intended, paints it.[61] Of particular interest though are the political implications of his argument. Recall that Cohen claims somewhat pre-emptively at the outset of the essay that his position has no truck with conservative politics more generally; fortunately, these issues get a fuller treatment towards the essay's end.

Social change and conservatism seem uneasy bedfellows. In times of revolutionary upheaval, heritage artefacts – monuments, churches and grand houses – are often wilfully destroyed, with little sense of any tragic loss, at least by those doing the destroying. Marx goes so far as to celebrate the destructive forces unleashed by capitalism itself. In the *Communist Manifesto*, Marx and Engels famously offer a paean to the bourgeoisie for its tremendous achievements:

> Subjection of Nature's forces to man, machinery, application of chemistry to industry and agriculture, steam-navigation, railways, electric telegraphs, clearing of whole continents for cultivation, canalisation of rivers, whole populations conjured out of the ground – what earlier century had even a presentiment that such productive forces slumbered in the lap of social labour?[62]

The bourgeoisie, likened to 'the sorcerer who is no longer able to control the powers of the nether world whom he has called up by his spells', does not have full control over the forces it has unleashed, the 'weapons' which will be turned against it. Thus, Marx's enthusiasm for the mastery of nature achieved by the capitalist class suggests that the devastating potential of bourgeois progress might not be so easily tamed.

'All that is solid melts into air'

The critique of capitalism reveals that ever-changing social forces will wipe out, not just ancient tyranny and prejudice, but also all that is deemed sacred and precious:

> All fixed, fast-frozen relations, with their train of ancient and venerable prejudices and opinions, are swept away, all new-formed ones become antiquated before they can ossify. All that is solid melts into air, all that is holy is profaned, and man is at last compelled to face with sober senses, his real conditions of life, and his relations with his kind.[63]

Leon Trotsky went further, eagerly anticipating a future where technology can 'cut down mountains and move them', on an 'immeasurably larger scale' than before, 'according to a general industrial and artistic plan'. Man will have 'rebuilt the earth, if not in his own image, at least according to his own taste', adding preposterously that he did not have 'the slightest fear that this taste will be bad'.[64] Some thinkers on the Left, such as Cohen's old friend Marshall Berman, recognize the complex role of modernism in Marxist thought. The celebration of revolutionary social change towards equality seems at the same time to betray a nihilism destructive of human value, a 'tension between Marx's critical insights and radical hopes'.[65]

The modernist, capitalist idea of progress has the upshot of what Henri Lefebvre calls the 'completely urbanized' society, a society of bureaucratic, controlled consumption, that debases and expropriates the common, producing anxiety and isolation.[66] Never-ending economic development rips apart and destroys cultural heritage, community, shared values, nature and other creatures in the natural world. And the 'productivist socialism' of the Soviet Union, which ultimately so disappointed Cohen, must shoulder part of the blame.[67] 'Both planning and the market' he ventured, are hostile to the 'conservative truth' that valuable things should be cherished.[68]

Green progressivism

There is thus an affinity between an enlightened, green progressivism and Cohen's conservatism. We saw that bioethicists advance, contra Cohen, that genetic manipulation could awaken an ethical consciousness committed to stringent environmental protections. Yet it is certainly the case that environmental ethics are, in their essence, a kind of 'conservation' of value – the etymological link with conservatism is no accident. Among the reasons for Cohen's disenchantment with Marxist historical materialism, articulated elsewhere, is its promethean arrogance, its confidence that the earth would perpetually yield a surplus that could be marshalled for socialist goals.[69] Cohen invokes the warnings of his Oxford colleague David Wiggins about our 'self-righteous insatiability' that does not permit the natural world to set any limits on our desires.[70] Central to Wiggins's position is an environmental consciousness, the idea that it is wrong to deprive future generations of resources they can 'reasonably expect to share' and, moreover, that 'the human scale of values is not uniformly human centred'.[71] It is striking, however, that Cohen's green politics are not much in evidence in this essay, except by implication in his discussion of biotechnologies.[72] Humility towards nature, a commitment to the preservation of other species, respect for the habitus of human and other life, is a conservative attitude that is apposite for those concerned with wanton disregard for the impact of our actions on the earth.

Cohen underscored that his conservatism did not mean an opposition to change to correct injustice. He suggests the paradox of a Left-winger endorsing conservatism may be resolved with the insight that, sometimes, social change is required to protect those things of value, 'to revolutionize our situation'. His former doctoral student Nicholas Vrousalis goes so far as to say that it is 'Cohen's radicalism that explains his particular brand of conservatism'.[73] Cohen recalls that 'one thing Karl Marx said about the socialist revolution was that that revolution was necessary to preserve the fruits of civilization against the ravages of capitalism'.[74]

Against 'market mania'

The socialist can thus find common cause with the conservative in their shared abhorrence for the commodification of human values. Cohen's argument shows how socialists and conservatives share a disaffection with the 'market mania' of 'Thatcherite Toryism'. That 'great betrayal of conservatism' failed to recognize what Marx saw so well: that 'capitalism so comprehensively transforms everything', including itself. Unlike traditional conservatives, British large-C Conservatives since Thatcher, Cohen sneers, 'blather on about warm beer and sturdy spinsters cycling to church and then they hand Wal-Mart the keys to the kingdom'. This is why working-class communities will find that, as Cohen puts it, 'small-c conservatism is a buffer against *in*equality'.[75] Indeed, in a chapter entitled 'The Truth in Socialism', the conservative Roger Scruton (with whom Cohen had many disagreements but whose politics were strongly anti-Thatcher) applauded Marx for his insight into the relentless commodification inflicted by the market.[76]

As the cultural theorist Slavoj Žižek (an unlikely ally for our analytical philosopher) remarks, 'only a radical Leftist' can be a 'true conservative' who is 'attentive to the dark obverse of progress'.[77] Cohen notes in passing the perspective of William

Morris, the nineteenth-century socialist aesthete, well known for his call for traditional craftsmanship in the face of capitalist mechanization.[78] Morris's route to socialism began in fact with his work for the Society for the Preservation of Ancient Buildings, including penning its manifesto which declared that 'the claims of poetry and history' require that historic architecture be handed down as 'instructive and venerable' to those that come after us.[79] Dubbed a 'conservative radical',[80] Morris bemoaned the 'shortsighted, reckless brutality of squalor', the 'ugly surroundings' confronting ordinary people since the decline of traditional crafts under capitalism.[81]

If you're an egalitarian, how come you're in favour of All Souls College?

Cohen's position on existing value faces the challenge that some valuable things are implicated in an unjust social order and can only be conserved in the context of such an order. Cohen's key example and arguably the inspiration for his argument is his beloved All Souls College. Indeed, the paper offers the following joke: '"Professor Cohen, how many Fellows of All Souls does it take to change a light bulb?" "Change?!?"'[82] Cohen relates how the fellows at All Souls wrestled with a controversial proposal, that the college become more integrated with external funding bodies, thereby risking the loss of its distinctive character.[83] All Souls, as discussed in chapter 1, is a particularly distinctive example of a venerable institution with a long history that involves privilege and exclusion. Upon his retirement, Cohen recalls how deeply saddened he was by the task of packing up and saying farewell to the beautiful rooms he had inhabited for 23 years. His experience poignantly exemplifies our connection with the past.[84]

Cohen was persuaded, as Otsuka puts it, that talk of preserving All Souls unchanged would 'expose his defense of conservatism to ad hominem mockery as a parochial concern bound up with an elite establishment of which he was a member'. Thus, in a subsequent version of the essay, Cohen replaced the references to All Souls with a fictional liberal arts college, 'Kenora Rainy River College' (doubtless strategically, since Kenora is a city in a rural area in northeast Ontario with no elite connotations). In the revised version the issue is whether Kenora College should expand and admit graduate students.[85] In deciding to include the original essay in the volume of essays produced after Cohen's death, Otsuka offers that the original essay conveys the personal roots of Cohen's ideas; his decision to include that version was made less difficult upon the realization that he would thereby be 'preserving a thing of value that might otherwise be lost'.[86] All Souls is a thing of particular value, and a thing of personal value to Cohen, as was the essay in which it figured.

Conservation and social justice

This background indicates Cohen's unease about the implications of his position. Although Cohen's conservative bias involves progressive themes, there remain potential tensions with his egalitarian ideals. Often conserving the old entails sacrificing other projects with egalitarian value, not just in the realm of futuristic genetic experimentation, but in the world we know.

Heritage conservation is a good example: policies that aim to conserve the heritage integrity of a historic property can conflict with making it accessible for disabled persons. Moreover, conservation requirements mean that repair and maintenance can be expensive, out of the reach of low-income people, fuelling a process of gentrification where the original inhabitants risk being unable to afford to live in their communities. Well-conserved older properties, often located in desirable neighbourhoods, tend to be more expensive than new. Debate frequently rages in municipalities about the relative merits of high-density affordable housing pitted against the conservation of historic houses. True, the issue of affordability is often disingenuously deployed by developers who argue that restrictions should be loosened to address a low-income housing crisis, when the projects in question turn out be relatively exclusive – for example, high-end condominium towers in old neighbourhoods. Nonetheless, there remain genuine good-faith dilemmas of principle here that do not feature in Cohen's discussion.

The All Souls example is telling. Like many very old institutions, its existence is bound up with relations of inequality. All Souls enjoys a significant concentration of wealth, a portion of which is the fruits of the slave trade,[87] and as with other institutions and practices at Oxford, the college has a history of exclusivity and privilege, many features of which are in tension with principles of social justice.[88] (To coin a phrase, if you're an egalitarian, how come you're in favour of All Souls?) The All Souls example demonstrates the idea that to conserve something in its essence, often change must be undertaken;[89] thus, as Cohen relates with approval, All Souls College now has women fellows.[90] Oxford and All Souls are currently seeking to rectify and reverse many of their traditions of privilege, and it may be that not only is this the right thing to do, but also that their very survival depends on it.

Things of beauty and sites of conscience

Perhaps there is a threshold of injustice: the evils of an existing thing's constitution could on the one hand be minimal, on the other so egregious that the claim to value is undermined. These issues can be illustrated with a thought experiment. Imagine a beautiful, very old painting, a portrait, that is highly valued. Art conservationists discover that the red pigment of the paint was made of the blood of the person depicted in the painting, who was tortured and killed. It turns out, therefore, that the beautiful painting has an abominable history. What should be our attitude to this painting? Its existing, particular value is now inextricably bound up with the horrendous moral wrong that created it. Indeed, the evil of the work's creation is such that we can no longer look at it the same way. Some might cease to find the painting beautiful. Yet perhaps we owe a duty to the woman whose blood was spilled to conserve this manifestation of her suffering existence.

There are real-world dilemmas of this kind. In Canada, the colonization of Indigenous peoples caused immeasurable harm that persists to this day: abysmal living conditions, low rates of education, poor health, as well as the deep-seated psychological and cultural effects of intergenerational trauma. One dimension of this colonial history is how Indigenous children were forcibly taken, removed from their families and brought to residential schools to ensure they lost all connection with their culture, language and traditions (thereby destroying many things of existing value). Children at these schools suffered from a myriad of ills: abuse, poor medical facilities, crowding and cruelty. A day of reckoning came in June 2021 for settler peoples in Canada when it was made public that hundreds of children died and were buried on the grounds of these institutions.

Many of the buildings where atrocities took place, like prisons and insane asylums, are characterized by beautiful architecture: Georgian or Victorian in design, with elegant proportions, excellent materials, and displaying superb artisanship. Such 'sites of conscience' raise important questions about their existing value and how that value might be understood and conserved in such a way that nonetheless honours these institutions' tragic past.[91]

Cohen's case should be pressed further on these points. In the case of All Souls, it could not exist in the way so beloved by Cohen without it continuing to be an elite institution that gives its members advantages not enjoyed by people elsewhere, even within the limited and already privileged context of higher education.[92] Presumably there are some valuable existing things whose value, in the All Souls sense (community, tradition), will lose out to their disvalue if the injustice they continue to perpetuate is serious enough. Cohen's former graduate student Paula Casal points to bullfighting as an example of a tradition whose cruelty disqualifies it from conservation.[93] Noteworthy are Scanlon and Scheffler's diverging views on tradition: the former noting that a tradition's value depends on its content, the latter contending content-based judgements are at odds with tradition's value.[94]

Cohen's Philosophical Tool Box

Fact independence

Cohen may have been able to address this dilemma with philosophical resources developed in his earlier work; for example, the idea of the ultimately independent nature of values in relation to facts. That is, the conservative bias in favour of existing value can be understood as a fact-independent ethical principle that might be compromised in the face of real-world factors. Cohen contends that his concern for existing value could be trumped by countervailing considerations: 'its particular value for anyone' is 'not the only considerations that should govern our decisions' he says of his central example, the financial autonomy of All Souls.[95]

However, the idea of carving out a fact-independent principle of conservatism that steers clear of fact-oriented considerations seems hard to sustain; arguably it's not the sordid world of regulation that is at issue when it comes to the impact of the conservative bias, but rather that the principles at stake confront other, conflicting principles. Though the essay entertains the idea that conservatism is an expensive taste because of its opposition to maximization,[96] Cohen does not go so far as to propose that conserving value figures as an illegitimate expensive taste if exclusivity is intrinsic to why the existing thing is valued (which might be said of All Souls, for example).[97]

Competing values

Cohen thus has another philosophical commitment that might help in working out the relative weight of justice and conservatism. As we saw in previous chapters, Cohen subscribes to value pluralism, the idea that there is not a single political value but many, often incommensurable, ones. In the face of competing principles – for example conserving value as opposed to equality or justice – often one must be sacrificed for another. Cohen states that an egalitarian would likely want to put justice lexically prior to other values or take a position of 'deference to justice' given that it would take something 'as momentous as justice' to trump 'the value that we seek to conserve'.[98] But conservation of value might still win out:

> I do not say that I am myself so uncompromising an egalitarian, so lexically pro-justice. I am not sure that we should regret the production of all the wonderful material culture that we have inherited and that was produced at the expense of gross injustice. Of course we regret that it was produced in that way, but would we be happier if it had not been produced, on the assumption that there would have been no non-unjust way of producing it?[99]

Egalitarian values are of great importance, but Cohen is not prepared to say they should triumph over all other goals, conservatism included. It seems that if the value is significant enough, the artefacts of our past are owed conservation and care despite their unjust origins and history, and indeed potentially the injustice their existence continues to perpetuate. His remark, 'something that merits destruction because it is unjust might nevertheless be of great value, all things considered' is elusive.[100]

Vrousalis suggests that Cohen sought solace in things of existing value as a kind of 'break' from the struggle for justice.[101] But this seems to make light of the deeply held commitments of this essay. True, we would expect that conservative values, which Cohen admits are defeasible, would take a back seat given the preeminent value of equality articulated in earlier work. Other values – for example, efficiency – were typically ascribed secondary importance, entering largely in connection with fact-conditioned regulatory rules. In other cases, such as justice and community, the relative weight is unclear with both values vying for priority in Cohen's egalitarian philosophy. Certainly Cohen's conservative bias does not seem easily overridden. The essay suggests that conservative values are of fundamental ethical importance, much like equality, justice and community are in Cohen's other writings.

Responsibility and the given

Cohen's conservative position indicates a tension with his progressive views in another, suggestive sense. The idea of accepting the given and thus the flaws in one's corporeal, mortal nature, is in tension with elements of the luck egalitarian creed, which stresses how individuals' choices are paramount in determining whether they are eligible for the remedy of disadvantage. Cohen's emphasis on accepting the given downplays the idea of individuals as fully autonomous choosers, masters of their destiny, and thus casts doubt on whether a person who is disadvantaged due to their choices should truly be held responsible.

Here I am picking up on the bioethicist argument we encountered earlier, yet not to endorse the case for genetic enhancement according to luck egalitarian criteria, but quite the contrary, to cast doubt on luck egalitarianism given the conservative bias. We noted in the last chapter that Sher purports, contra luck egalitarianism, that events in a life are difficult to separate into the categories of the chosen and unchosen. Sher contends that for people to live effectively, they must 'cope with contingency', the 'innumerable surprises, obstacles, windfalls, shocks and reversals that together make up a human life'. Society should ensure that its members can increase their stock of resources and opportunities given the inevitable limitations we will all encounter.[102] Sher's critique of luck egalitarianism entails a modest metric for redistribution, but the critique could also entail the forgoing of luck egalitarianism to achieve a more ambitious metric, in keeping with Cohen's socialist ideals.

Conservatism and perfectionism

There is another sense in which Cohen's conservatism may help elaborate or expand his egalitarian aims, rather than conflict with them. This is the idea of the constituents of a life well lived that emerges in this essay. Cohen's conservative analysis brings to the fore the perfectionist elements in his philosophical outlook. As we saw in the last chapter, Cohen's idea of 'access to advantage', which draws on Sen's idea of capabilities and functionings, lends itself to a view about the role of living well in egalitarian theory.

For Cohen, what counts as advantage includes preference satisfaction, but also involves some objective account of what is good for human beings. Being adequately nourished is an obvious, uncontroversial example, but we saw that Cohen also emphasizes non-material dimensions of living well, for example, the contribution of cheerfulness to human wellbeing. Also to be added, perhaps, are our connections with the past, with artefacts of our history, the 'eloquence of stone' that 'enthralled' Cohen whilst in Edinburgh for the Gifford Lectures.[103]

Cohen's case for conservatism involves the idea that human beings' lives are enriched by existing things, and that capitalism's ills involve not just the unequal distribution of the means of life but also a process of relentless commodification that destroys things of value. This is consistent with Cohen's commendation of fellowship and community (which he unexpectedly found in college life) over the market's 'greed and fear'. Cohen's foray into conservatism tells us that cathedrals, All Souls College, acceptance of one's corporeal nature, are all constituents of the good life, whereas 'plasticization' of the human body, Walmart, an 'attitude of universal mastery over everything'[104] are not.

Cohen is not monistic about what counts as worthy and valuable: there are many good things, and no one person is likely to enjoy all good things equally, as illustrated by Cohen's examples of Hockney and Filippo Lippi paintings, Byzantine icons and Frank Gehry architecture.[105] Thus Cohen, in deploying the conservative outlook, is able to dispatch a common prejudice against perfectionism that it dictates a single way of life, that it is concerned with, literally, '*the* good'.[106] The emphasis on the appreciation for variety which Cohen says is inherent in the conservative position encapsulates the pluralist idea that what makes a life good is diverse and multi-faceted, that one person's good may not be endorsed by another. Given the incommensurability of many goods, often one good may have to be sacrificed for another, or a potential good forgone for the preservation of an existing one.[107]

Rigour and insight

Proposing that Cohen was sympathetic to perfectionist ideas may seem an extravagant claim, and the evidence adduced for this here is modest. Moreover, as noted in earlier chapters, in all his critiques of liberal egalitarianism, Cohen did not target directly the 'neutralism' of liberals like Dworkin and Rawls, that is, their insistence that society should not seek to promote conceptions of the good, and their egalitarian arguments for the state abstaining from perfectionist policy. Perhaps Cohen's parsimonious method, deployed to interrogate the egalitarianism of liberal philosophy, did not permit him to stray into other controversial debates. His austere analytical strategy, the preference for the micro, was for him a matter of argumentative integrity, a methodology he both practised and preached.[108]

Yet in these final reflections we can discern some pulling back from his emphasis on austerity in argumentation, from the rejection of holism, or the injunction on the poetic or non-literal in one's philosophical writing. Thus, an intriguing dimension of Cohen's essay is methodological, what it tells us about how to do philosophy. This suggests another paradox of the many paradoxes in Cohen's thought that is worth exploring. We have noted how the conservatism essay's approach is to offer some considerations about existing value that should have weight, without elaborating further on their implications. Some critical responses to the essay sought to tease out the logical conundrums of Cohen's view, though with the admission that such efforts 'may seem objectionably untethered from our actual valuing attitudes and practices'.[109] True, many of Cohen's earlier writings did not yield definitive conclusions, for example, the question of the rich egalitarian. But typically the uncertainty came after a rigorous analytical scrutiny of the arguments for and against. That is not the flavour of the writing here.

The limits of the analytical

Cohen admits that claims about existing value might not win out, but he does not specify how conflicts would be resolved. Whereas in other essays he made analytical distinctions about ultimate, fact-independent values as opposed to values conditioned by facts, or pure principles as opposed to rules of regulation, no such moves are made here. In juxtaposing this newly articulated conservative disposition with Cohen's longstanding egalitarianism, it is difficult to come up with a resolution that would not undermine the essay's distinctive contribution. As a progressive Cohen did not want to insist on the priority of conserving things that exist but nor did he want to give carte blanche to the goals of social change trumping conservative considerations. The analytical philosopher may search for a formula or criterion, but in this case Cohen only navigates and negotiates in the face of difficult, complex considerations.

Cohen's work on Marx called for analytical tools to bring rigour to a field of study that lacked them, a project that defined his philosophical approach thereafter. However, in Cohen's final writings a different picture emerges. The tone of this essay is tentative and modest, but also deeply personal, communicating sage reflections as he concludes his career. That Cohen wrote this essay when he did evokes considerations of what Edward Said calls 'late style' where the intellectual possesses 'a mature subjectivity, stripped of hubris and pomposity, unashamed either of its fallibility or of the modest assurance it has gained as a result of age and exile'.[110]

Cohen's very final, unfinished essay on spirituality 'celebrates life', counsels humility and affirms the beauty of the world as it exists. Cohen's sympathy for religious ideas came as a surprise to many of Cohen's colleagues and students. However, in his Gifford Lectures, Cohen the ambivalent Marxist revealed himself to be an agnostic, not an atheist, and a lifelong reader of both the Old and New Testaments.[111] Moreover, Cohen admitted that the increasing focus in his work on personal moral engagement was 'so near to Christianity that it would have shocked his younger self'.[112] In these final ruminations Cohen speaks of the importance of looking for good and being grateful for 'what some think of as God's bounty', suggesting some profound attachments that, if deferred, should be done with great care.[113] And Cohen imparts wisdom to counter cleverness. The idea that life is beautiful as we find it, he says, might tempt a philosopher to reach for a case that disproves the claim. But, Cohen concludes, 'old analytical philosophers should understand when not to use the counterexample machine'.[114]

Conclusion

Cohen leaves us with a vital insight: that things in the world have existing value that, other things being equal, call upon us to respect and conserve, whatever might follow from the weighing of competing considerations. Yet with only one late essay on conservativism against a large career-long corpus on egalitarianism, it is difficult to know how to assess the significance of the conservative view for Cohen's overall philosophical position. Although this essay poses a particularly striking paradox when considered against Cohen's larger political and philosophical commitments, ultimately it reminds us of Cohen's value pluralism, that is, the license he gave himself to profess a range of competing values, even if equality is preeminent.

It is indisputable that there are respects in which the call for conserving 'existing value' such as traditional ancient institutions like All Souls College sits uneasily with radical calls for equality and justice. However, it is also the case that there are some surprising affinities here with socialist ideals, particularly the theme of community that emerges forcefully in his last published volume, *Why Not Socialism?* and his critique of the ethos of the market. Moreover, one might say that Cohen's conservatism, expounded at the end of his career, accounts for why he wrote his book on Marx at his career's start: to conserve the communist ideals with which he had been raised. 'Loyalty to his former self', noted in chapter 1, is a conservative attitude too. Cohen's conservatism essay focuses on loyalty to things, but there is a profound sense in which things embody or represent persons, practices, communities, even nature, loyalty to which were features of his work and life too.

Finally, the conservatism essay suggests some fascinating ways in which Cohen's other commitments, be they methodological or substantive, might need a more complex reading. Cohen's commitment to avoiding 'bullshit' meant perhaps that he felt compelled to utilize the resources of his analytical toolbox to pursue the idea of conserving value, wherever it may lead. Yet, that Cohen the radical should also be a conservative, Cohen the analytical philosopher should also be stepping back, albeit very gently, from the brash confidence of no-bullshit to a domain of spirituality and tradition, simply confirms the rich, paradoxical legacy – incisive, surprising, witty and wise – of Jerry Cohen's contribution to political thought.

7
Conclusion: Paradox and Legacy

'A day will come when no one will be able to defend a form of society in which a minority profit from the dispossession of the majority.'[1]

G. A. Cohen's philosophy was distinguished by formidable rigour, originality of thought and analytical acumen. But perhaps above all, his thought was shaped by several deeply felt and profoundly personal emotions – a passion for justice, equality and community, an abiding nostalgia and loyalty to the past, and a deep love for family and friends. It is hardly surprising, then, that his untimely and tragic death precipitated such exceptional feelings of grief among so many. Philosophers around the world mourned the loss of a person who was a great thinker and a beloved friend. Solace could be taken in the fact that, as he remarked at his retirement conference to his many former students, he faced this stage of his career, 'yielding' to the 'end of striving', with equanimity, gratitude and peace, even if the people in his life wished for much more time with him.[2]

This book has characterized Cohen's political philosophy in terms of several paradoxes. Indeed, Cohen's memorable essay title about personal responsibility for remedying inequality is a suggestive way of reflecting on his thought more broadly. Thus: If Cohen was a Marxist how come he was an analytical philosopher? If Cohen was a Leftist, how come he was exercised by libertarianism? If Cohen was a socialist, how come he considered principles of justice to be independent of material conditions? If Cohen was a radical egalitarian, how come he was a luck egalitarian? If Cohen was a progressive, how come he was a conservative?

Conclusion: Paradox and Legacy 165

By 'paradoxes' I mean puzzles or tensions in Cohen's thought that make for surprising juxtapositions, original insights and potentially inconsistent views or claims. It may seem that describing a thinker's work as paradoxical suggests a defect or weakness, but that would be the wrong inference to make of Cohen's contribution.[3] Some paradoxes, such as the use of 'bourgeois' analytical philosophy to argue for radical political claims, or the Marxist interest in libertarianism, are easily dispelled considering the compelling arguments they generated. Cohen's pathbreaking contributions settle the matter. Some paradoxes, however, make for unresolved tensions.

Perhaps the most challenging paradox is at the heart of Cohen's radical egalitarianism, the focus of chapter 5. Cohen understands justice to demand, not just institutional change, but personal contributions to the amelioration of inequality. This principle sits alongside another which seems to pull in the opposite direction: that only inequalities that result from circumstance or brute luck are entitled to remedy. Cohen sought to resolve the paradox himself by reference to the principle of community, where fellow feeling would attend to disadvantages ineligible for redress at the bar of justice. However, he was uncomfortable with the possible upshot that community and justice are at odds. A resolution to the paradox, we saw, may lie in an understanding of the egalitarian community as requiring that we be accountable for our actions, not expecting our fellows to shoulder the burden of our irresponsible choices. Yet that ideal of accountability on the part of the individual still leaves open the possibility that the community is nonetheless obligated to attend to disadvantage, whatever its cause. Indeed, it is possible that it is precisely the shortfall in remedy for disadvantage that results from Cohen's luck egalitarianism that prompted the demanding expectation that individuals assume personal responsibility for the promotion of equality.

Of course, paradoxes abound in the most important and influential of texts. Cohen was in good company with the Bible, which he read avidly and occasionally cited. Thus Thessalonians 3:10, states 'we commanded you, that if any would not work, neither should he eat'. Yet Acts 2:44–5 relays that 'all that believed were together and had all things in common; and sold their possessions and goods, and parted them to all men, as every man had need'.[4] Some of the most powerful and persuasive ideas are not fully reconcilable with each other. The complexity with which Cohen addressed questions of freedom, equality and justice attests to the rich and stimulating character of his thought.

Scientific and Utopian

One way of linking all these paradoxes is with the idea, noted in earlier chapters, that Cohen's thought was both utopian and scientific.[5] The distinction between utopian and scientific socialism was first made by Marx and Engels, who disparaged previous socialist thought for being utopian, unlike their own, scientific, approach. For Marx and Engels, socialist argument had hitherto been insufficiently revolutionary, guilty of overestimating the role of ideas and blueprints, and failing to understand the crucial role of historical circumstances. According to their scientific doctrine of historical materialism, in contrast, socialist revolution is not merely an act of revolutionary will or the realization of good ideas. Instead, emancipation requires that a particular agent, the working class, seize the opportunities presented by crises in capitalism that occur as part of the inevitable progress towards socialist transformation.

The seeds of the scientific in Cohen's philosophy were planted early. Cohen had grown up with the communist belief in the scientific credentials of Marxism as a single explanatory theory. He saw his first task as a mature philosopher to be to show that Marx's historical materialism was sound. However, he did so by means of a scientific approach extrinsic to Marxism. Just as Marx and Engels conceived historical materialism as a new, superior methodology for the critique of capitalism, Cohen can be said to have consciously employed a new scientific approach. Only this time the approach was informed by the methods and standards of analytical philosophy and, moreover, producing a form of analysis critically to bear on the claims of Marxism itself.

Nonetheless, the scrupulous insistence on analytical method, which indeed Cohen likened to modern science, hearkened back to Marx and Engels's belief in the superiority of their methodology.[6] In fact, as we saw in chapter 2, Cohen invited the analogy with Marx and Engels on the matter of being scientific, noting Engels's tribute to Marx as the founder of 'scientific socialism' which, like Cohen and his colleagues, used 'the most advanced resources of social science ... within the frame of a socialist commitment', and which 'exploited ... what was best in the bourgeois social science of his day'.[7]

In Cohen's case, arguably that hard-headed outlook pertained to, not just method, but also substantive commitments. Cohen backed away from classical Marxist tenets that he believed could

Conclusion: Paradox and Legacy

no longer be defended, for example the quasi-libertarian understanding of workers' exploitation, or the assumption of socialist abundance. Indeed, Cohen ultimately denigrated Marxism for its claims to be scientific because of its lack of predictive power. The need for a radical, normative philosophy followed from Cohen's conclusion that socialism would not come about due to inevitable historic processes. This insistence on facing up to challenging ethical realities also made for a tough line on issues that socialists had wished away in the past. This is why, perhaps, Cohen targets free riders in his embrace of luck egalitarianism – no-bullshit Marxism thus dictates no-sucker socialism.

Yet Cohen was undeniably a utopian thinker – insistent that facts should not fetter one's ideals, that we stay loyal to the vision and artefacts of the past, that a bucolic camping trip among friends be a model for the just society. Whether it be riling against Rawls's principles of justice for their concessions to the baser parts of people's nature, lambasting the UK Labour Party's opportunistic move to the right, or invoking the spirit of community and self-sacrifice that characterized the British war effort, Cohen imagined that human beings could aspire to a world beyond selfishness and inequality.

Cohen's Impact

It is difficult to overestimate Cohen's impact. His arrival as the Chichele Chair in 1980s Oxford was highly anticipated and much celebrated, and he left an indelible mark on the philosophical character and culture of both the university and his beloved college, All Souls. Students, especially progressive ones, flocked to his lectures and sought his supervision. Cohen thus shaped, not only the themes and ideas of his generation, but of those who came after him. Furthermore, there is no doubt about Cohen's importance in contemporary political philosophy: 'the cleverest among us'[8] yet 'the most serious and intense of philosophers',[9] 'the best political philosopher in the UK',[10] 'one of the greatest philosophers of our time',[11] indeed, 'a genius',[12] who provided a defence of 'the most thoroughgoing and radical egalitarianism to be found among analytical philosophers',[13] 'second to none'.[14]

Cohen has left an impressive corpus of highly influential writings which engendered several trends, themes, indeed even schools in political thought. As we saw in chapter 6, even his single and arguably most eccentric essay on conservatism had an impact, generating debate about the nature of value, conservation and our relation to the past.

However, first, and perhaps foremost, there is the work on Marx and Marxism identified in chapter 2, beginning with his book on historical materialism and the ensuing body of creative work – by Cohen and his Analytical Marxist colleagues – on questions of social explanation, historical materialism, exploitation, class and social change. Cohen's analysis of difficult problems such as the relationship of capitalist material conditions and social institutions, the nature of workers' unfreedom, the role of labour in the value of commodities, is unparalleled. The influence of this body of writing was enormous, forever changing the way socialist and Marxist ideas are understood and conceptualized.

Second, related to this, as we saw in chapter 3, Cohen's critique of capitalism, and in particular his powerful assault on the libertarian ideas of Nozick, was innovative and inspiring. In his immanent critique, Cohen carefully dissected the assumptions and steps of this right-wing anarchist position to show, not that equality mattered more than liberty (although that was probably in fact his view), but rather that in libertarian hands, the value of liberty loses out to private property. Again, Cohen's refusal to take an easy route and his strict eschewal of left-wing platitudes and blithe assumptions was tremendously refreshing.

Third, Cohen's turn to egalitarianism was highly influential. The expensive tastes debate between Cohen and Dworkin, discussed in chapter 5, was a significant contribution. And arguably Cohen's turn to luck egalitarianism was crucial in giving the doctrine broad appeal, influencing left-wing egalitarians as well as liberals. As we saw in chapter 4, Cohen's radical critique of Rawls, his challenge to think about egalitarian principles as applicable beyond institutions, continues to reverberate. Indeed, the important and influential work of contemporary political philosophers about the justice of the family – childrearing practices, children's autonomy, the transmission of advantage, has much to do with Cohen putting on the philosophical agenda the question of how our private lives intersect with our public commitments.

Finally, there is Cohen's concept of access to advantage, or 'midfare', a theme in chapter 5. The idea of a metric that melded material resources and wellbeing promised to offer an original, important egalitarian approach. Moreover, the perfectionist intimations of the view, which come through in Cohen's critique of the

Conclusion: Paradox and Legacy 169

attitudes of the market and his turn to conservatism, would have been worth exploring.[15] Not only would the idea of access to advantage constitute a radical critique of the neutralist liberals,[16] but it would also have brought back into focus socialist, if not Marxist, ideals about living well. It seems regrettable that Cohen did not develop this view further. Perhaps he was daunted by Amartya Sen's highly influential, similar approach. Or Cohen worried that he could not muster a view that would withstand the analytical scrutiny he would exact of himself. Or he had other, more tempting fish to fry – in particular, the critique of Rawls. Nonetheless, this seems a missed opportunity.

Hedgehog or Fox?

Two of Cohen's former students, Nicholas Vrousalis and Jonathan Wolff, came to different conclusions about their teacher's contribution. For Vrousalis, though the contribution was 'piecemeal', there was a unity in Cohen's thought which could be captured with the phrase, 'secular egalitarian theodicy'. 'Theodicy' signals the Manichean sense of a battle of good against evil that Vrousalis found at the heart of Cohen's work. Just as traditional theodicies seek to reconcile the existence of evil with the existence of God, Cohen's work centred on the possibility of banishing the evil of capitalism and the ushering forth of a 'fully emancipated humanity'. Vrousalis contended that this substantive commitment, summed up in Cohen's phrase of 'back to socialist basics', coupled with the unified methodological approach of analytical philosophy, made for a powerful unity in Cohen's thought. Moreover, Vrousalis finds that Cohen's project possessed 'an existential urgency' that is 'rare among contemporary political thinkers'.[17]

Wolff, in contrast, claimed that Cohen's skills – 'unrivalled' though they were – lay in being more of a 'reactive' than a 'creative' thinker, something that, as we saw in chapter 1, Cohen understood about himself.[18] For Cohen, philosophical engagement involved taking on an opponent, and his career can be understood in terms of tackling one opponent after the other, from Marx, to Nozick, to Dworkin and Rawls. Certainly, that one of Cohen's YouTube videos is the hilarious 'Marxist boxing match' tells us something about how he understood philosophy.[19]

Thus, though there are 'a large number of distinctive arguments and insightful positions', Cohen's 'reluctance to engage in big picture thinking of his own' meant he never put them together in an 'overarching structure'. Wolff agreed that there is unity of a 'moral and motivational' kind, and of course a methodological unity in Cohen's analytical approach. However, he was unconvinced by Vrousalis's claim that there is a unity of project in either a general conception or even a link among the different components of Cohen's thought.[20]

Cohen's diverse philosophical interests no doubt reflect the variety of influences on his thought – his Montreal childhood and communist upbringing, the discovery of Oxford philosophy, the cut and thrust of the 'Star Wars' seminars (again the language of battle), the politics of Thatcher's Britain, the rarefied world of All Souls. It is true that Cohen did not provide a coherent, systematic theory, but rather responded to a range of theoretical positions current in his time. This made for principles that were in tension with each other.

In this Cohen might be said to be a 'fox' rather than a 'hedgehog'. His mentor Isaiah Berlin famously elaborated this metaphor from the Ancient Greek poet Archilochus, who said 'the fox knows many things, but the hedgehog knows one big thing'. Berlin proposed that there were thinkers whose thought was animated by a single idea, who buried themselves in one project, and others who darted from idea to idea, seeing the world from a variety of views.[21] There is certainly the hedgehog in Cohen's work – a constant purpose in the defence of a radical, far-reaching and inspiring idea of equality.

Yet Cohen, with his consideration of different thinkers, his value pluralism, his diverse positions and interests, could also be thought a fox. Although well known for his classes on Marx and liberal egalitarianism, Cohen also lectured throughout his career on a range of political thinkers, and not just what was deemed the canon among British philosophers (Plato, Aristotle, Hobbes, Locke, etc.), but even, surprisingly, Nietzsche. As conveyed to him by his teacher Gilbert Ryle, his approach in these lectures tended to be to subject thinkers to exacting critical scrutiny rather than to consider them in context.[22]

Although Cohen was humble in his self-estimation as one who targeted others' work rather than forged a systematic theory of his own, he also saw his approach as a philosophical virtue, the product of his Oxford (versus Harvard) schooling, 'the only way to go'. Whereas Rawls provides a theory, Cohen's approach was to determine what principles to endorse by investigating one's individual normative judgements on particular cases, with

Conclusion: Paradox and Legacy   171

the result that one's ethical commitments 'present themselves in competitive array'. They cannot all be satisfied all the time, nor is there a systematic method to bring them together.[23] But that is, Cohen thought, as it should be.

Analytical and Particular

Cohen's embrace of the analytical might therefore help explain the absence of a systematic philosophical position. In his exhortations against bullshit, he insisted that a defining feature of cogent thought was that it eschew broad, sweeping views. He decried holism, understood as the view that 'social formations and classes' obey 'laws of behaviour that are not a function of the behaviours of their constituent individuals'. Of course, there are certainly many systematic, anti-holist philosophies. However, in Cohen's work, his anti-holism helped buttress his confidence that he could provide fruitful analyses of political phenomena. For Cohen, 'micro-analysis is always desirable and always *in principle* possible'.[24] Indeed, to return to an earlier theme, Cohen unabashedly deployed scientific vocabulary on this point, urging 'resolution to a more atomic level'. Pre-analytical Marxism was 'scientifically undeveloped', according to Cohen:

> ... rather in the way that thermodynamics was before it was supplemented by statistical mechanics, and, in each case, because of failure to represent molar level entities (such as quantities of gas, or economic structures) as arrangements of their more fundamental constituents. It is one thing to know, as phenomenological thermodynamics did, *that* the gas laws hold true. It is another to know *how* and *why* they do, and that further knowledge requires analysis, in the narrow sense, which statistical mechanics provided by applying Newton's laws to the molecular constituents of gases. Partly similarly, to claim that capitalism must break down and give way to socialism is not yet to show how behaviours of individuals lead to that result. And nothing else leads to that result, since behaviours of individuals are always where the action is, in the final analysis.[25]

The drive for specificity, the effort to isolate a single question from more general themes or ideas, was where Cohen's prodigious analytical talents lay, and he often spoke of his enjoyment in working out, as he put it, the 'curlicues and twirly bits' rather than the big picture in philosophy.[26] In an interview published near the end of his life, Cohen related that he read 'very slowly' and as a consequence 'I don't read as many things as I should'.[27] The comment is self-effacing, but the flipside is, befitting his methodological principles, what he read, he read with great care.

Perhaps Cohen's political outlook also prevented him from looking for a systematic theory. As we saw in chapter 1, growing up and well into his adulthood, Cohen was confident that historical materialism provided the tools to give an exhaustive account of human society. He may therefore have thought there was no need to come up with a systematic theory of his own. The exception to this in Cohen's corpus, though it too involved analysing the work of another, was his magisterial book on Marx, which sought a thorough defence of the very creed he had long assumed to be true.

Yet the tough-minded approach whereby socialist commitments were parsed into distinct premises and conclusions and tested for their validity was uncongenial to carving out a new sweeping and systematic theory to supplement or replace the old. In the face of theoretical dead ends, the setbacks of history, and Marxism's waning influence in the academy, Cohen abandoned key Marxist commitments. However, he did not look for a replacement theoretical system. Arguably his experience with Marxism and its disappointments confirmed his suspicion that such an account was unavailable and foolhardy to pursue.

Analytical and Ethical

It is worth reflecting on the ethical significance of Cohen's Analytical Marxism. The emphasis on clarity in both his writings and teaching had a bracing effect on political philosophy, setting a standard for all of us – students, teachers and scholars. His students were exceptionally fortunate to have the benefits of, not just his example, but also Cohen's counsel on how to do political philosophy which was formally shared at the first meeting of his Oxford graduate seminar.[28] Cohen's ability to carefully work out and expose the weaknesses of an argument earned him the epithet of 'expert demolition worker'.[29] As discussed in chapter 1, Cohen was especially hard on himself. He was not content to leave his work be, but would write, revise and refine, addressing objections and rethinking his position. His papers and chapters often had long addenda where he would answer criticisms, thereby sacrificing elegance of presentation for assiduous scholarship.

Conclusion: Paradox and Legacy 173

In earlier chapters we noted how the apolitical character of much postwar philosophy indicated that political convictions had no place in philosophical thinking. Cohen himself – under the tutelage of Gilbert Ryle and imbibing the culture of the positivist Oxford philosophical scene – chose not to challenge this view until his career as a philosopher was well under way. When Cohen did engage with political philosophy, he turned to Marxism, realizing that to truly pay homage to the teachings of his family and community, he should not insulate them from philosophical reflection, but subject them to disciplined scrutiny. And so Cohen paid the greatest tribute of all to the politics of his origins in his analytical, no-bullshit, Marxist writings.

Cohen's model of demanding self-scrutiny is particularly valuable for theorists on the Left. This is because, first, many on the Left had wrongly assumed that there was no intellectual home for them in the Anglo-American philosophical tradition, and second, as Cohen knew so well from the inside, radicals are especially prey to bullshit to avoid interrogating their deeply felt political convictions. For thinkers in the socialist tradition, tempted to blithely conclude that their noble ends justify any means, be they in action or argument, these were salutary lessons.

Moreover, there were in fact moral implications at stake in the very Oxford philosophy that Cohen had been schooled in. Cohen was taught the virtues of responsible speech, that one be accountable for what one says. To learn to stand by what one has said, until one can no longer mean it, was a lesson in responsibility. Integrity went along with clarity. Thus for all the ordinary language philosophers' suspicion of moral and political value, Cohen was doubtless attracted to the strong ethical conviction that underlay the emphasis on clear, straightforward communication.[30]

The Personal Is Political – Humanity and Wit

Cohen's example of how personal convictions could inspire penetrating political thought also had a substantive aspect, insofar as he argued, against the grain of most liberal and socialist thinking, that one's personal choices should reflect one's public commitments to justice. Thus, he contended that the person who professes egalitarian principles should live by them, forgoing salary incentives or tax breaks, making socially useful occupational choices, raising one's children in ways that don't privilege them over others. As discussed, this position was extremely influential, with a whole corpus of contemporary political philosophy interrogating the matter of the obligations of well-off egalitarians, particularly when it came to weighing one's special interests in, and obligations to, family.[31]

Cohen's distinctive voice made a difference. Not only was there the joke of his essay title – if you're an egalitarian how come you're so rich? – that inspired the personal turn in political theorizing and spawned so many imitations. But also, Cohen's philosophical interactions in general, be they on the page or in person, were so very entertaining. An encounter with Cohen was likely to be both edifying and amusing. He was one of a kind, of course, and few of us could hope to match Cohen's wit. However inimitable, though, his example was important. Cohen made philosophy fun, as one enjoyed his sense of humour and mischief, and in the sheer pleasure one could take in aspiring to analytical acuity.

Alongside his humour was Cohen's kindness and fellowship. The humanity that underlay his philosophical interests often came to the surface in anecdotes about anti-communist repression, or mistreatment of family members by factory bosses, union songs and utopian poetry, throwing into sharp relief the ethical issues and dilemmas at stake. For all his no-bullshit austerity, Cohen was also a romantic. His final writings on conservatism and spirituality, as explored in chapter 6, give voice to that romantic side.

Those writings also show Cohen's suspicion of following a 'party line' when truth might lie elsewhere. Cohen would invoke the words of sources that he knew were reactionary, but which he nonetheless found of value, such as the British imperialistic poetry of his school days, as noted in chapter 1. He once quoted to me the fascist sympathizer and celebrated poet, Ezra Pound, acknowledging the dubious pedigree, but nonetheless treasuring the wisdom of the eloquent lines: 'what thou lovest well remains, the rest is dross'.[32]

Conclusion

Of the many paradoxes in Cohen's work, the one that perhaps best sums them all up is the one with which this closing chapter began: the combination of austere analytical thinking and passionate political belief. It made for a unique and compelling contribution. The political context of Cohen's writings – the rise of Reagan,

Conclusion: Paradox and Legacy

Thatcher and the New Right, the collapse of the Soviet Union, the waning of Marxism as a theoretical world view, the tendency of left-wing parties to move to the centre – made for a crisis in socialist thought. A lack of confidence beset many radical thinkers and organizations. Yet Cohen's socialist convictions were unwavering throughout. 'Justice just is justice' as he was fond of pronouncing.[33] Today, with a yawning gap between rich and poor, a monumental cost of living crisis, the ever more fragile state of socialized medicine in many countries, and a global environmental emergency in a context of geopolitical turmoil, the capitalist market's capacity to meet human needs is shown to be ever more inadequate. Many are turning to radical ideas for inspiration. To think through, with rigour and discipline, the ideas and arguments for a socialist alternative, seems imperative. We need Jerry Cohen more than ever.

Notes

Preface

1 Philippe Van Parijs says this in his endorsement on the cover of *Finding Oneself in the Other*, edited by Michael Otsuka.
2 I quote these laudatory remarks from the endorsements from, respectively, Philippe Van Parijs, Andrew Williams, Seana Shiffrin, Marshall Berman, Andrew Williams, Philippe Van Parijs, John Roemer, on the covers of the collections of Cohen's work, *On the Currency of Egalitarian Justice* and *Finding Oneself in the Other*, both edited by Michael Otsuka, and *Lectures on the History of Moral and Political Philosophy*, edited by Jonathan Wolff.

Chapter 1: The Political is Personal: G. A. Cohen's Philosophical Journey

1 G. A. Cohen, 'Valedictory Lecture: My Philosophical Development (and impressions of philosophers whom I met along the way)', 175–6.
2 Michael Otsuka, 'Remarks at G. A. Cohen's Funeral'.
3 G. A. Cohen, 'Politics and Religion in a Montreal Communist Jewish Childhood', 21.
4 Conversation with Michael Cohen, 17 January 2023.
5 Cohen, 'Paradoxes of Conviction', 9.
6 Cohen, 'Politics and Religion in a Montreal Communist Jewish Childhood', 22.
7 As summed up by Merrily Weisbord, *The Strangest Dream: Canadian Communists, The Spy Trials and the Cold War*, 31. Weisbord consulted Cohen when conducting her research and upon the book's publication,

Cohen went on record with his praise. A later edition includes Cohen's letter which states, 'I shall be grateful to you for the rest of my life'. 'Letter from G. A. Cohen, 1984', 312–13.
8   Hillel Steiner, 'G. A. Cohen, "Where the Action Was"', also conversation with Hillel Steiner, 10 December 2019.
9   Cohen, 'Politics and Religion in a Montreal Communist Jewish Childhood', 23–31.
10 Weisbord, *The Strangest Dream*, 278–80.
11 Weisbord describes this vividly in *The Strangest Dream*, 279–89. See also Cohen, 'Politics and Religion in a Montreal Communist Jewish Childhood', 26.
12 Conversation with Michael Cohen, 17 January 2023.
13 Among his interesting cases was defending professional ice hockey players in a lockout of the National Hockey League in 2012; conversation with Michael Cohen, 17 January 2023.
14 Conversation with Michael Cohen, 17 January 2023.
15 Cohen, 'Politics and Religion in a Montreal Communist Jewish Childhood', 32.
16 Conversation with Michael Cohen, 17 January 2023.
17 Cohen, 'Valedictory Lecture', 177.
18 Cohen, 'Valedictory Lecture', 178.
19 Cohen, 'Valedictory Lecture', 178.
20 Another comment was that 'this essay reveals that you have unusual philosophical ability' but 'I disagree violently with much of what you say'. G. A. Cohen, Personal Archive.
21 The B.Phil. is a two-year graduate degree in philosophy in which students prepare to write examination papers in a range of subjects followed by a thesis. Other subjects, under pressure from overseas students, adopted the nomenclature of M.Phil. for the equivalent postgraduate degree. However, the Philosophy Faculty (then Sub-faculty) took the view that the Oxford B.Phil. in Philosophy was so respected and well known that the name should be retained; the B.Phil. continues to this day in Oxford.
22 Conversation with Michael Cohen, 17 January 2023.
23 Cohen, 'Politics and Religion in a Montreal Communist Jewish Childhood', 37.
24 It is surprising how intellectual insecurity and unease about being Jewish in Oxford combined to produce self-doubt in even the most accomplished people; for a powerful example, see Nicola Lacey, *A Life of H.L.A. Hart: The Nightmare and the Noble Dream*.
25 G. A. Cohen, 'Isaiah's Marx, and Mine', 2.
26 Marshall Berman, 'Gerald Cohen (1941–2009)'.
27 Cohen, 'Valedictory Lecture', 181, G. A. Cohen, 'Preface', *History, Labour, and Freedom: Themes from Marx*, xi. Michael Kremer, however, notes that Ryle himself disliked the term 'analytical philosophy'

and did not use it. Indeed, it would be wrong to portray analytical philosophers as uniformly hostile, for example, to the history of philosophy. See Gilbert Ryle, *Critical Essays*, which include papers on historical figures such as Plato, Locke and Hume. I'm grateful to Michael Kremer and Alice Crary for these insights.
28 Gilbert Ryle, *The Concept of Mind*.
29 Nikhil Krishnan, *A Terribly Serious Adventure: Philosophy and War at Oxford 1900–1960*, 28–9.
30 Michael Rosen, 'Jerry Cohen – An Appreciation'.
31 Nicholas Vrousalis, *The Political Philosophy of G. A. Cohen: Back to Socialist Basics*, 3.
32 Cohen, Personal Archive.
33 Tariq Ali, '*Isaac and Isaiah: The Covert Punishment of a Cold War Heretic* by David Caute – a Review'. Isaiah Berlin published his studies of Marx in *Karl Marx: His Life and Environment*.
34 Cohen, 'Isaiah's Marx, and Mine', 4–15.
35 G. A. Cohen, 'Freedom and Money', 166–7.
36 The word 'McCarthyite' owes its origins to U.S. Senator Joseph McCarthy, who in 1950 gave a speech alleging that 'the State Department is infested with Communists', thereby unleashing a series of American government inquiries with the mandate to identify and dismiss communists from their roles in public and social life and prevent them from finding future employment. Robert Griffin, *The Politics of Fear: Joseph R. McCarthy and the Senate*, 49.
37 Isaiah Berlin, 'Two Concepts of Liberty', 217, 168. James Tully is critical of the neoliberal implications of the essay; see his critique, '"Two Concepts of Liberty" in Context' and George Crowder's defence, 'In Defence of Berlin: A reply to James Tully'. For another sympathetic consideration of the essay in context, see Ian Shapiro and Alicia Steinmetz, 'Negative Liberty and the Cold War'.
38 Anthony Arblaster, 'Vision and Revision: A Note on the Text of Isaiah Berlin's *Four Essays on Liberty*'.
39 See Berlin's letters to the editor of *Political Studies* on the matter; *Isaiah Berlin Building: Letters 1960–1975*, 454–5.
40 See Berlin's July 1971 correspondence with Cohen and Geoffrey Marshall on the matter in 'Papers of Sir Isaiah Berlin, 1897–1998, with some family papers, 1903–72', [hereafter MS. Berlin] Oxford, Bodleian Libraries, MS. Berlin 194, fols. 164, 123, 194, Bodleian Library. Cohen supplied a possible explanation that Berlin found gratifying, that Arblaster thought himself performing a 'service for the revolution'.
41 Steven Lukes, 'The Cold War on Campus'.
42 Berlin deemed Deutscher 'the only man whose presence in the same academic community as myself I would find morally intolerable', though it seems the blackballing was due to a personal slight – a critical book review – rather than Deutscher's communist politics.

Berlin's role in this was long suspected but vehemently denied by Berlin. See David Caute, *Isaac and Isaiah: The Covert Punishment of a Cold War Heretic*, 4, 64–8, 290.
43 G. A. Cohen, 'Freedom, Justice and Capitalism', 288.
44 Cohen letter to Berlin, 26 June 1979, MS. Berlin 213, fol. 114; see also 7 July 1971 letter to Berlin, MS. Berlin 194, fol. 164.
45 Cohen letter to Berlin, 14 May 1984, MS. Berlin 219, fol. 79.
46 Cohen, 'Freedom and Money', 166. The essay is highly critical of Berlin's freedom argument; Cohen waited until after Berlin's death before publishing an explicit disavowal of his former teacher's views.
47 Cohen did not take a doctoral degree; at the time the Oxford B.Phil. was considered more than sufficient qualification for an academic post in philosophy.
48 Rosen, 'Jerry Cohen – An Appreciation'.
49 See Ted Honderich, *Philosopher: A Kind of Life*, 147, 191, 237. These three dimensions were at work in Honderich's critical review of Cohen's Marx book; Honderich admitted he was 'not proud of its origins in my passions', 250–1. See Ted Honderich, 'Against Teleological Historical Materialism'. See also Honderich, *Philosopher*, 346.
50 G. A. Cohen, *Rescuing Justice and Equality*, 142.
51 Conversation with Maggie Cohen, 16 October 2022; conversation with Miriam Cohen, 16 October 2022.
52 Conversation with Maggie Cohen, 16 October 2022; conversation with Miriam Cohen, 16 October 2022; Honderich remarks on his colleague's superior work ethic in Honderich, *Philosopher*, 247. Cécile Fabre notes this continued at All Souls; conversation 9 June 2022.
53 Conversation with Maggie Cohen, 16 October 2022.
54 Conversation with Gideon, Miriam and Sarah Cohen, 27 May 2022; conversation with Arnold Zuboff, 27 May 2022.
55 Correspondence with Sarah Cohen, 8 March 2023.
56 Deighton, J., 'Michael Seifert obituary', *The Guardian*, 9 August 2017.
57 In 1931 Carr was imprisoned for 30 months for being an officer in the Communist Party; upon his release he helped organize the 1935 On-to-Ottawa Trek, a mass protest movement sparked by unrest among unemployed single men in federal relief camps during the Great Depression. In 1949 Carr was convicted for espionage and imprisoned in Kingston Penitentiary for 7 years; Weisbord discusses the Soviet spy network in Canada in *The Strangest Dream*, 179–81.
58 Conversation with Maggie Cohen, 16 October 2022.
59 Conversation with Maggie Cohen, 16 October 2022 and Michael Cohen, 17 January 2023.
60 Conversation with Arnold Zuboff, 27 May 2022.
61 Cohen, 'Preface', *History, Labour, and Freedom*, xii.
62 See G. A. Cohen, 'Preface', *Self-Ownership, Freedom and Equality*, v. Conversation with Arnold Zuboff, 27 May 2022 and 7 June 2022.

63 Cohen, 'Preface', *History, Labour, and Freedom*, xi.
64 G. A. Cohen, 'The Future of a Disillusion', 249–50; and 'Prague Preamble to "Why Not Socialism?"', 16–17.
65 G. A. Cohen, 'Beliefs and Roles' and 'The Workers and the Word: Why Marx Had the Right to Think He Was Right'.
66 G. A. Cohen, 'On Some Criticisms of Historical Materialism'.
67 See Jonathan Wolff, 'G. A. Cohen: A Memoir', 330–1.
68 Letter to Berlin, 5 February 1979, MS. Berlin 213, fol. 35.
69 In 1988, forty-four reviews were tallied by Jack Pitt, a PhD student at California State University, with Cohen's assistance. Cohen, Personal Archive.
70 Letter 16 November 1982, Cohen, Personal Archive; Maurice Mandelbaum, 'G. A. Cohen's Defences of Functional Explanation', 285–7.
71 *Canadian Jewish Outlook*, April 1979 in Cohen, Personal Archive; Eric Hobsbawm, 'Points of Departure: Review of G. A. Cohen, *Karl Marx's Theory of History*' (also filed in Cohen, Personal Archive). Arnold Zuboff relates how gratifying it was, at a UCL seminar, to hear the famous logician Carl Hempel express admiration for Cohen's concept of functional explanation; Conversation 7 June 2022.
72 Cohen letter to Bill [surname unknown], 25 July 1989, in Cohen, Personal Archive.
73 26 June 1979, MS. Berlin 213 fol. 113. Cohen states this in published work too; see Cohen, 'Preface', *History, Labour, and Freedom*, xi.
74 Conversation with Maggie Cohen, 16 October 2022.
75 Who also had a Canadian connection: his father, a victim of McCarthyism, was exiled with his family in Saskatchewan, helping to construct the first socialized medicine system in North America; Roemer describes this time as a high point in his parents' lives. Conversation with Roemer, 10 February 2023.
76 Nicholas Vrousalis contends no-bullshit was for the British, non-bullshit for the Americans.
77 As Van Parijs's wife Sue relates, upon the invitation, her husband was 'like an excited little kid'; conversation 18 October 2022.
78 Philippe Van Parijs, 'Address at G. A. Cohen Memorial Service'.
79 G. A. Cohen, *Karl Marx's Theory of History: A Defence*, xix. Philippe Van Parijs conversation, 17 October 2022.
80 Letter to an Eastern European correspondent, 21 July 1999, Cohen, Personal Archive.
81 Philippe Van Parijs conversation, 17 October 2022.
82 Philippe Van Parijs conversation, 17 October 2022; correspondence with Hillel Steiner, 22 July 2023, Philippe Van Parijs, Personal Archive. Steiner recalls that he made it clear that he intended replacing the welfare state with something like unconditional basic income; also, among the demands of the manifesto was a demand for open borders,

which he thought ought to be endorsed by his fellow Septembrists (email correspondence 22 July 2023).
83 Cohen letter to Steiner 19 May 1982, Van Parijs, Personal Archive. However much scepticism Steiner harboured about state beneficence, he was particularly kind to the Cohen family, according to Maggie (conversation 16 October 2022).
84 John Roemer, 'Address at G. A. Cohen Memorial Service'.
85 Van Parijs, 'Address', 3.
86 Roemer, 'Address', 9.
87 A salutation frequently employed by Cohen in his correspondence with the group.
88 Conversation with Maggie Cohen, 16 October 2022.
89 Conversation with Hillel Steiner, 10 December 2019; conversation with Philippe Van Parijs, 17–18 October 2022; conversation with John Roemer, 10 February 2023. Cohen contends the collapse of the USSR was a 'major factor' in both cases; see Simon Tormey, 'Simon Tormey Interviews Gerald Cohen', 352.
90 John Roemer, 'Socialism's Future: An Interview with John Roemer'.
91 Roemer, conversation, 10 February 2023. Roemer noted, though, that Wright (1947–2019) remained a Marxist 'to the bone to the end'.
92 Jonathan Wolff, conversation, 1 June 2022.
93 22 May 1984 letter to Philippe Van Parijs, Van Parijs, Personal Archive; Steiner, 'G. A. Cohen: Where the Action Was'.
94 Paul Levy, 'Professor Jerry Cohen: Maverick Philosopher who Subjected Marxism to the Rigours of Analytical Philosophy'.
95 Clipping in Van Parijs, Personal Archive; Jonathan Wolff also notes this in 'G. A. Cohen: A Memoir', 327.
96 See Christine Sypnowich, 'Introduction: G. A. Cohen's Egalitarian Conscience', 1.
97 G. A. Cohen, 'Rescuing Conservatism: A Defense of Existing Value', 146.
98 See David Edmonds, *Parfit: A Philosopher and his Mission to Save Morality*, 88–91.
99 Pulzer led the campaign to deny Margaret Thatcher an honorary degree at Oxford; see Peter Pulzer, 'The Oxford Vote'.
100 The college's very existence drew the ire of the student Left in late 1960s Oxford, evident in an article in the student paper *The Cherwell* and a letter to the then Warden, John Sparrow. See Edmonds, *Parfit*, 93.
101 Cohen's famous skit about the encounters between a British and an American philosopher, available on YouTube, suggests that even he might have encountered reticence about 'full social engagement' from some fellows; see G. A. Cohen, 'British vs. American Philosopher'.
102 David Edmonds, 'Why Have So Many of the Giants of Moral Philosophy Been Jews?'
103 See Edmonds, *Parfit*, 218, 221, 322.
104 Derek Parfit, 'Kant's Arguments for His Formula of Universal Law',

56. Parfit ventured into egalitarianism with his essay 'Equality or Priority' which he claimed 'owed much to the ideas of' Cohen, among others, note, 121.
105. Conversation with Hillel Steiner, 10 December 2019.
106. Conversation with Maggie Cohen, 16 October 2022; conversation with Avner Offer, 31 May 2022.
107. Conversation with Miriam Cohen, 16 October 2022.
108. Jane O'Grady, 'Obituary: G. A. Cohen'.
109. A theme in conversations with Michael Cohen, 17 January 2023, and Hillel Steiner, 10 December 2019.
110. Thomas Scanlon, 'Address at G. A. Cohen Memorial Service'.
111. Scanlon in his 'Address' insisted that Cohen's humour was not a 'defense mechanism'. That may be true, but it was still his modus operandi on social occasions.
112. Wolff, 'G. A. Cohen: A Memoir', 343.
113. Conversation with Maggie Cohen, 16 October 2022.
114. Cohen, Personal Archive.
115. Often calling friends at inconvenient times to try out the latest versions; Hillel Steiner, conversation, December 2019.
116. Gideon Cohen, 'Address at G. A. Cohen Memorial Service'; conversation with John Roemer, 10 February 2023.
117. 'John Dunn analyses the funniest political philosopher in the world' was a heading for his review of *If You're an Egalitarian How Come You're So Rich*; see Dunn, 'Capitalism Kills the Soul'.
118. Related by Miriam Cohen, conversation, 16 October 2022 and correspondence with Sarah Cohen, 8 March 2023.
119. Edmonds, *Parfit*, 220.
120. Conversation with Cécile Fabre, 9 June 2022.
121. Conversation with Maggie Cohen, 16 October 2022; conversations with Arnold Zuboff, 27 May 2022 and 7 June 2022.
122. It is worth recalling the formidable group of political philosophers in Oxford at the time; along with Cohen, it included Ronald Dworkin, David Miller, Derek Parfit, Joseph Raz, Amartya Sen and Bernard Williams. See Edmonds, *Parfit*, 217–21.
123. For ideas and arguments, but also dialogue from Hollywood movies, showtunes, postwar popular songs, socialist hymns or jingoistic British poetry.
124. Cohen was the 'fourth great political philosopher' according to Otsuka; address 19 June 2010. I observed these traits in my encounters with Cohen; they also emerged in conversations with Arnold Zuboff, Avner Offer, Cécile Fabre and Jonathan Wolff. See Edmonds, *Parfit*, 217–21.
125. Conversation with Cécile Fabre, 9 June 2022.
126. This phrase was coined by H. H. Asquith to describe the ethos of his former college, Balliol, though for present purposes it will suffice to describe the culture of Oxford philosophy. See H.H. Asquith, 'Political Notes', 12.

Notes to pp. 21–23 183

127 As noted above, a very different personality, but another brilliant (Jewish) Oxford thinker, had such feelings; see Lacey, *A Life of H.L.A. Hart*. It is interesting that both men were concerned about Ronald Dworkin; in Hart's case, that Dworkin's work constituted a refutation of his own; in Cohen's case, largely that Dworkin's status eclipsed his! Conversation with Arnold Zuboff, 27 May 2022.
128 Letter from Cohen, 29 June 1989 in Van Parijs, Personal Archive.
129 Rosen, 'Jerry Cohen – An Appreciation'.
130 Conversation with Cohen in March 2006. Indeed, in print he modestly refers to himself as an 'interlocuteur valable' in the philosophical community created by John Rawls; Cohen, *Rescuing Justice and Equality*, 14. Left-wing critics had their own reasons for making little of his post-Marxist contributions – Sean Sayers complained in his later work Cohen was writing mere 'footnotes to Rawls', 'Whatever Happened to Analytical Marxism?', 41.
131 Cohen, Personal Archive.
132 The author of this monograph was one of the co-founders, along with fellow graduate students Robin Archer, who led the enterprise, and Adam Swift. The group held a conference, publishing the papers in the collection *Out of Apathy: Voices on the New Left Thirty Years On*.
133 G. A. Cohen, 'Two Weeks in India'.
134 Cohen, *Rescuing Justice and Equality*, 268; and G. A. Cohen, 'How to do Political Philosophy', 227–9. A longstanding preoccupation it seems: an unpublished typescript dated 2 May 1968 entitled 'Utopian Proposals and Theoretical Perspectives', calls for 'Ruminations on socialist programme that would ask the left not only to act, but act in concert, and it asks the Left not only to act but to think'.
135 As Honderich, who lived on the more favoured street, ruefully recalls; see *Philosopher*, 191.
136 7 December 1969; it appears that Cohen prepared for such appearances by ascribing a letter to each theme, and then memorizing the letters. Cohen, Personal Archive.
137 See G. A. Cohen, 'A Black and White Issue', 'Casting the First Stone: Who Can and Who Can't, Condemn the Terrorists?', 'Ways of Silencing Critics'. The latter two, occasioned by conflict in the Middle East, were especially controversial. See Daniel Statman, 'Casting the First Stone: Did Cohen Have Standing to Condemn Israel's Condemnation of Terrorism?'
138 Conversation with David Parkin, 10 June 2022.
139 Materials in Cohen, Personal Archive.
140 G. A. Cohen, 'Anti-Anti-Racism'.
141 G. A. Cohen, 'On the Currency of Egalitarian Justice'; see also chapter 5 in this book.
142 Michael Cohen used the term in conversation, 27 January 2023.
143 Jonathan Wolff spoke of Cohen 'wasting his talent' on these themes, conversation, 1 June 2022.

144 G. A. Cohen, 'Rescuing Justice from Constructivism and Equality from the Basic Structure Objection', *Rescuing Justice and Equality*, ch. 1.
145 G. A. Cohen, 'Justice, Incentives and Selfishness'.
146 Scanlon, 'Address'.
147 G. A. Cohen, 'Envoi'.
148 Cohen, 'Prague Preamble to "Why Not Socialism?"', 19.
149 Cohen, Personal Archive.
150 Cohen, 'The Future of a Disillusion', 250.
151 Cohen, 'The Future of a Disillusion', 252–65; Cohen rebukes Thomas Nagel on this point in 'Mind the Gap', 209–10.
152 G. A. Cohen, 'Closing Comments'; Rosen, 'Jerry Cohen – An Appreciation'.
153 As Rosen put it in 'Jerry Cohen – An Appreciation'.
154 Conversation with Michael Cohen, 17 January 2023.
155 Conversation with Miriam Cohen, 16 October 2022.
156 Conversation with Miriam Cohen, 16 October 2022.
157 Conversation with Miriam Cohen, 16 October 2022.
158 Cohen was impressed with Sarah's hotel and healing centre in India, for example, and recommended it to friends; see Philippe Van Parijs, Personal Archive.
159 Conversation with Michael Cohen, 17 January 2023.
160 Correspondence with Sarah Cohen, 8 March 2023.
161 Conversation with Gideon, Miriam and Sarah Cohen, 27 May 2022, and Miriam Cohen, 16 October 2022 and conversation with Michael Cohen, 17 January 2023.
162 Conversation with Miriam Cohen, 27 May 2022.
163 Honderich, *Philosopher*, 346, and conversation with Michael Cohen, 17 January 2023.
164 Conversation with Philippe Van Parijs, 17 October 2022.
165 Conversation with Maggie Cohen, 16 October 2022.
166 Conversation with Miriam Cohen, 16 October 2022.
167 Conversation with Michèle Cohen, 2 May 2022, correspondence, 7 March 2023.
168 Paula Casal, 'Marx, Rawls, Cohen and Feminism', 811.
169 Cohen, 'Preface', *Self-ownership, Freedom, and Equality*, ix.
170 Conversation with Cécile Fabre, 9 June 2022.
171 Conversation with Cécile Fabre, 9 June 2022.
172 Cohen, 'How to do Political Philosophy', 226.
173 Conversation with Avner Offer, 19 May 2022.
174 Sypnowich, 'G. A. Cohen's Socialism: Scientific but also Utopian', 27.
175 Gerald Dworkin, 'In Memoriam G. A. (Jerry) Cohen'.
176 Chris Bertram, 'Jerry Cohen, A Personal Appreciation'.
177 See Paula Casal's post at the time of Cohen's death replying to Bertram, 'Jerry Cohen, A Personal Appreciation'.
178 Cohen, 'Closing Comments'.
179 Cohen defended his use of 'she' in his writing, contending that

though economic forces would be important to generate sexual equality, 'sometimes the superstructure needs a separate push or jolt', G. A. Cohen, 'Housewives are expendable'.

180 They include Cohen's beloved friend, the left-libertarian Michael Otsuka, who published Cohen's work posthumously in two excellent volumes, a tribute to the 'sheer brilliance' ('Address at G. A. Cohen Memorial Service') of his teacher; fellow Canadian and celebrated theorist of multicultural and animal citizenship, Will Kymlicka; the influential egalitarian political philosopher Jonathan Wolff, Cohen's last graduate student at UCL, who edited the third posthumous collection; Rajeev Bhargava, the eminent Indian political theorist who hosted Cohen's India trip; the wide-ranging and accomplished political philosopher Cécile Fabre, who followed in her teacher's footsteps and took up a fellowship at All Souls; Nicholas Vrousalis, the Greek Marxist based in the Netherlands whose uploading of the Cohen YouTube videos rivals his significant work on exploitation as an homage to his teacher; the distinguished theorists of distributive justice in Barcelona, Paula Casal and Serena Olsaretti; Seana Shiffrin, a leading legal and political philosopher at UCLA; his last doctoral student, the moral and political philosopher and fellow Canadian, Kerah Gordon-Solmon; and the egalitarian political theorist and current editor of *Mind*, Kasper Lippert-Rasmussen. There are many more.

181 Gideon Cohen, 'Address'.

182 John Roemer, conversation, 10 February 2023. Gerald Dworkin called Cohen his 'closest friend', relating that on even a brief acquaintance, 'it was clear that we would be friends. We were close in age, both political philosophers of an analytic bent, and we were both "red-diaper" children [as was John Roemer – author], i.e. raised by Communist mothers to believe that historical progress was inevitable and that its engine was the working-class. As important a factor was that we shared a sense of humor; knowing a funny joke, or making a clever pun, was as natural and important for us as making a good argument or knowing the details of a text. Last, and least, we were both Gerald's who were always, and only, called Jerry's.' 'In Memoriam G. A. (Jerry) Cohen'.

183 Gideon Cohen, 'Address'. The matter of relating across the boundaries of social class is pursued as a philosophical question in G. A. Cohen, 'Notes on Regarding People as Equals'.

184 Berman, 'Gerald Cohen (1941–2009)'.

185 Cohen, 'Two Weeks in India', 29.

186 Conversation with Gideon, Miriam and Sarah Cohen, 27 May 2022.

187 Mark 8:36, quoted in Cohen, 'Envoi', 181.

188 Rosen, 'Jerry Cohen – An Appreciation'.

189 Cohen, 'Closing Comments'.

190 Cohen, 'Closing Comments'.

191 Preserved by his daughter Miriam.

Chapter 2: 'No-Bullshit' Marxism and the Fate of Historical Materialism

1. G. A. Cohen, 'Isaiah's Marx, and Mine', 1–3.
2. Michael Rosen, 'Jerry Cohen – An Appreciation'.
3. G. A. Cohen, 'Preface', *History, Labour, and Freedom: Themes from Marx*, xi.
4. G. A. Cohen, 'Beliefs and Roles'. A more explicit Marxist investigation of such themes can be found in 'Being, Consciousness, and Roles' and 'Human Nature and Social Change in the Marxist Conception of History'.
5. G. A. Cohen, 'Isaiah's Marx, and Mine', 2.
6. Isaiah Berlin, 'Does Political Theory Still Exist?', 143.
7. Iris Murdoch, 'A House of Theory', 224; John Plamenatz, 'The Use of Political Theory', cited in Peter Laslett; 'Introduction', x; see David Miller's fascinating discussion of the relationship of Chichele professors to the social sciences over the past 100 years in 'Political Theory, Philosophy and the Social Sciences: Five Chichele Professors', 168–9.
8. G. A. Cohen, *Karl Marx's Theory of History: A Defence*, xxi.
9. See Louis Althusser, *For Marx*, and Rosen, 'Jerry Cohen – An Appreciation'.
10. Sudhir Hazareesingh, *How the French Think: An Affectionate Portrait of an Intellectual People*, 158.
11. G. A. Cohen, 'Complete Bullshit', 94–5.
12. See Harry Frankfurt, *On Bullshit*.
13. Cohen, 'Complete Bullshit', 104–5.
14. Cohen, *Karl Marx's Theory of History*, xxvi.
15. Cohen, 'Complete Bullshit', 106–7, note 26.
16. Cohen, *Karl Marx's Theory of History*, xi, and 'Complete Bullshit', 105.
17. Cohen, 'Complete Bullshit', 108–14.
18. Cohen, 'Complete Bullshit', 113.
19. See G. A. Cohen, 'Politics and Religion in a Montreal Communist Jewish Childhood', 188, note 11.
20. G. A. Cohen, 'The Workers and the Word'.
21. Cohen, 'Preface', *History, Labour, and Freedom*, xi.
22. Charles Taylor, 'The Politics of Recognition', 68–70.
23. Cohen, *Karl Marx's Theory of History*, xxii, note 1.
24. Karl Marx, *A Contribution to the Critique of Political Economy*, 20.
25. Cohen, *Karl Marx's Theory of History*, 158.
26. Cohen, *Karl Marx's Theory of History*, 160.
27. Nicholas Vrousalis, *The Political Philosophy of G. A. Cohen: Back to Socialist Basics*, 23.
28. Vrousalis, *The Political Philosophy of G. A. Cohen*, 2.
29. Cohen, *Karl Marx's Theory of History*, ch. VI–VIII.

30 Cohen, *Karl Marx's Theory of History*, 163.
31 Cohen, *Karl Marx's Theory of History*, ch. VI.
32 Cohen, *Karl Marx's Theory of History*, 258–72.
33 Charles Taylor, 'Critical Notice', 327–8.
34 Alan Carling, 'Rational Choice Marxism', 31.
35 Alex Callinicos, 'Introduction', 8.
36 Eric Hobsbawm, 'Points of Departure: Review of G. A. Cohen, *Karl Marx's Theory of History*'.
37 Cohen expressed his delight with his customary wit in a letter: 'our views on functional explanation are not similar, unless identity is a form of similarity'. Moreover, he added, 'and I am sure there is between us the further agreement that what explains the agreements already listed is that we are both right', 2 November 1978, in Philippe Van Parijs, personal archive on G. A. Cohen and conversation, 17–18 October 2022. See Philippe Van Parijs, *Evolutionary Explanation in the Social Sciences. An Emerging Paradigm*.
38 Thomas F. Mayer, *Analytical Marxism*, 18.
39 Jon Elster, *Explaining Technical Change*, 59–61; see Jon Elster, 'Cohen on Marx's Theory of History'; 'Marxism, Functionalism, and Game Theory: The Case for Methodological Individualism'.
40 Jon Elster, *Making Sense of Marx*, 4.
41 Henry Laycock, 'Critical Notice', 355.
42 G. A. Cohen, 'Functional Explanation: A Reply to Elster', 132; see also 'Reply to Elster on "Marxism, Functionalism, and Game Theory"'. I am grateful to Nicholas Vrousalis for stressing this in 'Commentary'; and also John Roemer in conversation on 10 February 2023.
43 Richard Miller, *Analysing Marx*, 205–16, 225–7.
44 Jonathan Wolff, 'Review, Nicholas Vrousalis, *The Political Philosophy of G.A Cohen: Back to Socialist Basics*'.
45 Vrousalis, *The Political Philosophy of G. A. Cohen*, 38–9.
46 Terrell Carver and Paul Thomas, 'Introduction'.
47 Mayer, *Analytical Marxism*, 15.
48 Ellen Meiksins Wood, 'Rational Choice Marxism: Is the Game Worth the Candle?', 82.
49 Wood, 'Rational Choice Marxism: Is the Game Worth the Candle?' 108–9, 111–12.
50 Callinicos, 'Introduction', 16. But as Mayer argued, if a theoretical perspective is to remain relevant in the face of significant and unanticipated social change, it must 'possess both a stable intellectual core and ample conceptual flexibility'. Mayer, *Analytical Marxism*, 16.
51 See Marcus Roberts, *Analytical Marxism: A Critique*.
52 William Clare Roberts, *Marx's Inferno: The Political Theory of Marx's Capital*, 239.
53 Gareth Stedman Jones, *Karl Marx: Greatness and Illusion*.
54 Taylor, 'Critical Notice', 332–3.

55 Vrousalis, *The Political Philosophy of G. A. Cohen*, 23.
56 Joshua Cohen, 'Book Review of "Karl Marx's Theory of History"'. See also Vrousalis, *The Political Philosophy of G. A. Cohen*, 29. Cohen took up this problem in a subsequent essay he wrote with Will Kymlicka, 'Human Nature and Social Change in the Marxist Conception of History'; see also G. A. Cohen, 'Historical Inevitability and Revolutionary Agency'.
57 Paula Casal, 'Marx, Rawls, Cohen and Feminism', and 'G. A. Cohen's Historical Materialism: A Feminist Critique'.
58 Callinicos, 'Introduction', 2. See John Roemer (ed.), *Analytical Marxism*, which collected essays from different exponents of what Roemer called an 'analytically sophisticated Marxism'; 'Introduction', 1.
59 Cohen, 'Complete Bullshit', 95. Although some thought the bullshit reference too arrogant and the September Group appellation became preferred (conversation with Philippe Van Parijs, 17 October 2022), the group went so far as to design a logo, complete with defecating bull, for stationery; see 'Complete Bullshit', 94.
60 Cohen, *Karl Marx's Theory of History*, xvii.
61 Mayer, *Analytical Marxism*, 23.
62 See chapter 7 for further discussion of Cohen's critique of holism.
63 Cohen, Personal Archive, 12 February 1986. I believe these ruminations were never published.
64 Cohen, 'Preface', *History, Labour, and Freedom*, xii. After the Marx book, Cohen also wrote some essays clarifying and defending the main themes of the Marx book. See 'Forces and Relations of Production', 'Base and Superstructure', 'Fettering', 'On an Argument for Historical Materialism', 'Reconsidering Historical Materialism', 'Restricted and Inclusive Historical Materialism'.
65 Although it might be said that is unclear why we should suppose that the methodologies of continental Europe are no less 'bourgeois'. Cohen invokes the example of the character, Fulvia Morgana, an Italian Marxist who justifies her life of luxury in David Lodge's satirical novel of academic life, *Small World*; see Cohen, 'Political Philosophy and Personal Behavior', 151–4.
66 Cohen's view is thus more in line with John Roemer's likening the approach of Analytical Marxism to appreciating that a good tool should not be thrown away even if it might fail in certain applications and that the Analytical Marxist project is thus an effort to clarify and elucidate Marxism's 'valid core'; see Roemer (ed.), *Analytical Marxism*, 'Introduction', 2.
67 Elster, *Making Sense of Marx*, xiv.
68 Mayer, *Analytical Marxism*, 315.
69 Cohen, *Karl Marx's Theory of History*, xxvi.
70 Cohen, *Karl Marx's Theory of History*, xxii.
71 Borne out by David Leopold's substantive entry on Analytical

Marxism published in 2022 in the *Stanford Encyclopedia of Philosophy*; see David Leopold, 'Analytical Marxism'. Leopold identifies the crux of the school to be how it parted with 'true believers' by proposing a philosophical division of labour – non-Marxist analytical methods on the one hand, and Marxist concerns and commitments, on the other. In 'Afro-Analytical Marxism and the Problem of Race', Tommie Shelby affirms the continuing relevance of Analytical Marxism and discusses how the school's inattention to questions of race can be remedied.
72 David Caute, *Isaac and Isaiah: The Covert Punishment of a Cold War Heretic*, 115. See the discussion in chapter 1.
73 Cohen, 'Isaiah's Marx, and Mine', 7.
74 G. A. Cohen, 'The Labour Theory of Value and the Concept of Exploitation', 231–4.
75 Cohen, 'Reconsidering Historical Materialism', 132. See also 'On an Argument for Historical Materialism'.
76 Cohen, 'Reconsidering Historical Materialism', 138–40.
77 Cohen, 'Restricted and Inclusive Historical Materialism', 158–66.
78 Cohen, 'Restricted and Inclusive Historical Materialism', 171.
79 Marx, *Capital, Volume 1*, Pt. 3, Ch. 7, §1, 284.
80 See David Leopold, *The Young Karl Marx*, and Jan Kandiyali, 'The Importance of Others: Marx on Unalienated Production'.
81 G. A. Cohen, 'The Future of a Disillusion', 250.
82 Simon Tormey, 'Simon Tormey Interviews Gerald Cohen', 352.
83 Frederic Jamieson, 'The Politics of Utopia', 35.
84 Cohen, 'The Future of a Disillusion', 253–65.
85 G. A. Cohen, 'Mind the Gap', 209–10.
86 Tormey, 'Simon Tormey Interviews Gerald Cohen', 352.
87 G. A. Cohen, 'Prague Preamble to "Why Not Socialism?"', 19.
88 Cohen, *Karl Marx's Theory of History*, 389–95. See also Vrousalis, *The Political Philosophy of G. A. Cohen*, 30–1.
89 G. A. Cohen, 'Hegel in Marx: The Obstetric Motif in the Marxist Conception of Revolution', 75.
90 Cohen, 'Hegel in Marx: The Obstetric Motif in the Marxist Conception of Revolution', 75–7.
91 Or, in an 'extraordinary alliance' with society's 'oppressed outcasts', that philosophers' role is simply to explicate and become realized in the inevitable activism of that class. G. A. Cohen, 'The Opium of the People: God in Hegel, Feuerbach and Marx', 93–100; see also G. A. Cohen, 'Hegel in Marx: The Obstetric Motif in the Marxist Conception of Revolution', 77; 'Equality: From Fact to Norm'; 'Historical Inevitability and Revolutionary Agency'.
92 G. A. Cohen, 'Back to Socialist Basics', 214–15. See also 'Historical Inevitability and Revolutionary Agency'. My thanks to Nicholas Vrousalis who supplied this insight.

93 G. A. Cohen, 'Introduction: History, Ethics, and Marxism', 7.
94 Allen Wood, 'The Marxian Critique of Justice'; see also Allen Wood, *Karl Marx*, 127–42.
95 Robert Tucker, *Philosophy and Myth in Karl Marx*, 20; Allen Wood, *Karl Marx*, 127–42; see also Steven Lukes, *Marxism and Morality*.
96 G. A. Cohen, 'Self-Ownership, Communism and Equality: Against the Marxist Technological Fix', 139; 'Equality: From Fact to Norm', 101–4. See also G. A. Cohen, 'Review of *Karl Marx* by Allen Wood'; Norman Geras, *Marx and Human Nature: Refutation of a Legend*. Raymond Geuss argues that the standard understanding of ethics in English-speaking philosophy as concerning what we ought to do has little purchase in German philosophy in general. See his 'Outside Ethics'.
97 Although as noted Cohen came to dispute the labour theory of value; see Cohen, 'The Labour Theory of Value and the Concept of Exploitation', 212.
98 This theme is explored in Christine Sypnowich, 'G. A. Cohen's Socialism: Scientific, but also Utopian'.
99 Cohen, *Karl Marx's Theory of History*, xxvii, note 1.
100 G. A. Cohen, 'The Development of Socialism from Utopia to Science'.
101 Cohen, *Karl Marx's Theory of History*, xxv–xxvi.
102 Karl Marx and Friedrich Engels, 'Manifesto of the Communist Party', 498–9.
103 Cohen, 'Future of a Disillusion', 265.
104 Isaiah Berlin took Cohen to task for not being more critical in his analysis of Marcuse; remarked by Cohen in letter to Berlin, 7 October 1969, Papers of Sir Isaiah Berlin, 1897–8, with some family papers, 1903–72, MS Berlin 184, Sept.–Oct. 1969, 606678721, folio 164.
105 G. A. Cohen, 'Critical Theory: The Philosophy of Herbert Marcuse' and Cohen, *Karl Marx's Theory of History*, 317–25; 245.
106 Cohen, 'Complete Bullshit', 106.
107 Cohen, 'Complete Bullshit', 104, note 22. Cohen not only discussed Hegel's philosophy in connection with Marx, he also lectured on Hegel; see 'Hegel: Minds, Masters, and Slaves'. The YouTube pastiche can be found at G. A. Cohen, 'The German Idea of Freedom'.
108 G. A. Cohen, 'How to do Political Philosophy', 226.
109 See especially Charles Taylor, 'Interpretation and the Sciences of Man', and David Miller, 'Political Theory, Philosophy and the Social Sciences: Five Chichele Professors', 178–82.
110 Murdoch, 'A House of Theory', 228–33.
111 John Stuart Mill, *On Liberty*, 57, 81.
112 Allen Buchanan, 'Marx, Morality, and History: An Assessment of Recent Analytical Work on Marx', 104.
113 Mayer, *Analytical Marxism*, 23.
114 Think what analytical criticism would do, and inappropriately, Cohen

noted, to 'Keats's identification of truth and beauty, or to Sartre's identification of hell with other people', 'Complete Bullshit', 111.

Chapter 3: Rescuing Freedom from Nozick

1. G. A. Cohen, 'Introduction: History, Ethics, and Marxism', 4.
2. Jan Narveson, *The Libertarian Idea*, 7.
3. Emma Goldman, 'Anarchism: What it Really Stands For', 5–6.
4. Jason Brennan, *Libertarianism: What Everyone Needs to Know*, 1. Though Stephen Wall proposes that the anti-paternalism of libertarianism, particularly in its self-ownership versions, is a weakness, not a strength. See Steven Wall, 'Self-Ownership and Paternalism'.
5. Randy Barnett, 'The Moral Foundations of Modern Libertarianism', 73–4.
6. Narveson, *The Libertarian Idea*, 8. See also Gerald Gaus, 'Coercion, Ownership, and the Redistributive State: Justificatory Liberalism's Classical Tilt'. Jeffrey Paul describes Nozick as a 'twentieth century successor to the great classical liberals of the seventeenth century'; 'Introduction', *Reading Nozick*, 4. Interestingly Jeremy Waldron contended that the best piece of critical engagement with the Wilt Chamberlain argument was missing from this collection, that is Cohen's essay originally published in *Erkenntnis*, 'Robert Nozick and Wilt Chamberlain: How Patterns Preserve Liberty'. See Jeremy Waldron, 'Ours by Right: Review of *Reading Nozick*', 1277.
7. Brennan stresses libertarianism's hands-off approach to a range of social issues in *Libertarianism*.
8. Jonathan Wolff, *Robert Nozick: Property, Justice and the Minimal State*, 133.
9. Robert Nozick, *Anarchy, State and Utopia*, 163.
10. Nozick, *Anarchy, State and Utopia*, 149–53.
11. I'm grateful to Colin Macleod for noting this.
12. Nozick, *Anarchy, State and Utopia*, 26–30, 149–64.
13. Nozick, *Anarchy, State and Utopia*, 160–4.
14. Cohen, 'Introduction: History, Ethics, and Marxism', 4.
15. At various points Cohen had lectured on Locke, though often with Nozick in mind; see G. A. Cohen, 'Marx and Locke on Land and Labour' and 'Locke on Property and Political Obligation'.
16. G. A. Cohen, 'Are Freedom and Equality Compatible?'
17. A play on Kant's remark about his encounter with Hume; Cohen, 'Introduction: History, Ethics, and Marxism', 4.
18. Michael Otsuka, 'Commentary'; and also John Roemer in conversation on 10 February 2023.
19. Cohen, 'Robert Nozick and Wilt Chamberlain: How Patterns Preserve Liberty', 25–6.

20 Nozick, *Anarchy, State and Utopia*, 28–35.
21 Cohen, 'Robert Nozick and Wilt Chamberlain: How Patterns Preserve Liberty', 31–3.
22 G. A. Cohen, 'Justice, Freedom, and Market Transactions', 55.
23 Cohen, 'Robert Nozick and Wilt Chamberlain: How Patterns Preserve Liberty', 34.
24 Cohen, 'Justice, Freedom, and Market Transactions', 60.
25 Jan Narveson, 'Libertarianism vs. Marxism: Reflections on G. A. Cohen's *Self-Ownership, Freedom and Equality*', 26.
26 Nicholas Vrousalis, *The Political Philosophy of GA Cohen: Back to Socialist Basics*, 57.
27 Cohen, 'Robert Nozick and Wilt Chamberlain: How Patterns Preserve Liberty', 12.
28 Cohen, 'Robert Nozick and Wilt Chamberlain: How Patterns Preserve Liberty', 37.
29 Jeremy Waldron, 'Mr. Morgan's Yacht'.
30 Otsuka, 'Commentary'.
31 G. A. Cohen, 'Freedom and Money', 186, note 40.
32 G. A. Cohen, 'Freedom, Justice and Capitalism'.
33 G. A. Cohen, 'The Structure of Proletarian Unfreedom', 255–6.
34 Cohen, 'The Structure of Proletarian Unfreedom', 256.
35 Cohen, 'The Structure of Proletarian Unfreedom', 256–9.
36 See Cohen, 'The Structure of Proletarian Unfreedom', 259–61, 261 note 10; quoting Karl Marx, *Capital, Volume 1*, 1079.
37 The economist Thomas Piketty elaborates workers' lack of mobility in *Capital in the Twenty-first Century*.
38 Cohen, 'The Structure of Proletarian Unfreedom', 260.
39 Cohen, 'The Structure of Proletarian Unfreedom', 261–2. Cohen proposes a modification to increase workers' chances of escape – two doors and two keys – to show that even if one leaves, it is still the case that no subsequent person's egress is blocked by another. The complexity of individual human behaviour and collective action is an important theme in the analysis of the obstacles to social change, which Cohen considered in other essays written in the 1980s, for example, regarding historical inevitability and revolutionary agency, or how workers are forced to take hazardous jobs. See G. A. Cohen, 'Historical Inevitability and Revolutionary Agency', 'Are Disadvantaged Workers Who Take Hazardous Jobs Forced to Take Hazardous Jobs?' See also G. A. Cohen, 'The Dialectic of Labour in Marx'.
40 Cohen, 'The Structure of Proletarian Unfreedom', 263.
41 Cohen, 'The Structure of Proletarian Unfreedom', 264.
42 Cohen, 'The Structure of Proletarian Unfreedom', 264.
43 Cohen, 'The Structure of Proletarian Unfreedom', 272.
44 Cohen, 'The Structure of Proletarian Unfreedom', 271.

45 Cohen, 'The Structure of Proletarian Unfreedom', 272–5.
46 John Gray, *Post-Liberalism: Studies in Political Thought*, 134–7.
47 Cohen, 'The Structure of Proletarian Unfreedom', 278–80.
48 Isaiah Berlin coined the term 'positive freedom' to contrast it unfavourably with a classical liberal conception of 'negative freedom' in which the individual is unimpeded or unobstructed. See 'Two Concepts of Liberty', but also Charles Taylor's powerful case for positive freedom, 'What's Wrong with Negative Liberty', 211–29.
49 Vrousalis, *The Political Philosophy of G. A. Cohen*, 51. A more recent effort to focus on the place of liberty in Marx's critique of capitalism can be found in Ernesto Screpanti, *Libertarian Communism: Marx, Engels and the Political Economy of Freedom*.
50 See G. A. Cohen, 'Marxism and Contemporary Political Philosophy, or: why Nozick Exercises some Marxists more than he does any Egalitarian Liberals'. Though many left liberals were determined to dissociate Nozickian libertarianism from the liberal creed. Freeman, for example, contends that, contra Nozick's argument for the inviolability of private economic agreements, it is 'because contract and property are matters of publicly enforceable right imposing uniform duties upon everyone that liberals do not respect the outcome of just any given private agreement as a valid enforceable contract'; moreover, equality of opportunity, the provision of public goods, are other key points of disagreement. See Samuel Freeman, 'Illiberal Libertarians: Why Libertarianism Is Not A Liberal View'.
51 Richard Arneson, 'Lockean Self-Ownership: Towards a Demolition', 54.
52 Thomas Scanlon, 'Nozick on Rights, Liberty, and Property' 123.
53 Thomas Nagel, 'Libertarianism without Foundations', 197.
54 Judith Jarvis Thomson, 'Some Ruminations on Rights', 146.
55 Thomas Nagel, 'Libertarianism without Foundations', 200.
56 Note, however, Bas Van der Vossen contends that it is not obvious that self-ownership figures as a premise for Nozick, given that *Anarchy, State and Utopia* invokes the idea only once, and, moreover, that the concept does not figure in many of his arguments against distributive conceptions of justice. See Bas Van der Vossen, 'Libertarianism'.
57 Indeed, as Cohen notes, they tend to find the self-ownership thesis a mere unargued assertion; see Cohen, 'Marxism and Contemporary Political Philosophy', 163, and Nagel, 'Libertarianism without Foundations'. Dworkin's concern for mitigating the effects of 'brute luck' focuses on inequality of talent; I discuss this issue in connection with Cohen in chapter 5.
58 Cohen, 'Introduction: History, Ethics, and Marxism', 13.
59 Something that Eric Mack contended was a significant vulnerability in Nozick's theory. See his 'Nozick on Unproductivity: The Unintended Consequences'.

60 Cohen, 'Introduction: History, Ethics, and Marxism', 13. Although Locke's interpretation of this proviso ends up permitting significant disadvantage; see C.B. Macpherson, *The Political Theory of Possessive Individualism*, part 5.
61 Cohen, 'Self-Ownership, World Ownership, and Equality', 78.
62 Cohen, 'Self-Ownership, World Ownership, and Equality', 78–82.
63 Cohen, 'Self-Ownership, World Ownership, and Equality', 90.
64 Eric Mack, 'Robert Nozick's Political Philosophy'.
65 Cohen, 'Self-Ownership, World Ownership, and Equality', 83–4.
66 Cohen, 'Are Freedom and Equality Compatible?', 94–6.
67 Cohen, 'Introduction: History, Ethics, and Marxism', 14.
68 Cohen, 'Are Freedom and Equality Compatible?', 105.
69 Cohen, 'Self-Ownership: Delineating the Concept' and 'Marxism and Contemporary Political Philosophy', 148–50; Cohen makes a powerful case for this position in his 'Review of *Karl Marx* by Allen Wood'.
70 Cohen, 'Marx and Locke on Land and Labour', 182–6; 169. Cohen's position can be contrasted with the view of James Tully, *A Discourse on Property*, 164. Tully contends, contra much Locke scholarship, that the state is established in order to put all possessions in the hands of the community.
71 Cohen, 'Marxism and Contemporary Political Philosophy', 151.
72 See Marx, 'A Critique of the Gotha Programme', 531.
73 Simon Tormey, 'Simon Tormey Interviews Gerald Cohen', 351.
74 Cohen, 'Self-Ownership, Communism and Equality: Against the Marxist Technological Fix', 122–3.
75 Cohen, 'Self-Ownership, Communism and Equality', 132.
76 Cohen, 'Introduction: History, Ethics, and Marxism', 7. Philippe Van Parijs proposes, however, three concepts of abundance – absolute, strong and weak – and purports that weak abundance is possible, and consistent with at least some of the premises of socialist society, such as the satisfaction of needs; 'In Defence of Abundance', 486–93.
77 Cohen, 'Marxism and Contemporary Political Philosophy', 159–60.
78 Cohen, 'Marxism and Contemporary Political Philosophy', 161.
79 Cohen, 'Marxism and Contemporary Political Philosophy', 163–4.
80 Allen Buchanan, *Marx and Justice: The Radical Critique of Liberalism*, 133.
81 Vrousalis, *The Political Philosophy of G. A. Cohen*, 57.
82 Michael Otsuka, *Libertarianism without Inequality*. See also Hillel Steiner, *An Essay on Rights*.
83 Hillel Steiner, 'Self-Ownership and Conscription'.
84 Cohen, 'Are Freedom and Equality Compatible?', 104.
85 Cohen, 'Are Freedom and Equality Compatible?', 102.
86 G. A. Cohen, 'Exploitation in Marx: What Makes It Unjust?' 197–204.
87 Cohen, 'Exploitation in Marx', 203.

88 Cohen, 'Introduction: History, Ethics, and Marxism', 18.
89 Cohen, 'Self-Ownership: Assessing the Thesis', 234.
90 Dworkin, *Taking Rights Seriously*, 184–206; John Rawls, *Theory of Justice*, 244–50.
91 Although Michael Otsuka claims that violations of self-ownership best capture the idea of both the idea of the inviolability of persons and also the injustice of unequal ownership of resources; see his 'Self-Ownership and Equality: A Lockean Reconciliation'.
92 John Roemer, *A General Theory of Exploitation and Class*.
93 Neil Levy, 'Self-Ownership: Defending Marx against Cohen'.
94 Paul Warren, in his 'Self-Ownership, Reciprocity, and Exploitation, or Why Marxists Shouldn't Be Afraid of Robert Nozick'. See also 'In Defense of the Marxian Theory of Exploitation: Thoughts on Roemer, Cohen, and Others'. Cohen offered a mixed appraisal of Warren's argument; see 'Marxism and Contemporary Political Philosophy, 164, note 34.
95 See Jeffrey Reiman, 'An Alternative to "Distributive" Marxism: Further Thoughts on Roemer, Cohen and Exploitation'.
96 Nicholas Vrousalis, 'Exploitation, Vulnerability and Social Domination', and *Exploitation as Domination: What Makes Capitalism Unjust*, 1.
97 Cohen, 'The Labour Theory of Value and the Concept of Exploitation'.
98 Cohen, 'Are Disadvantaged Workers Who Take Hazardous Jobs Forced to Take Hazardous Jobs?'
99 Marx, 'Economic and Philosophic Manuscripts', 77.
100 John Locke, *Second Treatise on Government*, ch. 5, § 27, 19.
101 Cohen, Personal Archive.
102 G. A. Cohen, 'Bourgeois and Proletarians'.
103 Cohen, 'The Structure of Proletarian Unfreedom', 262. See also 'Capitalism, Freedom and Proletariat'. George C. Brenkert criticizes Cohen for not appreciating the domination inflicted by capitalism more generally in 'Cohen on Proletarian Unfreedom'. See Cohen's response in 'Are Workers Forced to Sell their Labor Power?'
104 Jon Elster, *Making Sense of Marx*.
105 This is discussed in more detail in the previous chapter. See G. A. Cohen, 'Complete Bullshit', 104–5.
106 Arthur Ripstein, 'Rationality and Alienation', 466. Although Cohen's former doctoral student Cécile Fabre provocatively defends the right to commercialize one's body; see *Whose Body is it Anyway?*
107 Cohen, 'Self-ownership: Delineating the Concept', 211, 215, 223. These points were stressed by Serena Olsaretti in a comment she made at *Freedom, Equality, and Justice: G. A. Cohen's Lasting Relevance*, conference on Sypnowich book manuscript, Universitat Pompeu Fabra, Barcelona, 6 May 2022.
108 Jan Kandiyali, 'The Importance of Others: Marx on Unalienated Production'.

109 Iris Murdoch, *The Sovereignty of Good*, 10–11.
110 Murdoch, *Sovereignty of Good*, 65.
111 Midgley, *The Solitary Self: Darwin and the Selfish Gene*, 64. The challenge that Murdoch and Midgley posed to the moral philosophy orthodoxy in Oxford is brought to life in Clare Mac Cumhaill and Rachael Wiseman, *Metaphysical Animals: How Four Women Brought Philosophy Back to Life*; see especially 262–76.
112 Murdoch, *Sovereignty of Good*, 84.

Chapter 4: Rescuing Justice from Rawls

1 Thomas Nagel discusses the different meanings of liberalism in the contemporary context, from the defence of an unfettered market economy to the call for greater social and economic equality in 'Rawls and Liberalism'.
2 Matthew Clayton and Andrew Williams, 'Some Questions for Egalitarians', 2.
3 See Alistair Macleod, 'The Domain of Distributive Justice: Personal Choices, Institutions, States of Affairs'.
4 G. A. Cohen, *Rescuing Justice and Equality*, 11–13.
5 About whose *Leviathan* Rawls concurred with Cohen's assessment, calling it 'the greatest work in political philosophy in English'; John Rawls, *Lectures on the History of Political Philosophy*, 23.
6 John Rawls, *Theory of Justice*, 15–19; ch. 3.
7 John Rawls, *Justice as Fairness: A Restatement*, 18–29.
8 Rawls, *Justice as Fairness*, 29–31.
9 Rawls, *Theory of Justice*, ch. 2.
10 Rawls, *Theory of Justice*, 64–5.
11 Rawls, *Theory of Justice*, 13, 68–9, 130–1, 135–6, 246. In *Justice as Fairness*, Rawls refers in passing to the 'need' for inequalities in light of their role as incentives, 67–9, 77, 78. Cohen lays out Rawls's claims about incentives in Cohen, *Rescuing Justice and Equality*, 28–30, 68–86.
12 Cohen puzzles over a shift in Rawls's thinking on this, from his 1958 essay, 'Justice as Fairness' and *Theory of Justice*; see Cohen, *Rescuing Justice and Equality*, 177–80. Philippe Van Parijs counters that the most cogent case for capitalist inequality is not that the expectation of reward induces productivity, but rather that those who are most innovative or efficient find market success, taking wealth and economic power from their less capable rivals; see his 'Difference Principles', 203–4.
13 Cohen, *Rescuing Justice and Equality*, 119–23. Cohen notes parenthetically that 'talent' can be manifest in low-paying work.
14 Cohen, *Rescuing Justice and Equality*, 29. See also an earlier version of this argument in 'Justice, Incentives and Selfishness'.
15 Cohen, *Rescuing Justice and Equality*, 27, quoting Jan Narveson, 'Rawls

on Equal Distribution of Wealth', 287–8. As a libertarian, Narveson did not accept the premisses of Rawls's case for incentives, which he saw as unnecessarily 'legitimizing our perfectly normal behavior in markets and other contexts of social life', 'Cohen on Rawls on Incentives and Equality', 53; but he shared Cohen's complaint that Rawls is inconsistent; see Jan Narveson, 'Cohen's Rescue'.

16 Cohen, *Rescuing Justice and Equality*, 40, 48. Cohen recalls this analogy is captured in the Hollywood movie, *Ruthless People*.
17 R.H. Tawney, *Equality*, 29.
18 Cohen, *Rescuing Justice and Equality*, 42–5
19 Cohen, *Rescuing Justice and Equality*, 35–48.
20 See Thomas Scanlon, *What We Owe to Each Other*; Stephen Darwall, *The Second-Person Standpoint, Morality, Respect and Accountability*; Elizabeth Anderson, 'The Fundamental Disagreement between Luck Egalitarians and Relational Egalitarians', 19.
21 Cohen, *Rescuing Justice and Equality*, 170–6.
22 Cohen, *Rescuing Justice and Equality*, 173.
23 From the German, *Gemeinschaft* means a traditional community where members relate to each other with bonds of sentiment and personal connection, in contrast with *Gesellschaft*, civil society, where members are citizens whose relations are impersonal and formal. The sociologist Ferdinand Tonnies deployed this distinction to capture the difference between traditional and modern societies; see Ferdinand Tonnies, *Community and Civil Society*.
24 Cohen, *Rescuing Justice and Equality*, 45. Certainly, more ambitious ideas about community and our connections with others do play a role in other parts of Cohen's view, as we will see.
25 Cohen, *Rescuing Justice and Equality*, 128.
26 Cohen, *Rescuing Justice and Equality*, 171.
27 Rawls, *Justice as Fairness*, 3, 21, 32.
28 Cohen, *Rescuing Justice and Equality*, 45, 76–81; Adam Cureton, 'Justice and the Crooked Wood of Human Nature', 93–4.
29 Cohen, *Rescuing Justice and Equality*, 302–5.
30 John Roemer laments that the extent to which 'selfish optimisation' has penetrated our thinking is borne out by how 'even the most influential left-wing political philosophy of the twentieth century, that of Rawls, is deeply infected by it'; John Roemer, 'Ideology, Social Ethos and the Financial Crisis', 292.
31 Cohen, *Rescuing Justice and Equality*, 19–21, 253–4, 263–72.
32 Cohen, *Rescuing Justice and Equality*, 3.
33 Kyle Johannsen, *A Conceptual Investigation of Justice*, 81–3.
34 Cohen, *Rescuing Justice and Equality*, 84.
35 Nicholas Vrousalis, *The Philosophy of G. A. Cohen: Back to Socialist Basics*, 7.
36 Cohen, *Rescuing Justice and Equality*, 283–5.

37 Simon Tormey, 'Simon Tormey Interviews Gerald Cohen', 357–8.
38 Martin O'Neill, 'The Radicalism of Equality of Opportunity'.
39 Rawls, *Theory of Justice*, 197–200.
40 Rawls, *Justice as Fairness*, 135.
41 Rawls, *Justice as Fairness*, 135–6.
42 Rawls, *Lectures on the History of Political Philosophy*, 365–72. See Martin O'Neill and Thad Williamson (eds), *Property-Owning Democracy: Rawls and Beyond*. O'Neill stresses Rawls's opposition to welfare state capitalism and the radical implications of his idea of a property-owning democracy in 'Free (and Fair) Markets without Capitalism; Political Values, Principles of Justice, and Property-Owning Democracy'.
43 William Edmundson, *John Rawls: Reticent Socialist*.
44 Rawls, *Political Liberalism*.
45 Rawls, *Lectures on the History of Political Philosophy*, 153, note 27.
46 Rawls, *Lectures on the History of Political Philosophy*, 153, note 27.
47 Joseph Raz, *Ethics in the Public Domain*, 46.
48 See Brian Barry, 'John Rawls and the Search for Stability'; Susan Moller Okin, 'Book Review, John Rawls, *Political Liberalism*'; Bernard Williams, 'A Fair State'.
49 As I argue; see Christine Sypnowich, *Equality Renewed: Justice, Flourishing, and the Egalitarian Ideal*, 85–7. Cohen does address *Political Liberalism* in terms of whether its focus on legitimacy and consensus amounted to a principle of justice – his answer is yes, though not a principle of distributive justice; *Rescuing Justice and Equality*, 296–8.
50 See John Rawls, *The Law of Peoples*. The global justice literature is immense; a useful collection which contains some key thinkers is Gillian Brock and Harry Brighouse (eds), *The Political Philosophy of Cosmopolitanism*.
51 Simon Tormey, 'Simon Tormey Interviews Gerald Cohen', 359.
52 Rawls, *Theory of Justice*, 7.
53 Rawls, *Justice as Fairness*, 162–8.
54 Susan Moller Okin, *Justice, Gender and the Family*. Cohen's admiration for Okin meant that she was to contribute an essay to the volume in his honour in Christine Sypnowich (ed.), *The Egalitarian Conscience: Essays in Honour of G. A. Cohen*; alas her untimely death meant that was not possible.
55 See James Meade, *Theory of Economic Externalities: The Control of Environmental Pollution and Similar Social Costs*, 52; Cohen, *Rescuing Justice and Equality*, 173–4.
56 Cohen, *Rescuing Justice and Equality*, 174–5.
57 We will consider the implications of this view in the next chapter.
58 Cohen, *Rescuing Justice and Equality*, 133–4.
59 G. A. Cohen, 'Justice, Incentives and Selfishness', 123.
60 Cohen, *Rescuing Justice and Equality*, 140. Cohen's position received some qualified endorsement from feminists; see Clare Chambers,

'"The Family as a Basic Institution": A Feminist Analysis of the Basic Structure as Subject'.
61 Cohen, *Rescuing Justice and Equality*, 70, 143.
62 Cohen, *Rescuing Justice and Equality*, 184; see also Paula Casal, 'Occupational Choice and the Egalitarian Ethos', and Michael Otsuka, 'Freedom of Occupational Choice'.
63 Cohen, *Rescuing Justice and Equality*, 175. Harry Brighouse and Adam Swift pursue these issues in *Family Values: The Ethics of Parent–Child Relationships* and Adam Swift, *How Not to be a Hypocrite: School Choice for the Morally Perplexed Parent*. Matthew Clayton draws on the anti-paternalist themes of liberal egalitarians in his *Justice and Legitimacy in Upbringing*.
64 Cohen, 'Political Philosophy and Personal Behavior', 161.
65 Peter Singer, 'Famine, Affluence, and Morality'.
66 There is much literature on these questions, but Iris Marion Young's *Justice and the Politics of Difference* makes a pioneering contribution in criticizing the 'distributive' preoccupation of political philosophy, to the neglect of issues of, e.g., sexism and racism.
67 Recall, too, Cohen's point about the relevance of culture in his ideas about 'restricted historical materialism'; see 'Restrictive and Inclusive Historical Materialism'. Intriguingly, in his unpublished papers is an undated but yellowed typescript outlining 'a scheme of surnomen-clature for a post-sexist society', Cohen, Personal Archive.
68 Samuel Scheffler, 'Is the Basic Structure Basic?'
69 Thomas Scanlon, 'Justice, Responsibility, and the Demands of Equality'.
70 Seana Shiffrin, 'Incentives, Motives, and Talents', 113.
71 Ian Carter, 'Basic Equality and the Site of Egalitarian Justice'
72 Serena Olsaretti, 'The Inseparability of the Personal and the Political: Review of G. A. Cohen's *Rescuing Justice and Equality*'.
73 Michael Titelbaum, 'What Would a Rawlsian Ethos of Justice Look Like?'
74 Jonathan Quong, 'Justice Beyond Equality', 320–5.
75 Pablo Gilabert, 'Cohen on Socialism, Equality and Community'.
76 Loren King, 'Concepts, Conceptions and Principles of Justice'.
77 This discussion draws on the ideas in Christine Sypnowich, 'The Demands of Equality'.
78 Andrew Williams, 'Incentives, Inequality and Publicity', and 'Justice, Incentives and Constructivism'.
79 As noted in chapter 2; see Paula Casal, 'Marx, Rawls, Cohen and Feminism', and 'G. A. Cohen's Historical Materialism: A Feminist Critique'.
80 Williams, 'Incentives, Inequality and Publicity', 238–9; Casal, 'Marx, Rawls, Cohen and Feminism', 820–4 and 'Gender, Social Justice and Publicity', 177–9.

81 Casal, 'Gender, Social Justice and Publicity', 181.
82 Cohen, *Rescuing Justice and Equality*, 132–43.
83 Cohen, 'Justice, Incentives and Selfishness', 127.
84 Cohen, *Rescuing Justice and Equality*, 141–2.
85 Cohen, *Why Not Socialism?*
86 Cohen, *Rescuing Justice and Equality*, 353.
87 Cohen, *Rescuing Justice and Equality*, 143.
88 Cohen, *Rescuing Justice and Equality*, 142.
89 Cohen, *Rescuing Justice and Equality*, 353.
90 Cohen, *Rescuing Justice and Equality*, 220.
91 Cohen, *Rescuing Justice and Equality*, 219.
92 Marx, 'A Critique of the Gotha Programme', 531.
93 Cohen, *Rescuing Justice and Equality*, 219–22; see also Joseph Carens, 'The Egalitarian Ethos as a Social Commitment'. There is an extensive literature on the extent to which such prerogatives are compatible with Cohen's views about personal obligations; see for example, David Estlund, 'Liberalism, Equality and Fraternity in Cohen's Critique of Rawls'; Michael Otsuka, 'Prerogatives to Depart from Equality'; Scheffler, 'Is the Basic Structure Basic?'; Scanlon, 'Justice, Responsibility, and the Demands of Equality'.
94 Will Kymlicka, 'Left-Liberalism Revisited', 22.
95 Cohen, *Rescuing Justice and Equality*, 73.
96 See Sypnowich, *Equality Renewed*, 122–8.
97 Cohen, *Why Not Socialism?*, 10, 80–1.
98 Joshua Cohen, 'Taking People as They Are?', 377.
99 Joshua Cohen, 'Taking People as They Are?', 378.
100 Jonathan Wolff, 'Fairness, Respect and the Egalitarian Ethos', 104–5; 111–19. See also Jonathan Wolff, 'Fairness, Respect and the Egalitarian "Ethos" Revisited', 338.
101 Elizabeth Anderson, 'What is the Point of Equality?', 321–31. See also Ian Carter, 'Respect and the Basis of Equality'; Timothy Hinton, 'Must Egalitarianism Choose Between Fairness and Respect?'
102 Cohen, *Why Not Socialism?*, 44.
103 Nicholas Vrousalis, 'G. A. Cohen's Vision of Socialism', 211.
104 Cohen, *Rescuing Justice and Equality*, 353.
105 John Roemer, 'Jerry Cohen's *Why Not Socialism?* Some Thoughts', 260–1.
106 Cohen, *Why Not Socialism?*, 57–8.
107 Cohen, *Why Not Socialism?*, 51–2.
108 Roemer, 'Jerry Cohen's *Why Not Socialism?*', 259.
109 Roemer, 'Jerry Cohen's *Why Not Socialism?*', 260–1.
110 Evgeny Pashukanis, *The General Theory of Law and Marxism*, 160; see also Tom Campbell, *The Left and Rights: A Conceptual Analysis of the Idea of Socialist Rights* and Christine Sypnowich, *The Concept of Socialist Law*, ch. 1 and 5.

Notes to pp. 100–104   201

111 G. A. Cohen, 'Self-Ownership, Communism and Equality: Against the Marxist Technological Fix', 134–5.
112 Karl Marx, 'Circular Against Kriege', 41.
113 Bernard Williams, 'Egoism and Altruism', 250. Williams was made a fellow of All Souls in 1996.
114 Thomas Nagel, *The Possibility of Altruism*, 16–17. Interestingly, Cohen faulted Nagel for being too concessive to selfishness on matters of distribution; G. A. Cohen, 'Mind the Gap'.
115 Karl Marx and Friederich Engels, 'Manifesto of the Communist Party', 491; Cohen, 'Self-Ownership, Communism and Equality', 122–3.
116 David Hume, *An Enquiry Concerning the Principles of Morals*, 36. Hume's idea of the circumstances of justice plays an important role in Rawls, *Theory of Justice*, 126–30.
117 See Tom Campbell, *The Left and Rights* and Christine Sypnowich, *The Concept of Socialist Law*, ch. 1 and 124–8; a more recent contribution to this debate is Igor Shoikhedbrod's *Revisiting Marx's Critique of Liberalism: Rethinking Justice, Legality and Rights*.
118 In 1995 the British Labour Party, under the leadership of Tony Blair, removed the reference to 'common ownership' in Clause IV of the *Labour Party Rule Book*. Just a few months earlier Cohen was on a BBC Radio 4 panel, 'Fairly Modern' (14 December 1994) with Blair, among others, in which he criticized the influence of a market mentality on the Labour Party as potentially 'making things worse for the worse off'. Programme typescript, Personal Archives.
119 Cohen, 'Back to Socialist Basics', 213.
120 Bernard Williams, 'Forward to Basics'.
121 An influential defence of market socialism in the 1980s was Alec Nove, *The Economics of Feasible Socialism*.
122 David Miller, 'Our Unfinished Debate About Market Socialism'; Miller, *Market, State and Community: Theoretical Foundations of Market Socialism*. Miller also published a paper in the *Equality* volume, in which he refers to market socialism, though within a discussion about the importance of including considerations of desert; Miller, 'What Kind of Equality Should the Left Pursue?'
123 G. A. Cohen, 'David Miller on Market Socialism and Distributive Justice', 10–13.
124 Joseph Carens, *Equality, Moral Incentives and the Market*.
125 Cohen, *Why Not Socialism*, 53–82. See also Cohen, *Rescuing Justice and Equality*, 82, 189–91, 369; Cohen, 'The Future of a Disillusion', 255–65.
126 Cohen, *Rescuing Justice and Equality*, 269–70.
127 Cohen, *Rescuing Justice and Equality*, 229.
128 See Thomas Pogge, 'Cohen to the Rescue!'; Kyle Johannsen, 'Explanation and Justification: Understanding the Functions of Fact-Insensitive Principles'.
129 Thomas Pogge, 'Cohen to the Rescue!', 108.

130 Lea Ypi, 'Facts, Principles and the Third Man', 198, 201–14.
131 Cohen, *Rescuing Justice and Equality*, 291.
132 Kai Nielsen, 'Rescuing Political Theory from Fact-Insensitivity'.
133 David Miller, *Justice for Earthlings*, 232.
134 Miller, *Justice for Earthlings*, ch. 10; see also Ingrid Robeyns, 'Ideal Theory in Theory and Practice', 343.
135 Miller, *Justice for Earthlings*, 2, 232.
136 Adam Swift, 'The Value of Philosophy in Non-ideal Circumstances', 364.
137 Ingrid Robeyns, 'Ideal Theory in Theory and Practice', 343.
138 David Estlund, 'Utopophobia', 130.
139 Christine Sypnowich, 'G. A. Cohen's Socialism: Scientific, but also Utopian'.

Chapter 5: Taking Responsibility for Egalitarianism

1 G. A. Cohen, 'Prospectus', 1.
2 Cohen published an article of that name which was then included as 'Political Philosophy and Personal Behavior', ch. 10 in *If You're an Egalitarian, How Come You're So Rich?*. Others have replicated the title in papers, blogs, reviews, etc., for example: *'If you're an egalitarian how come* you're trying to sell an undergraduate arts degree that costs more than an MBA?', '... how come you're a philosopher?', '... how come you claimed so much in expenses?', '... how come you wanna be so poor?', '... how come you don't believe in genetic enhancement?', '... how come you read bedtime stories to your children?', '... how come you're so inegalitarian about your body?', '... how come you send your children to private school?' Colin Macleod argues that more intractable is the 'rich libertarian' problem; see his 'If You're a Libertarian, How Come You're So Rich?'
3 See Joseph Raz, *The Morality of Freedom*, ch. 9 and Larry Temkin, *Inequality*, and Harry Frankfurt, 'Equality as a Moral Ideal'. But see also Martin O'Neill, 'What Should Egalitarians Believe?' and Christine Sypnowich, 'Equality: From Marxism to Liberalism (and back again)'.
4 See Harry Frankfurt, 'Equality as a Moral Ideal', and Derek Parfit, 'Equality or Priority?'
5 R.H. Tawney, *Equality*, 113.
6 Jeffrey Noonan, 'G. A. Cohen and the Ethical Core of Socialism: Equality or Life-Sufficiency?', 133.
7 Pablo Gilabert, 'Cohen on Socialism, Equality, and Community'. David Rondel suggests that any inequality that persists in a context of well-designed institutions of justice is unlikely to be 'morally serious'; see 'G. A. Cohen and the Logic of Egalitarian Congruence'.
8 G. A. Cohen, *Rescuing Justice and Equality*, 319–20.

9   Amartya Sen, *Inequality Reexamined*, ch. 1. The idea of a plateau is widely acknowledged, arguably attributed first to Ronald Dworkin; see Will Kymlicka, *Contemporary Political Philosophy: An Introduction*, 3–4.
10 See Richard Arneson, 'Equality and Equal Opportunity for Welfare'.
11 Sen, *Inequality Reexamined*, ch. 3; see Christine Sypnowich, *Equality Renewed: Justice, Flourishing and the Egalitarian Ideal*, chs. 6–8.
12 Ronald Dworkin, *Sovereign Virtue: The Theory and Practice of Equality*, 65–119.
13 Sen, *Inequality Reexamined*, 42, 54–5.
14 G. A. Cohen, 'On the Currency of Egalitarian Justice', 42. Sen, *Development as Freedom*, 62–3. Thomas Scanlon concurs that welfare's subjectivism should be qualified by the discrimination between important and unimportant interests in 'Value, Desire, and the Quality of Life'.
15 G. A. Cohen, 'Equality of What? On Welfare, Goods and Capabilities', 59–60; see also G. A. Cohen, 'Sen on Capability, Freedom, and Control'. Colin Macleod argues that Dworkin fails to achieve equality with market mechanisms in *Liberalism, Justice and Markets: A Critique of Liberal Equality*.
16 Cohen, 'On the Currency of Egalitarian Justice', 40–2.
17 Cohen, 'On the Currency of Egalitarian Justice', 42–3.
18 G. A. Cohen, 'Equality of What?', 48.
19 Cohen, 'On the Currency of Egalitarian Justice', 20, 18, 28. Although Cohen later conceded that his position amounted, not to a theory, but to a 'repository of considerations with which an acceptable theory must come to terms', he continued to believe that there is not a single thing which must be equalized, and that both resources and welfare should be taken into account when devising an egalitarian distribution, G. A. Cohen, 'Afterword to Chapters One and Two', 61–4.
20 Cohen, 'Afterword to Chapters One and Two', 64; 'Expensive Taste Rides Again', 113.
21 See Sypnowich, *Equality Renewed*.
22 I draw this example in Christine Sypnowich, 'The Demands of Equality'.
23 Cohen, 'On the Currency of Egalitarian Justice', 28.
24 Cohen, 'Afterword to Chapters One and Two', 62.
25 Cohen, *Rescuing Justice and Equality*, 200–1.
26 Cohen, *Rescuing Justice and Equality*, 293.
27 Cohen, *Rescuing Justice and Equality*, 368.
28 Steven Wall, 'Perfectionism in Moral and Political Philosophy'.
29 Kasper Lippert-Rasmussen devised an egalitarian metric not dissimilar from Cohen's access to advantage, which deems that 'what really matters', people's 'concerns', should exclude those that are 'brute' or 'badly misinformed'. Here, too, we see hints of a perfectionist view. See Kasper Lippert-Rasmussen, *Luck Egalitarianism*, 98–101.
30 John Rawls, 'Social Unity and Primary Goods', 168–9; see also Rawls,

'Justice as Fairness: Political not Metaphysical', 243–4. See Cohen 'On the Currency of Egalitarian Justice', 9–10.
31 Dworkin, *Sovereign Virtue*, 51.
32 Cohen, *Rescuing Justice and Equality*, 55–8; see Sypnowich, *Equality Renewed*, 119–20.
33 Indeed, Dworkin himself stressed the importance of treating people with 'equal concern and respect' rather than treating people the same, in his defence of preferential hiring as an egalitarian policy. See Dworkin, *Sovereign Virtue*, ch. 11 and Dworkin, *A Matter of Principle*, ch. 14–16.
34 Cohen, 'On the Currency of Egalitarian Justice', 24–5.
35 Cohen, 'On the Currency of Egalitarian Justice', 12–13.
36 Cohen, 'Expensive Taste Rides Again', 98.
37 David Miller counters this in *Principles of Social Justice*, ch. 9.
38 Dworkin, *Sovereign Virtue*, 73–8.
39 Dworkin rejects the luck egalitarian label in 'Equality, Luck and Hierarchy'. Luck egalitarian views can be found in, for example, John Roemer, *Egalitarian Perspectives* and *Theories of Distributive Justice*; Eric Rakowski, *Equal Justice*; Richard Arneson, 'Equality and Equal Opportunity for Welfare', 'Egalitarianism and Responsibility', 'Equality of Opportunity for Welfare Defended and Recanted', 'Luck Egalitarianism – A Primer'; Larry Temkin, *Inequality* and 'Egalitarianism Defended'. See Carl Knight and Zofia Stemplowska (eds), *Responsibility and Distributive Justice*, and their 'Responsibility and Distributive Justice: An Introduction' in that volume.
40 See Lippert-Rasmussen, *Luck Egalitarianism*, 23.
41 Cohen credits this formulation to Larry Temkin, 'Inequality', 101 and a modified version, 'no fault or choice', in Larry Temkin, *Inequality*, 13. See G. A. Cohen, 'Fairness and Legitimacy in Justice, and: Does Option Luck Ever Preserve Justice?', 139, note 7.
42 Cohen, 'On the Currency of Egalitarian Justice', 5; see also Cohen, *Rescuing Justice and Equality*, 7–8.
43 Cohen, 'On the Currency of Egalitarian Justice', 29.
44 Cited in 'On the Currency of Egalitarian Justice', 31–2; see Will Kymlicka, *Contemporary Political Philosophy: An Introduction*, 74.
45 Cohen, *Rescuing Justice and Equality*, 7.
46 Cohen, 'On the Currency of Egalitarian Justice', 32.
47 I consider how luck egalitarian considerations might be brought to bear on the decision to give to beggars in Christine Sypnowich, 'Begging', 182–4.
48 Andrew Williams, 'How Gifts and Gambles Preserve Justice', 82. Anne Phillips is particularly scathing about the liberal emphasis on choice in 'Beyond Choice'.
49 Why not, then, blow one's pay on a Saturday night to compensate for the drudgery of the week even if it leaves nothing for a rainy day – a

theme evocatively rendered in the song, 'Sudbury Saturday Night' by Stompin' Tom Connors (Sudbury is a mining town in northern Ontario). See Christine Sypnowich, 'What's Wrong with Equality of Opportunity (2020)' and *Equality Renewed*, 146–51.
50 Tawney, *Equality*, 41–2.
51 Thomas Hurka, *Perfectionism*, 170. See Michael Harrington, *The New American Poverty* and Guy Standing, *The Precariat: The New Dangerous Class*, 3–25.
52 See Samuel Scheffler, 'What is Egalitarianism?' 17–19, and 'Choice, Circumstance, and the Value of Equality', 10–14.
53 George Sher notes examples of 'unhappy outcomes that are the results of people's choices, yet are not themselves chosen', in *Equality for Inegalitarians*, 30.
54 Thomas Scanlon says that the 'legitimating effect' that opportunity to choose can have on disadvantage depends on 'sufficiently good conditions'. Scanlon, *Why Does Inequality Matter?*, 156. Sometimes our conditions are such that our choices are not our own and we should be absolved of the responsibility for making them or for the negative outcomes that ensue; Sypnowich, 'What's Wrong with Equality of Opportunity' (2020). See also Christine Sypnowich, 'What's Wrong with Equality of Opportunity' (2023) and 'Equality Matters' and several incisive critical responses in Deborah Chasman and Joshua Cohen (eds) *Is Equal Opportunity Enough?*.
55 Richard Arneson notes this in 'Egalitarianism and the Undeserving Poor', 332.
56 Indeed, this was Rawls's thinking in his notion of the natural lottery in *A Theory of Justice*, 64: 'Even the willingness to make an effort, to try, and so to be deserving in the ordinary sense is itself dependent on happy family and social circumstances'. Keith Dowding, 'Luck, Equality and Responsibility', invokes 'relative parenting pushiness' as an example that tracks cultures, but also diversity within cultures, that suggest it's 'hard to disentangle luck and responsibility'.
57 G. A. Cohen, 'The Future of a Disillusion', 253–5. See also Cohen, 'On the Currency of Egalitarian Justice', 14–15.
58 Cohen, 'Equality of What? On Welfare, Goods and Capabilities', 60.
59 Michael Otsuka directed his critique at Dworkin in 'Luck, Insurance, and Equality'; see also David Miller, 'The Incoherence of Luck Egalitarianism'.
60 Cohen, 'Fairness and Legitimacy in Justice, and: Does Option Luck Ever Preserve Justice?', 143.
61 I'm grateful to Colin Macleod for this point.
62 Bernard Williams and Thomas Nagel, 'Moral Luck', 140.
63 Cohen, *Rescuing Justice and Equality*, 404–5.
64 Susan Hurley, *Justice, Luck, and Knowledge*.
65 Susan Hurley, 'Choice and Incentive Inequality', 151–2.

66 Bernard Williams, 'Moral Luck: A Postscript', 241.
67 Sher, *Equality for Inegalitarians*, 125.
68 Bernard Williams and Thomas Nagel, 'Moral Luck', 115–36.
69 Cohen, 'Luck and Equality', 121. The phrase 'corporate welfare bums' was coined by David Lewis, former leader of the New Democratic Party of Canada. See his *Louder Voices: Corporate Welfare Bums*, also Jonathan Wolff, 'Fairness, Respect, and the Egalitarian "Ethos" Revisited', 340.
70 Cohen, 'Casting the First Stone: Who Can, and Who Can't, Condemn the Terrorists?', 118–19. See also 'Ways of Silencing Critics'. It might also be asked whether terrorists who commit atrocities lose their standing to blame.
71 I am grateful to Nicholas Vrousalis for suggesting this point.
72 Nicholas Vrousalis, *The Philosophy of G. A. Cohen: Back to Socialist Basics*, 65.
73 Jonathan Wolff argues that the deleterious influence of the libertarian Nozick on liberal egalitarianism accounts for this misguided focus on choice and responsibility; see Jonathan Wolff, 'Equality: The Recent History of an Idea'.
74 Cohen, 'Expensive Taste Rides Again', 102.
75 As Roemer contended in conversation with me on 10 February 2023, remarking that there may be 'very few circumstances where disadvantaged people are responsible'. The left-libertarian Peter Vallentyne stresses the role of luck egalitarianism as a theory of the duties we owe each other given the inequalities that result from brute luck; see Peter Vallentyne, 'Justice, Interpersonal Morality and Luck Egalitarianism'. Kasper Lippert-Rasmussen also argues that on an appropriate understanding of luck egalitarianism, 'precious little inequality – whether generated by differential option luck or otherwise – would be unobjectionable'; Kasper Lippert-Rasmussen, 'Egalitarianism, Option Luck and Responsibility', 579.
76 John Roemer, *Equality of Opportunity*.
77 Paul Hufe, Andreas Peichl, John Roemer, Martin Ungerer, 'Inequality of Income Acquisition: The Role of Childhood Circumstances', 500–1. See John Roemer, 'Designing for Outcomes'.
78 Lippert-Rasmussen, 'Egalitarianism, Luck and Responsibility'.
79 Serena Olsaretti, 'Responsibility and the Consequences of Choice', 167; 'Rescuing Justice and Equality from Libertarianism'.
80 Zofia Stemplowska, 'Making Justice Sensitive to Responsibility'.
81 See the discussion in Michael Otsuka and Andrew Williams, 'Equality, Ambition and Insurance'.
82 Tom Parr and Andrew Williams, 'Fair Insurance Defended, Amended, and Extended', 70.
83 Zofia Stemplowska, 'No Equality Without Liberal Equality', and 'Responsibility and Respect: Reconciling Two Egalitarian Visions'.
84 Thomas Scanlon, *Why Does Inequality Matter?*, 5.

85 Marc Fleurbaey, *Fairness, Responsibility, and Welfare*, 256.
86 Philippe Van Parijs, 'Why Surfers Should be Fed: The Liberal Case for an Unconditional Basic Income'. See also Philippe Van Parijs and Yannick Vanderborght, *Basic Income: A Radical Proposal for a Free Society and a Sane Economy*. Studies indicate remarkable results; see Evelyn Forget, 'The Town with No Poverty: The Health Effects of a Canadian Guaranteed Annual Income Field Experiment'.
87 Parr and Williams, 'Fair Insurance Defended, Amended, and Extended', 73.
88 Cohen, *Rescuing Justice and Equality*, 184–9.
89 Cohen, *Rescuing Justice and Equality*, 220, 123. Nonetheless, this is more demanding than the position ventured in *If You're an Egalitarian, How Come You're So Rich?* which focuses on obligations due to inadequate institutions.
90 Joseph Carens, 'The Egalitarian Ethos as a Social Commitment', 71–8.
91 Cohen, *Rescuing Justice and Equality*, 219–22.
92 Patrick Tomlin, 'Survey Article: Internal Doubts about Cohen's Rescue of Justice'.
93 Jonathan Quong, 'Justice Beyond Equality'.
94 Cohen, *Rescuing Justice and Equality*, 199.
95 See also Paula Casal, 'Occupational Choice and the Egalitarian Ethos'.
96 Cohen, 'Thanks', 249.
97 Conversation with Cohen, March 1999.
98 Cohen, 'Prospectus', 6.
99 I discuss these issues in Sypnowich, 'The Demands of Equality'.
100 Cohen, *Rescuing Justice and Equality*, 10; 213–14; 'Political Philosophy and Personal Behavior', 168.
101 Daniel Weinstock, 'Review: G.A. Cohen, *If You're an Egalitarian, How Come You're so Rich?*'
102 Oscar Wilde, 'The Soul of Man Under Socialism', 915. Interestingly, Cohen alludes to Wilde's point in 'Political Philosophy and Personal Behavior', 217, note 32.
103 Cohen, 'Political Philosophy and Personal Behavior', 168.
104 Bernard Williams, 'Critique of Utilitarianism', 116–17.
105 See Kok-Chor Tan, 'Justice and Personal Pursuits' and *Justice, Institutions and Luck*, 53, 19–49.
106 Cohen, *Rescuing Justice and Equality*, 271.
107 Jonathan Wolff, 'Fairness, Respect, and the Egalitarian Ethos', 104–5; 111–19. See also Timothy Hinton, 'Must Egalitarianism Choose Between Fairness and Respect?'
108 G. A. Cohen, *Why Not Socialism?* See Christine Sypnowich, 'G. A. Cohen's Socialism: Scientific but also Utopian', 28; Nicholas Vrousalis, 'Jazz Bands, Camping Trips and Decommodification: G. A. Cohen on Community', 152, note 29 and 154, note 32.
109 Elizabeth Anderson, 'What is the Point of Equality?', 287.

110 Anderson, 'What is the Point of Equality?', 321.
111 Contending that 'Cohen might have been a luck egalitarian, but he was also a relational egalitarian', Lippert-Rasmussen argues that the two doctrines are best brought together. Kasper Lippert-Rasmussen, *Relational Egalitarianism: Living as Equals*, 232.
112 G. A. Cohen, 'Notes on Regarding People as Equals'.
113 Bernard Williams, 'The Idea of Equality', 239–49. Cohen draws on the ideas of Williams in his essay.
114 G. A. Cohen, *Rescuing Justice and Equality*, 122–4.
115 Cohen, *Why Not Socialism?*
116 John Roemer, 'Address at G. A. Cohen Memorial Service'.
117 Cohen, *Why Not Socialism?*, 40–1, 77.
118 Cohen, *Why Not Socialism?*, 44, 34–5. Again Lippert-Rasmussen sees affinities with his relational egalitarian view here. See *Relational Egalitarianism: Living as Equals*, 230–4.
119 Miriam Ronzoni doubts that a camping trip can tell you what societal justice requires; see her 'Life is Not a Camping Trip – On the Desirability of Cohenite Socialism'. Other critics hold that the example is prejudicial; see Richard Arneson, 'Why Not Capitalism?'; Jason Brennan, *Why Not Capitalism?*.
120 See Alex Sager, 'Review of Jason Brennan, *Why Not Capitalism*'.
121 Jonathan Wolff, 'Fairness, Respect and the Egalitarian Ethos', 104–5.
122 Nicholas Vrousalis, *Back to Socialist Basics: The Political Philosophy of G. A. Cohen*, 131.
123 Richard Miller, 'Relations of Equality: A Camping Trip Revisited', 231–2.
124 Cohen, *Why Not Socialism?*, 34–8. See also Cohen, 'On the Currency of Egalitarian Justice', 933.
125 David Miller is insightful on this point in 'The Incoherence of Luck Egalitarianism', 147–9. See also Richard Miller, 'Relationships of Equality: A Camping Trip Revisited'.
126 Pablo Gilabert, 'Cohen on Socialism, Equality and Community'. Michael Otsuka proposes that considerations of fairness animate both the egalitarian and non-egalitarian dimensions of Cohen's view, 'Justice as Fairness: Luck Egalitarian, not Rawlsian'.
127 Jonathan Wolff, 'Fairness, Respect and the Egalitarian "Ethos" Revisited', 338.
128 Cohen, *Rescuing Justice and Equality*: compare 64–5 and 7.
129 See Michael Sandel, *Liberalism and the Limits of Justice* and Charles Taylor, 'Atomism'.
130 See John Rawls, 'Justice as Fairness: Political not Metaphysical'; Bernard Williams, 'Pluralism, Community and Left-Wittgensteinianism', 34.
131 Miller, 'The Incoherence of Luck Egalitarianism', 146–50.
132 Zofia Stemplowska makes this point in 'Commentary'.
133 Cohen, *Why Not Socialism?*, 38–45. John Roemer offers solidarity

in a similar spirit; see John Roemer, 'Impartiality, Solidarity, and Distributive Justice', 219–24.
134 G. A. Cohen, 'Notes on Regarding People as Equals', 194.
135 Anne Phillips, *Unconditional Equals*.
136 I am grateful to Will Kymlicka and Andrew Lister for pressing these points.
137 Arneson, 'Egalitarianism and the Undeserving Poor', 350.
138 A point I make in Sypnowich, *Equality Renewed*, 149.
139 As Arneson says, 'for most poor people, having a job is good for you whether you think so or not.' 'Egalitarianism and the Undeserving Poor', 348.
140 John Stuart Mill, *Principles of Political Economy*, 955, quoted in Arneson, 'Egalitarianism and the Undeserving Poor', 335.
141 See Richard C. Fording and William D. Berry, 'The Historical Impact of Welfare Programs on Poverty: Evidence from the American States'. The findings regarding universal basic income also tell against such prejudices. See David Cox, 'Canada's Forgotten Universal Basic Income Experiment', Van Parijs and Vanderborght, *Basic Income*, and Forget, 'The Town with No Poverty'.
142 Note Jeremy Waldron's argument against paternalism: 'I wish … that I could be made a better chooser rather than having someone on high take advantage (even for my own benefit) of my current thoughtlessness and my shabby intuitions'; Jeremy Waldron, 'It's All for Your Own Good'.
143 Will Kymlicka, 'Left-Liberalism Revisited', 25–32.
144 Katrina Forrester, *In the Shadow of Justice: Postwar Liberalism and the Remaking of Political Philosophy*, 223–7.
145 G. A. Cohen, 'Against Capitalism'.
146 Michael Otsuka, 'Editor's Preface' in G. A. Cohen, *Finding Oneself in the Other*, xi.

Chapter 6: Rescuing Existing Value – For or Against Socialism?

1 G. A. Cohen, 'Rescuing Conservatism: A Defence of Existing Value', 144.
2 The *Monist* devoted an issue to essays on conservatism, many of which, the editors Martin Beckstein and Francis Cheneval proclaimed, were 'indebted to Jerry Cohen's seminal paper on conservative value', which 'develops a sophisticated justification of what Michael Oakeshott … called the disposition to be conservative'. 'Conservatism: Analytically Reconsidered', 333.
3 Lionel Trilling, *The Liberal Imagination: Essays on Literature and Society*, xv.
4 Ted Honderich, *Conservatism*, 2; cited by Cohen, 'Rescuing Conservatism', 171.

5 *Online Etymological Dictionary*, 'Conservative'.
6 Richard Davenport-Hines also declares that Cohen 'cannot be called conservative' because he 'never reneged on the basic elements of his kiddies' Marxism'. *Conservative Thinkers from All Souls College*, 8.
7 Encyclopedia Britannica, 'Divine Right of Kings' https://www.britannica.com/topic/divine-right-of-kings
8 Burke, Edmund. *Reflections on the Revolution in France*. Burke did not in fact use the term conservative.
9 Geoffrey Brennan and Alan Hamlin, 'Conservative Value', 353.
10 Cohen, 'Rescuing Conservatism', 170.
11 Simon Tormey, 'Simon Tormey Interviews Gerald Cohen', 353.
12 Cohen, 'Rescuing Conservatism', 143. Of course, an old-fashioned socialist might also be substantively conservative in their resistance to change, for example, unhappy with the embrace of progressive views such as varieties of feminism that repudiate the relevance of social class.
13 George Sher, 'The Weight of the Past', 152–3.
14 As Anca Gheaus helpfully put it in 'Commentary'.
15 Cohen, 'Rescuing Conservatism', 144.
16 Jan Narveson, *You and the State: A Short Introduction to Political Philosophy*, 53.
17 Jacob M. Nebel defends this dimension of Cohen's argument in 'Status Quo Bias, Rationality, and Conservatism about Value'.
18 Cohen, 'Rescuing Conservatism', 144. (Note, though, that modern Egyptologists dispute the claim that the pyramids were built by slaves.)
19 Cohen, 'Rescuing Conservatism', 167.
20 Cohen, 'Rescuing Conservatism', 148, 153–5.
21 Cohen, 'Rescuing Conservatism', 156; Ralf Bader, 'Review of G. A. Cohen, *Finding Oneself in the Other*'.
22 David O'Brien, 'Conservatism Reconsidered', 166.
23 Cohen, 'Rescuing Conservatism', 156.
24 Bader, 'Review of G. A. Cohen, *Finding Oneself in the Other*'.
25 O'Brien, 'Conservatism Reconsidered', 163–4; Frances Kamm, 'The Purpose of My Death: Death, Dying, and Meaning', 734–5.
26 Samuel Scheffler, *Why Worry About Future Generations?*, 115.
27 Thomas Scanlon, *What We Owe to Each Other*, 97–9.
28 Scanlon, *What We Owe to Each Other*, 95.
29 Samuel Scheffler, 'Valuing', 28–31.
30 Cohen, 'Rescuing Conservatism', 163–4. This is in contrast to Sher's view in 'The Weight of the Past', which stresses our 'shared social world' (158) – something like the latter plays a role in some of Cohen's examples, but not all.
31 Erich Hatala Matthes, 'Impersonal Value, Universal Value, and the Scope of Cultural Heritage'.
32 Cécile Fabre, 'Territorial Sovereignty and Humankind's Common Heritage'.

Notes to pp. 144–149 211

33 Jonathan Pugh, Guy Kahane and Julian Savulescu, 'Cohen's Conservatism and Human Enhancement', 335.
34 Burke, *Reflections on the Revolution in France*, 106.
35 Cohen, 'Rescuing Conservatism', 156.
36 Bader, 'Review of G. A. Cohen, *Finding Oneself in the Other*'.
37 Cohen, 'Rescuing Conservatism', 158.
38 Pugh, Kahane and Savulescu, 'Cohen's Conservatism', 336.
39 G.K. Chesterton, 'The Thing: Why I Am a Catholic', 157.
40 Iris Murdoch, *The Sovereignty of Good*, 95. See Simon P. James, 'Why Old Things Matter'.
41 Think of the acceptance in our society of plastic surgery for cosmetic purposes, to reduce, lift, augment, tuck, shape, contour parts of the human form; the so-called 'mommy makeover' to remove the effects of pregnancy on women's bodies; the routine use of Botox to fill in wrinkles in order to look younger, and so forth.
42 Cohen, 'Rescuing Conservatism', 150–1.
43 Samuel Scheffler, *Death and the Afterlife*; Nico Kolodny, 'Introduction', 9.
44 Cohen, 'Rescuing Conservatism', 151.
45 Cohen, 'Rescuing Conservatism', 152.
46 Michael Sandel, *The Case against Perfection*, 99–100.
47 Pugh, Kahane and Savulescu, 'Cohen's Conservatism', 343–7.
48 Pugh, Kahane and Savulescu, 'Cohen's Conservatism', 351. See Bernard Williams, *Philosophy as a Humanistic Discipline*, 152.
49 Cohen, 'Rescuing Conservatism', 170.
50 Cohen, 'Rescuing Conservatism', 169; see Michael Oakeshott, 'The Voice of Poetry in the Conversation of Mankind', and Burke, *Reflections*, 108.
51 G.K. Chesterton, *Orthodoxy*, 30.
52 Cohen, 'Rescuing Conservatism', 168. This argument can apply to school buildings too, as is evident in an unsuccessful fight to save Ontario's oldest public high school, Kingston Collegiate, housed in a heritage-designated 'collegiate gothic' building. Those calling for closure of the school invoked the buzzword 'twenty-first century learning', a phrase one critic scorned as 'semi-literate, evidence-free gibberish' and 'warmed-over romantic progressivism – think *Summerhill* mixed with a jolt of *Future Shock*'; see Margaret Wente, 'The Brave New World of 21st Century Learning'.
53 G. A. Cohen, *Karl Marx's Theory of History*, 345.
54 John Ruskin, *The Seven Lamps of Architecture*, 183.
55 Ruskin, *The Seven Lamps of Architecture*, 201
56 Adolphus Riegl, 'The Modern Cult of Monuments: Its Essence and Its Development', 72–3; Carolyn Korsmeyer, 'Real Old Things'.
57 Friederich Nietzsche, *The Use and Abuse of History*, 20 and Beata Labuhn, 'Breathing a Moldy Air: Olfactory Experience, Aesthetics, and Ethics in the Writing of Ruskin and Riegl'.

58 Cornelius Holtorf, 'Perceiving the Past: From Age Value to Pastness'. See also Erich Hatala Matthes, 'History, Value and Irreplaceability'.
59 Cohen, 'Rescuing Conservatism', 159.
60 Cohen, 'Rescuing Conservatism', 159–60.
61 Cohen, 'Rescuing Conservatism', 162.
62 Karl Marx and Frederick Engels, 'Manifesto of the Communist Party', 476–7.
63 Marx and Engels, 'Manifesto of the Communist Party', 476.
64 Leon Trotsky, *Literature and Revolution*, 204.
65 Marshall Berman, *All That is Solid Melts into Air: The Experience of Modernity*, 120.
66 Henri Lefebvre, *The Urban Revolution*, 1–4; see also David Harvey, *Rebel Cities: From the Right to the City to the Urban Revolution*, 78.
67 Lefebvre, *The Urban Revolution*, 14.
68 Tormey, 'Simon Tormey Interviews Gerald Cohen', 355.
69 Cohen, 'Hegel in Marx: The Obstetric Motif in the Marxist Conception of Revolution'.
70 David Wiggins, *Sameness and Substance Renewed*, 242.
71 David Wiggins, 'A Reasonable Frugality', 178, and 'Presidential Address: Nature, Respect for Nature, and the Human Scale of Values', 8.
72 Sher explicitly separates considerations about the natural world from his account of conservatism; 'Weight of the Past', 157, 163–4.
73 Nicholas Vrousalis, *The Political Philosophy of G. A. Cohen*, 11.
74 Cohen, 'Rescuing Conservatism', 173.
75 Cohen, 'Rescuing Conservatism', 168–73.
76 Roger Scruton, *How to be a Conservative*. Scruton was on the other side of the debate on the issue of racism in Britain noted in chapter 1.
77 Nadya Tolokonnikova and Slavoj Žižek, *Comradely Greetings: The Prison Letters of Nadya and Slavoj*, 94–5.
78 Cohen, 'Rescuing Conservatism', 156.
79 William Morris, 'Manifesto, Society for the Protection of Ancient Buildings'.
80 Fiona MacCarthy, *William Morris*, 605.
81 William Morris, 'The Lesser Arts', 95.
82 Cohen, 'Rescuing Conservatism', 144.
83 Cohen explains the controversy as one where some Fellows wanted the college to 'establish a relationship with external sources of funding such as the Ford Foundation, and also that it should create short-term research associations between Fellows and academics in other institutions'. Cohen, 'Rescuing Conservatism', 146.
84 G. A. Cohen, 'One Kind of Spirituality: Come Back Feuerbach, All Is Forgiven!', 201.
85 G. A. Cohen, 'Rescuing Conservatism' (2011 version), 205.
86 Otsuka, 'Editor's Preface', in G. A. Cohen, *Finding Oneself in the Other*, ix.

87 Something which the college has taken steps to address; see All Souls College, 'The Codrington Legacy'.
88 To take one example, women weren't admitted to most colleges until the late 1970s; another is that Oxford has a long tradition of recruiting principally from fee-paying elite private schools. Cohen states that 'there was no case for preserving' that aspect of All Souls's identity which was that it excluded women. 'Rescuing Conservatism', 147, note 9.
89 Gheaus, 'Commentary'.
90 Cohen, 'Rescuing Conservatism', 147 note 9.
91 The Woodland Cultural Centre is an excellent example; it was established in October 1972, under the direction of the Association of Iroquois and Allied Indians upon the closure of the Mohawk Institute Residential School. It is now a museum and historic site. See Woodland Cultural Centre, 'Overview'. I explore these issues in Christine Sypnowich, 'Monuments and Monsters: Education, Cultural Heritage and Sites of Conscience'.
92 As one of my Oxford colleagues pointed out.
93 See Paula Casal, 'Whaling, Bullfighting, and the Conditional Value of Tradition'.
94 Scanlon, *What We Owe to Each Other*, 336–7; Samuel Scheffler, *Equality and Tradition*, 287–309.
95 Cohen, 'Rescuing Conservatism', 148.
96 Cohen, 'Rescuing Conservatism', 155.
97 Gheaus, 'Commentary'.
98 Cohen, 'Rescuing Conservatism', 172.
99 Cohen, 'Rescuing Conservatism', 172.
100 Cohen, 'Rescuing Conservatism', 172.
101 Vrousalis, *The Political Philosophy of G. A. Cohen*, 13–14.
102 George Sher, *Equality for Inegalitarians*, 124–5, 146–8.
103 G. A. Cohen, 'Preface', *If You're an Egalitarian, How Come You're So Rich?*, ix.
104 Cohen, 'Rescuing Conservatism', 149.
105 Cohen, 'Rescuing Conservatism', 156.
106 See John Rawls, *Justice as Fairness: A Restatement*, 153–7, note 27; see Christine Sypnowich, *Equality Renewed: Justice, Flourishing and the Egalitarian Ideal*, 156–7.
107 Joseph Raz, *The Morality of Freedom*, 395–6.
108 Similarly, in considering the possibility of an egalitarian perfectionism, Nicholas Vrousalis, insisted on the importance of 'economy' in one's philosophical method, commending the eschewal of perfectionism, and indeed even Marxist concepts of alienation, in order to avoid controversial propositions outside of those that are narrowly distributive. As I recall he invoked Cohen's example here. Personal conversation, 11 February 2021.
109 David O'Brien, 'Conservatism Reconsidered', 165.

110 Edward Said, 'Thoughts on Late Style'.
111 G. A. Cohen, 'Prospectus', 5–6.
112 Jane O'Grady, 'Obituary: G. A. Cohen'.
113 Cohen, 'One Kind of Spirituality', 206. It is interesting that there was some debate among Otsuka and Cohen's family as to the inclusion of this unfinished, religious essay, whether Cohen would have regarded it as representative of his corpus. Conversation with Miriam Cohen, 16 October 2022.
114 Cohen, 'One Kind of Spirituality', 207.

Chapter 7: Conclusion: Paradox and Legacy

1 G. A. Cohen, 'Against Capitalism'.
2 G. A. Cohen, 'Closing Comments'.
3 A less sympathetic though nonetheless laudatory source, an obituary in *The Financial Times*, in contrast, stressed 'contradictions' in Cohen's life and work. See John Lloyd, 'Marxist Philosopher Famed for His Intellect and Wit'.
4 I'm grateful to Danny Goldstick for pointing out these passages to me.
5 I propose this in Christine Sypnowich, 'G. A. Cohen's Socialism: Scientific but also Utopian'.
6 See G. A. Cohen, 'The Development of Socialism from Utopia to Science'.
7 G. A. Cohen, *Karl Marx's Theory of History: A Defence*, xxvii, note 1.
8 John Horton, 'The Smartest Guys in the Room: Cohen and Sen on Justice'.
9 Michael Rosen, 'Jerry Cohen – An Appreciation'.
10 Derek Parfit, quoted in David Edmonds, *Parfit: A Philosopher and his Mission to Save Morality*, 218.
11 J. Angelo Corlett, 'Editor-in-Chief's Introduction', 181–3.
12 Michael Otsuka, 'Remarks at G. A. Cohen's Funeral'.
13 Jonathan Wolff, 'G. A. Cohen: A Memoir', 342.
14 Brian Feltham, 'Introduction', 1.
15 Indeed, his former doctoral student, Kasper Lippert-Rasmussen, picked up some of these themes in his account of 'non-instrumental concern luck egalitarianism'; *Luck Egalitarianism*, 99–101. The theme's role in Marxist thought is fruitfully explored in the collection, Jan Kandiyali (ed.), *Reassessing Marx's Social and Political Philosophy: Freedom, Recognition, and Human Flourishing*. See Christine Sypnowich, 'Liberalism, Marxism, Equality and Living Well' in that volume.
16 Particularly his nemesis Dworkin; for a discussion of this issue see Matthew Clayton, 'Liberal Equality and Ethics'.
17 Nicholas Vrousalis, *The Political Philosophy of G. A. Cohen: Back to Socialist Basics*, 1–4.

18 Jonathan Wolff, 'Review, Nicholas Vrousalis, *The Political Philosophy of G.A Cohen: Back to Socialist Basics*' and 'G. A. Cohen: A Memoir', 337, 342.
19 G. A. Cohen, 'Marxist Boxing Match: Roemer vs. Habermas'.
20 Wolff, 'Review, Nicholas Vrousalis, *The Political Philosophy of G.A Cohen: Back to Socialist Basics*'.
21 Isaiah Berlin, *The Hedgehog and the Fox*.
22 Jonathan Wolff, 'Editor's Preface', viii–x.
23 Cohen, *Rescuing Justice and Equality*, 4–5.
24 Cohen, *Karl Marx's Theory of History*, xxiii.
25 Cohen, *Karl Marx's Theory of History*, xxiii–xxiv.
26 Rosen, 'Jerry Cohen – An Appreciation'.
27 Tormey, 'Simon Tormey Interviews Gerald Cohen', 357.
28 G. A. Cohen, 'How to do Political Philosophy' and Michael Otsuka, 'Editor's Preface' in *On the Currency of Egalitarian Justice*, xi.
29 Wolff, 'G. A. Cohen: A Memoir', 342.
30 Nikhil Krishnan, *A Terribly Serious Adventure: Philosophy and War at Oxford 1900–1960*, xvii–xxiii.
31 'What Does Egalitarianism Require?' was the subject of a conference and journal issue; see David Schmidtz, *Social Philosophy and Policy*.
32 Ezra Pound, 'Canto LXXXI'.
33 Cohen, 'Closing Comments'.

References

Works by G. A. Cohen

Cohen, G. A., 1966–7. 'Beliefs and Roles', *Proceedings of the Aristotelian Society*, 67.

Cohen, G. A., 1969. 'Critical Theory: The Philosophy of Herbert Marcuse', *New Left Review*, 57, September–October.

Cohen, G. A., 1970. 'On Some Criticisms of Historical Materialism', *Proceedings of the Aristotelian Society, Supplementary Volume*, 44.

Cohen, G. A., 1980. 'Functional Explanation: A Reply to Elster', *Political Studies*, 28, 1.

Cohen, G. A., 1983. 'Review of *Karl Marx* by Allen Wood', *Mind*, 92, 367, July.

Cohen, G. A., 1985. 'Are Workers Forced to Sell their Labor Power?', *Philosophy & Public Affairs*, 14, 1.

Cohen, G. A., 1986. 'Against Capitalism', *Opinions*, Channel 4, September, in two parts: https://www.youtube.com/watch?v=yA9WPQeow9c&t=6s and https://www.youtube.com/watch?v=oD1YEzd6QzQ

Cohen, G. A. 1987. 'Anti-Anti-Racism', Letters, *London Review of Books*, 9, 21, 26 November.

Cohen, G. A., 1988. 'Base and Superstructure', ch. 2 in *History, Labour and Freedom: Themes from Marx*, Oxford: Oxford University Press; reprints material from 'Reply to Four Critics', *Analyse und Kritik*, 5, 1983.

Cohen, G. A., 1988. 'Being, Consciousness, and Roles', ch. 3 in *History, Labour and Freedom: Themes from Marx*, Oxford: Oxford University Press; previously published in C. Abramsky (ed.), *Essays in Honour of E.H. Carr*, London: Macmillan, 1974.

Cohen, G. A., 1988. 'The Dialectic of Labour in Marx', ch. 10 in *History, Labour and Freedom: Themes from Marx*, Oxford: Oxford University Press;

References 217

revised version of 'Marx's Dialectic of Labour', in *Philosophy & Public Affairs*, 3, 3, Spring 1974.

Cohen, G. A., 1988. 'Are Disadvantaged Workers Who Take Hazardous Jobs Forced to Take Hazardous Jobs?', ch. 12 in *History, Labour, and Freedom: Themes from Marx*, Oxford: Oxford University Press; previously published in G. Ezorsky (ed.), *Moral Rights in the Workplace*, Albany, NY: SUNY Press, 1987.

Cohen, G. A., 1988. 'Fettering', ch. 6 in *History, Labour, and Freedom: Themes from Marx*, Oxford: Oxford University Press.

Cohen, G. A., 1988. 'Forces and Relations of Production', ch. 1 in *History, Labour, and Freedom: Themes from Marx*, Oxford: Oxford University Press; reprints material from 'Forces and Relations of Production' in B. Matthews (ed.), *A Hundred Years of Marxism*, London: Lawrence and Wishart, 1983 and 'Reply to Four Critics', *Analyse und Kritik*, 5, 1983.

Cohen, G. A., 1988. 'Freedom, Justice and Capitalism', ch. 14 in *History, Labour, and Freedom: Themes from Marx*, Oxford: Oxford University Press; previously published in *New Left Review*, 126, 1981.

Cohen, G. A., 1988. 'Historical Inevitability and Revolutionary Agency', ch. 4 in *History, Labour, and Freedom: Themes from Marx*, Oxford: Oxford University Press; revised version of 'Historical Inevitability and Revolutionary Agency', in Sir John Mason (ed.), *Predictability in Science and Society*, London: The Royal Society and the British Academy, 1986.

Cohen, G. A., 1988. *History, Labour, and Freedom: Themes from Marx*, Oxford: Oxford University Press.

Cohen, G. A., 1988. 'The Labour Theory of Value and the Concept of Exploitation', ch. 11 in *History, Labour, and Freedom: Themes from Marx*, Oxford: Oxford University Press; revised version of 'The Labour Theory of Value and the Concept of Exploitation', *Philosophy & Public Affairs*, 8, 4, Summer 1979.

Cohen, G. A., 1988. 'On an Argument for Historical Materialism', ch. 7 in *History, Labour, and Freedom: Themes from Marx*, Oxford: Oxford University Press; extended version of material previously published as 'Being, Consciousness, and Roles', in C. Abramsky (ed.), *Essays in Honour of E.H. Carr*, London: Macmillan, 1974 and 'Restricted and Inclusive Historical Materialism', *Irish Philosophical Journal*, 1, 1984.

Cohen, G. A., 1988. 'Preface', in *History, Labour, and Freedom: Themes from Marx*, Oxford: Oxford University Press.

Cohen, G. A., 1988. 'Reconsidering Historical Materialism', ch. 8 in *History, Labour, and Freedom: Themes from Marx*, Oxford: Oxford University Press; previously published in J. Roland Pennock and John W. Chapman (eds), *Marxism: Nomos XXVI*, New York: New York University Press, 1983.

Cohen, G. A., 1988. 'Restricted and Inclusive Historical Materialism', ch. 9 in *History, Labour, and Freedom: Themes from Marx*, Oxford: Oxford University Press; revised and expanded version of 'Restricted and Inclusive Historical Materialism', *Irish Philosophical Journal*, 1, 1984.

Cohen, G. A., 1988. 'The Structure of Proletarian Unfreedom', ch. 13 in *History, Labour, and Freedom: Themes from Marx*, Oxford: Oxford University Press; previously published in *Philosophy & Public Affairs*, 12, 1, Winter 1983 and reprinted in John Roemer (ed.), *Analytical Marxism*, Cambridge: Cambridge University Press, 1986.

Cohen, G. A., 1989. 'David Miller on Market Socialism and Distributive Justice' (unpublished paper).

Cohen, G. A., 1992. 'Housewives are expendable', Letters, *London Review of Books*, 14, 13, 9 July.

Cohen, G. A., 1995. 'Are Freedom and Equality Compatible?', ch. 4 in *Self-Ownership, Freedom and Equality*, Cambridge: Cambridge University Press; draws on material from 'Self-Ownership, World Ownership, and Equality: Part II', *Social Philosophy and Policy*, 3, 4, Spring 1986.

Cohen, G. A., 1995. 'Exploitation in Marx: What Makes It Unjust?', ch. 8 in *Self-Ownership, Freedom and Equality*, Cambridge: Cambridge University Press.

Cohen, G. A., 1995. 'The Future of a Disillusion', ch. 11 in *Self-Ownership, Freedom and Equality*, Cambridge: Cambridge University Press; previously published in Jim Hopkins and Anthony Savile (eds), *Psychoanalysis, Mind and Art: Perspectives on Richard Wollheim*, Oxford: Basil Blackwell, 1992. A version of the essay was also published in *New Left Review*, 190, November–December 1991.

Cohen, G. A., 1995. 'Introduction: History, Ethics, and Marxism', in *Self-Ownership, Freedom and Equality*, Cambridge: Cambridge University Press.

Cohen, G. A., 1995. 'Justice, Freedom and Market Transactions', ch. 2 in *Self-Ownership, Freedom and Equality*, Cambridge: Cambridge University Press.

Cohen, G. A., 1995. 'Marx and Locke on Land and Labour', ch. 7 in *Self-Ownership, Freedom and Equality*, Cambridge: Cambridge University Press; draws on material from 'Marx and Locke on Land and Labour', in *Proceedings of the British Academy*, 71, 1985, *Lectures and Memoirs*, 1986.

Cohen, G. A., 1995. 'Marxism and Contemporary Political Philosophy, or: why Nozick Exercises some Marxists more than he does any Egalitarian Liberals', ch. 6 in *Self-Ownership, Freedom and Equality*, Cambridge: Cambridge University Press; draws on material from 'Marxism and Contemporary Political Philosophy, or: why Nozick Exercises some Marxists more than he does any Egalitarian Liberals', *Canadian Journal of Philosophy*, Supplementary Volume 16, 1990.

Cohen, G. A., 1995. 'Robert Nozick and Wilt Chamberlain: How Patterns Preserve Liberty', ch. 1 in *Self-Ownership, Freedom and Equality*, Cambridge: Cambridge University Press; draws on material from 'Robert Nozick and Wilt Chamberlain: How Patterns Preserve Liberty', *Erkenntnis*, 11, 1977.

Cohen, G. A., 1995. 'Self-Ownership: Assessing the Thesis', ch. 10 in *Self-Ownership, Freedom and Equality*, Cambridge: Cambridge University Press.

Cohen, G. A., 1995. 'Self-Ownership, Communism and Equality: Against the Marxist Technological Fix', ch. 5 in *Self-Ownership, Freedom and Equality*, Cambridge: Cambridge University Press; draws on material from "Self-Ownership, Communism and Equality', *Proceedings of the Aristotelian Society*, Supplementary Volume 64, 1990.
Cohen, G. A., 1995. 'Self-Ownership: Delineating the Concept', ch. 9 in *Self-Ownership, Freedom and Equality*, Cambridge: Cambridge University Press.
Cohen, G. A., 1995. *Self-Ownership, Freedom and Equality*, Cambridge: Cambridge University Press.
Cohen, G. A., 1995. 'Self-Ownership, World Ownership, and Equality', ch. 3 in *Self-Ownership, Freedom and Equality*, Cambridge: Cambridge University Press; draws on material from 'Self-Ownership, World-Ownership, and Equality', in Frank Lucash (ed.), *Justice and Equality Here and Now*, Ithaca, NY: Cornell University Press, 1986.
Cohen, G. A., 2000. 'The Development of Socialism from Utopia to Science', ch. 3 in *If You're an Egalitarian, How Come You're So Rich?* Cambridge, MA: Harvard University Press.
Cohen, G. A., 2000. 'Envoi', in *If You're an Egalitarian, How Come You're So Rich?* Cambridge, MA: Harvard University Press.
Cohen, G. A., 2000. 'Equality: From Fact to Norm', ch. 6 in *If You're an Egalitarian, How Come You're So Rich?* Cambridge, MA: Harvard University Press; draws on material previously published as the Introduction and ch. 6 of *Self-Ownership, Freedom and Equality*, Cambridge: Cambridge University Press, 1995.
Cohen, G. A., 2000. 'Hegel in Marx: The Obstetric Motif in the Marxist Conception of Revolution', ch. 4 in *If You're an Egalitarian, How Come You're So Rich?* Cambridge, MA: Harvard University Press.
Cohen, G. A., 2000. *If You're an Egalitarian, How Come You're So Rich?* Cambridge, MA: Harvard University Press.
Cohen, G. A., 2000. 'Justice, Incentives and Selfishness', ch. 8 in *If You're an Egalitarian, How Come You're So Rich?* Cambridge, MA: Harvard University Press; previously published as part of 'Where the Action Is', *Philosophy & Public Affairs*, 26, 1, Winter 1997.
Cohen, G. A., 2000. 'The Opium of the People: God in Hegel, Feuerbach, and Marx', ch. 5 in *If You're an Egalitarian, How Come You're So Rich?* Cambridge, MA: Harvard University Press.
Cohen, G. A., 2000. 'Paradoxes of Conviction', ch. 1 in *If You're an Egalitarian, How Come You're So Rich?* Cambridge, MA: Harvard University Press.
Cohen, G. A., 2000. 'Political Philosophy and Personal Behavior', ch. 10 in *If You're an Egalitarian, How Come You're So Rich?* Cambridge, MA: Harvard University Press; previously published as 'If You're an Egalitarian, How Come You're So Rich?', *Journal of Ethics*, 4, 1/2, January–March, 2000.
Cohen, G. A., 2000. 'Politics and Religion in a Montreal Communist Jewish

Childhood', ch. 2 in *If You're an Egalitarian, How Come You're So Rich?* Cambridge, MA: Harvard University Press.

Cohen, G. A., 2000. 'Preface', in *If You're an Egalitarian, How Come You're So Rich?* Cambridge, MA: Harvard University Press.

Cohen, G. A., 2000. 'Prospectus', in *If You're an Egalitarian, How Come You're So Rich?* Cambridge, MA: Harvard University Press.

Cohen, G. A., 2000. 'Where the Action Is: On the Site of Distributive Justice', ch. 9 in *If You're an Egalitarian, How Come You're So Rich?* Cambridge, MA: Harvard University Press; previously published as part of 'Where the Action Is', *Philosophy & Public Affairs*, 26, 1, Winter 1997.

Cohen, G. A. 2000 (1978). *Karl Marx's Theory of History: A Defence*. Expanded edition, Princeton, NJ: Princeton University Press.

Cohen, G. A., 2006. 'Thanks', in Christine Sypnowich (ed.), *The Egalitarian Conscience: Essays in Honour of G. A. Cohen*, Oxford: Oxford University Press.

Cohen, G. A., 2008. *Rescuing Justice and Equality*, Cambridge, MA: Harvard University Press.

Cohen, G. A., 2009. 'Closing Comments' at Rescuing Justice and Equality: Celebrating the Career of G. A. Cohen – Conference at the Centre for the Study of Social Justice (CSSJ), Department of Politics and International Relations, University of Oxford, 23–24 January. https://podcasts.ox.ac.uk/cssj-cohen-conference-closing-comments

Cohen, G. A., 2009. *Why Not Socialism?* Princeton, NJ: Princeton University Press; a previous version was published in Edward Broadbent (ed.), *Equality: What Went Wrong?* University of Toronto Press, 2001.

Cohen, G. A., 2011. 'Afterword to Chapters One and Two', in *On the Currency of Egalitarian Justice* (ed. Michael Otsuka), Princeton, NJ: Princeton University Press.

Cohen, G. A., 2011. 'Back to Socialist Basics', ch. 10 of *On the Currency of Egalitarian Justice* (ed. Michael Otsuka), Princeton, NJ: Princeton University Press; part of the essay previously published in *New Left Review*, 207, September–October 1994 and reprinted in Jane Franklin (ed.), *Equality*, London: Institute for Public Policy Research, 1997.

Cohen, G. A., 2011. 'Capitalism, Freedom and the Proletariat', ch. 7 of *On the Currency of Egalitarian Justice* (ed. Michael Otsuka), Princeton, NJ: Princeton University Press; part 1 previously published in David Miller (ed.), *The Liberty Reader*, Edinburgh: Edinburgh University Press, 2006 and part 2 previously published as 'Illusions about Private Property and Freedom', in Steven Cahn (ed.), *Philosophy for the 21st Century: A Comprehensive Reader*, Oxford: Oxford University Press, 2002.

Cohen, G. A., 2011. 'Equality of What? On Welfare, Goods and Capabilities', ch. 2 of *On the Currency of Egalitarian Justice* (ed. Michael Otsuka), Princeton, NJ: Princeton University Press; previously published in Martha Nussbaum and Amartya Sen (eds), *The Quality of Life*, Oxford: Clarendon Press, 1993.

References

Cohen, G. A., 2011. 'Expensive Taste Rides Again', ch. 4 of *On the Currency of Egalitarian Justice* (ed. Michael Otsuka), Princeton, NJ: Princeton University Press; previously published in Justine Burley (ed.), *Dworkin and His Critics*, Oxford: Blackwell, 2004.

Cohen, G. A., 2011. 'Fairness and Legitimacy in Justice, and: Does Option Luck Ever Preserve Justice?', ch. 6 of *On the Currency of Egalitarian Justice* (ed. Michael Otsuka), Princeton, NJ: Princeton University Press; previously published in S. de Wijze, M.H. Kramer and I. Carter (eds), *Hillel Steiner and the Anatomy of Justice*, New York: Routledge, 2009.

Cohen, G. A., 2011. 'Freedom and Money', ch. 8 of *On the Currency of Egalitarian Justice* (ed. Michael Otsuka), Princeton, NJ: Princeton University Press; previously published in *Revista Argentina de Teoria Juridica*, 2, 2001.

Cohen, G. A., 2011. 'How to do Political Philosophy', ch. 11 of *On the Currency of Egalitarian Justice* (ed. Michael Otsuka), Princeton, NJ: Princeton University Press.

Cohen, G. A., 2011. 'Luck and Equality', ch. 5 of *On the Currency of Egalitarian Justice* (ed. Michael Otsuka), Princeton, NJ: Princeton University Press; previously published as 'Luck and Equality: A Reply to Hurley', *Philosophy and Phenomenological Research*, 72, 2006.

Cohen, G. A., 2011 (1991). 'British vs. American Philosopher', on YouTube (recorded by Eric Olin Wright, posted by Nicholas Vrousalis) https://www.youtube.com/watch?v=h5XNZ12SKkE

Cohen, G. A., 2011 (1991). 'The German Idea of Freedom', on YouTube (recorded by Eric Olin Wright, posted by Nicholas Vrousalis) https://www.youtube.com/watch?v=ey-hYJM7B3I

Cohen, G.A, 2011 (1991). 'Marxist Boxing Match: Roemer vs. Habermas', on YouTube (recorded by Eric Olin Wright, posted by Nicholas Vrousalis) https://www.youtube.com/watch?v=Eb1R3mjyZqc

Cohen, G. A., 2011. 'Mind the Gap', ch. 9 of *On the Currency of Egalitarian Justice* (ed. Michael Otsuka), Princeton, NJ: Princeton University Press; part of previously published essay in *London Review of Books*, 14, 9, 14 May 1992.

Cohen, G. A., 2011. 'On the Currency of Egalitarian Justice', ch. 1 of *On the Currency of Egalitarian Justice* (ed. Michael Otsuka), Princeton, NJ: Princeton University Press; previously published in *Ethics*, 99, 4, 1989.

Cohen, G. A., 2011. *On the Currency of Egalitarian Justice* (ed. Michael Otsuka), Princeton, NJ: Princeton University Press.

Cohen, G. A., 2011. 'Rescuing Conservatism', in Jay Wallace, Rahul Kumar and Samuel Freeman (eds), *Reasons and Recognition: Essays on the Philosophy of T. M. Scanlon*, Oxford: Oxford University Press.

Cohen, G. A., 2011. 'Rescuing Justice from Constructivism and Equality from the Basic Structure Objection', ch. 12 of *On the Currency of Egalitarian Justice* (ed. Michael Otsuka), Princeton, NJ: Princeton University Press; part of the essay is part of *Rescuing Justice and Equality*, Cambridge, MA; Harvard University Press, 2008.

Cohen, G. A., 2011. 'Sen on Capability, Freedom, and Control', ch. 3 of *On the Currency of Egalitarian Justice* (ed. Michael Otsuka), Princeton, NJ: Princeton University Press.

Cohen, G. A., 2013. 'A Black and White Issue', ch. 3 of *Finding Oneself in the Other* (ed. Michael Otsuka), Princeton, NJ: Princeton University Press; previously published in *Oxford Magazine*, 42, Second Week, Hilary Term, 1989.

Cohen, G. A., 2013. 'Casting the First Stone: Who Can, and Who Can't, Condemn the Terrorists?', ch. 6 of *Finding Oneself in the Other* (ed. Michael Otsuka), Princeton, NJ: Princeton University Press; previously published in Anthony O'Hear (ed.), *Political Philosophy*, Royal Institute of Philosophy Supplement, 58, Cambridge: Cambridge University Press, 2006.

Cohen, G. A., 2013. 'Complete Bullshit', ch. 5 of *Finding Oneself in the Other* (ed. Michael Otsuka), Princeton, NJ: Princeton University Press; part 1 previously published as 'Deeper Into Bullshit', in Sarah Buss and Lee Overton (eds), *Contours of Agency: Essays on Themes from Harry Frankfurt*, Cambridge, MA: MIT Press, 2002.

Cohen, G. A., 2013. *Finding Oneself in the Other* (ed. Michael Otsuka), Princeton, NJ: Princeton University Press.

Cohen, G. A., 2013. 'Isaiah's Marx, and Mine', ch. 1 of *Finding Oneself in the Other* (ed. Michael Otsuka), Princeton, NJ: Princeton University Press; previously published in Avishai Margalit and Edna Ullmann-Margalit (eds), *Isaiah Berlin: A Celebration*, London: Hogarth Press, Chicago: University of Chicago Press, 1991.

Cohen, G. A., 2013. 'Notes on Regarding People as Equals', ch. 10 of *Finding Oneself in the Other* (ed. Michael Otsuka), Princeton, NJ: Princeton University Press

Cohen, G. A., 2013. 'One Kind of Spirituality: Come Back, Feuerbach, All Is Forgiven!', ch. 11 of *Finding Oneself in the Other* (ed. Michael Otsuka), Princeton, NJ: Princeton University Press

Cohen, G. A., 2013. 'Prague Preamble to "Why Not Socialism?"' ch. 2 of *Finding Oneself in the Other* (ed. Michael Otsuka), Princeton, NJ: Princeton University Press

Cohen, G. A., 2013. 'Rescuing Conservatism: A Defense of Existing Value', ch. 8 of *Finding Oneself in the Other* (ed. Michael Otsuka), Princeton, NJ: Princeton University Press; a previous version was published in R. Jay Wallace, Rahul Kumar and Samuel Freeman (eds), *Essays on the Philosophy of T. M. Scanlon*, New York: Oxford University Press, 2011.

Cohen, G. A., 2013. 'Two Weeks in India', ch. 4 of *Finding Oneself in the Other* (ed. Michael Otsuka), Princeton, NJ: Princeton University Press.

Cohen, G. A., 2013. 'Ways of Silencing Critics', ch. 7 of *Finding Oneself in the Other* (ed. Michael Otsuka), Princeton, NJ: Princeton University Press.

Cohen, G. A., 2013. 'Valedictory Lecture: My Philosophical Development (and impressions of philosophers whom I met along the way)', ch.

9 of *Finding Oneself in the Other* (ed. Michael Otsuka), Princeton, NJ: Princeton University Press.

Cohen, G. A., 2014. 'Bourgeois and Proletarians', ch. 8 in *Lectures on the History of Moral and Political Philosophy* (ed. Jonathan Wolff), Princeton, NJ: Princeton University Press; previously published in *Journal of the History of Ideas*, 29, 2, April–June 1968.

Cohen, G. A., 2014. 'Hegel: Minds, Masters, and Slaves', ch. 6 in *Lectures on the History of Moral and Political Philosophy* (ed. Jonathan Wolff), Princeton, NJ: Princeton University Press.

Cohen, G. A. 2014. *Lectures on the History of Moral and Political Philosophy* (ed. Jonathan Wolff), Princeton, NJ: Princeton University Press.

Cohen, G. A., 2014. 'Locke on Property and Political Obligation', ch. 3 in *Lectures on the History of Moral and Political Philosophy* (ed. Jonathan Wolff), Princeton, NJ: Princeton University Press.

Cohen, G. A., 2014. 'Reply to Elster on "Marxism, Functionalism, and Game Theory"', ch. 10 in *Lectures on the History of Moral and Political Philosophy* (ed. Jonathan Wolff), Princeton, NJ: Princeton University Press; previously published in *Theory and Society*, 11, 1982.

Cohen, G. A., 2014. 'Review of *Karl Marx*, by Allen Wood', ch. 11 in *Lectures on the History of Moral and Political Philosophy* (ed. Jonathan Wolff), Princeton, NJ: Princeton University Press; previously published in *Mind*, 2, 1983.

Cohen, G. A., 2014. 'The Workers and the Word: Why Marx Had the Right to Think He Was Right', ch. 9 in *Lectures on the History of Moral and Political Philosophy* (ed. Jonathan Wolff), Princeton, NJ: Princeton University Press; previously published in *Praxis*, 3/4, 1968.

Cohen, G. A. and Kymlicka, Will, 1988. 'Human Nature and Social Change in the Marxist Conception of History', ch. 5 in *History, Labour, and Freedom: Themes from Marx*, Oxford: Oxford University Press.

Cohen, G. A., 2022. 'Letter from G. A. Cohen, 1984', in Merrily Weisbord, *The Strangest Dream: Canadian Communists, The Spy Trials and the Cold War*, revised third edn, Montreal: Vehicule Press.

Other sources

Ali, Tariq, 2013. '*Isaac and Isaiah: The Covert Punishment of a Cold War Heretic* by David Caute – a Review', *The Guardian*, 20 June.

All Souls College, 2023. 'The Codrington Legacy'. https://www.asc.ox.ac.uk/codrington-legacy

Althusser, Louis, 2005. *For Marx*, transl. B. Brewster, London: Verso, 2005.

Anderson, Elizabeth, 1999. 'What is the Point of Equality?', *Ethics*, 109, 2, January.

Anderson, Elizabeth, 2015. 'The Fundamental Disagreement between Luck Egalitarians and Relational Egalitarians', in Alexander Kaufman (ed.),

Distributive Justice and Access to Advantage: G. A. Cohen's Egalitarianism, Cambridge: Cambridge University Press.

Arblaster, Anthony, 1971. 'Vision and Revision: A Note on the Text of Isaiah Berlin's *Four Essays on Liberty*', *Political Studies*, 19, 1.

Arneson, Richard, 1989. 'Equality and Equal Opportunity for Welfare', *Philosophical Studies*, 56, May.

Arneson, Richard, 1991. 'Lockean Self-Ownership: Towards a Demolition', *Political Studies* 39, 1.

Arneson, Richard, 1997. 'Egalitarianism and the Undeserving Poor', *Journal of Political Philosophy*, 5, 4.

Arneson, Richard, 1999. 'Egalitarianism and Responsibility', *Journal of Ethics*, 3, 3.

Arneson, Richard, 1999. 'Equality of Opportunity for Welfare Defended and Recanted', *Journal of Political Philosophy*, 7, 4.

Arneson, Richard, 2011. 'Luck Egalitarianism – A Primer', in Carl Knight and Zofia Stemplowska (eds), *Responsibility and Distributive Justice*, Oxford: Oxford University Press.

Arneson, Richard, 2015. 'Why Not Capitalism?', in Alexander Kaufman (ed.), *Distributive Justice and Access to Advantage: G. A. Cohen's Egalitarianism*, Cambridge: Cambridge University Press.

Asquith, H.H., 1908. 'Political Notes', *The Times*.

Bader, Ralf, 2013. 'Review of G. A. Cohen, *Finding Oneself in the Other*', *Notre Dame Philosophical Reviews*, 3 April.

Barnett, Randy, 2004. 'The Moral Foundations of Modern Libertarianism', in Peter Berkowitz (ed.), *Varieties of Conservatism in America*, Stanford, CA: Hoover Institution Press.

Barry, Brian, 1995. 'John Rawls and the Search for Stability', *Ethics*, 105, 4.

Beckstein, Martin and Cheneval, Francis, 2016. 'Conservatism: Analytically Reconsidered', *The Monist*, 99, 4, October.

Berlin, Isaiah, 1939. *Karl Marx: His Life and Environment*, London: Thornton Butterworth; 5th edition published as *Karl Marx*, Princeton, NJ: Princeton University Press, 2013.

Berlin, Isaiah, 1953. *The Hedgehog and the Fox*, London: Weidenfeld and Nicolson.

Berlin, Isaiah, 1978. 'Does Political Theory Still Exist?', in *Concepts and Categories*, London: Hogarth Press.

Berlin, Isaiah, 2002 (1958). 'Two Concepts of Liberty', in *Four Essays on Liberty*, Oxford: Oxford University Press.

Berlin, Isaiah, 2013. *Isaiah Berlin Building: Letters 1960–1975* (ed. Henry Hardy and Mark Pottle), London: Chatto & Windus.

Berman, Marshall, 1982. *All That Is Solid Melts into Air: The Experience of Modernity*, Harmondsworth: Penguin.

Berman, Marshall, 2009. 'Gerald Cohen (1941–2009)', *Open Democracy*, 24 August. https://www.opendemocracy.net/en/remembering-jerry-cohen-marshall-berman/

References

Bertram, Chris, 2009. 'Jerry Cohen, A Personal Appreciation'. *Crooked Timber*, 6 August. https://crookedtimber.org/2009/08/06/jerry-cohen-a-personal-appreciation/
Brenkert, George G., 1985. 'Cohen on Proletarian Unfreedom', *Philosophy & Public Affairs*, 14, 1, Winter.
Brennan, Geoffrey and Hamlin, Alan, 2016. 'Conservative Value', *The Monist*, 99, 4, October.
Brennan, Jason, 2012. *Libertarianism: What Everyone Needs to Know*, Oxford: Oxford University Press.
Brennan, Jason, 2014. *Why Not Capitalism?* New York: Routledge.
Brighouse, Harry and Swift, Adam, 2014. *Family Values: The Ethics of Parent–Child Relationships*, Princeton, NJ: Princeton University Press.
Brock, Gillian and Brighouse, Harry (eds), 2005. *The Political Philosophy of Cosmopolitanism*, Cambridge: Cambridge University Press.
Buchanan, Allen, 1982. *Marx and Justice: The Radical Critique of Liberalism*, Totowa, NJ: Rowman and Littlefield.
Buchanan, Allen, 1987. 'Marx, Morality, and History: An Assessment of Recent Analytical Work on Marx', *Ethics*, 98, 1, October.
Burke, Edmund, 1890. *Reflections on the Revolution in France*, London: Macmillan.
Callinicos, Alex, 1989. 'Introduction', in Alex Callinicos (ed.), *Marxist Theory*, Oxford: Oxford University Press.
Campbell, Tom, 1983. *The Left and Rights: A Conceptual Analysis of the Idea of Socialist Rights*, London: Routledge and Kegan Paul.
Carens, Joseph, 1981. *Equality, Moral Incentives and the Market*, Chicago, IL: University of Chicago Press.
Carens, Joseph, 2015. 'The Egalitarian Ethos as a Social Commitment', in Alexander Kaufmann (ed.), *Distributive Justice and Access to Advantage: G. A. Cohen's Egalitarianism*, Cambridge: Cambridge University Press.
Carling, Alan, 1995. 'Rational Choice Marxism', in Terrell Carver and Paul Thomas (eds), *Rational Choice Marxism*, University Park, PA: Pennsylvania State University Press.
Carter, Ian, 2011. 'Respect and the Basis of Equality', *Ethics*, 121, 3, April.
Carter, Ian, 2013. 'Basic Equality and the Site of Egalitarian Justice', *Economics and Philosophy*, 29, 1, April.
Carver, Terrell and Thomas, Paul, 'Introduction', in Terrell Carver and Paul Thomas (eds), *Rational Choice Marxism*, University Park, PA: Pennsylvania State University Press.
Casal, Paula, 2013. 'Occupational Choice and the Egalitarian Ethos', *Economics and Philosophy*, 29, 1, April.
Casal, Paula, 2015. 'Marx, Rawls, Cohen and Feminism', *Hypatia*, 30, 4, Fall.
Casal, Paula, 2020. 'G. A. Cohen's Historical Materialism: A Feminist Critique', *Journal of Political Ideologies*, 25, 3.
Casal, Paula, 2021. 'Gender, Social Justice and Publicity', *Ethics & Politics*, 23, 3.

Casal, Paula, 2021. 'Whaling, Bullfighting, and the Conditional Value of Tradition', *Res Publica*, 27, 3.

Caute, David, 2013. *Isaac and Isaiah: The Covert Punishment of a Cold War Heretic*, New Haven, CT: Yale University Press.

Chambers, Clare, 2013. '"The Family as a Basic Institution": A Feminist Analysis of the Basic Structure as Subject', in Ruth Abbey (ed.), *Feminist Interpretations of John Rawls*, University Park, PA: Penn State University Press.

Chasman, Deborah and Cohen, Joshua (eds), 2023. *Is Equal Opportunity Enough?*, Cambridge, MA: Boston Review. https://www.bostonreview.net/forum/is-equal-opportunity-enough/

Chesterton, G.K., 1909. *Orthodoxy*, London: John Lane.

Chesterton, G.K., 1986 (1929). 'The Thing: Why I Am a Catholic', in G.K. Chesterton, *The Collected Works of G.K. Chesterton*, vol. 3, San Francisco, CA: Ignatius Press.

Clayton, Matthew, 2002. 'Liberal Equality and Ethics', *Ethics*, 113, 1, October.

Clayton, Matthew, 2006. *Justice and Legitimacy in Upbringing*, Oxford: Oxford University Press.

Clayton, Matthew and Williams Andrew, 2002. 'Some Questions for Egalitarians', in Matthew Clayton and Andrew Williams (eds), *The Ideal of Equality*, London: Palgrave Macmillan.

Cohen, Gideon, 2010. 'Address at G. A. Cohen Memorial Service', 19 June, All Souls College, Oxford.

Cohen, Joshua, 1982. 'Book Review of "Karl Marx's Theory of History: A Defence" by G. A. Cohen', *Journal of Philosophy*, 79, 5.

Cohen, Joshua, 2001. 'Taking People as They Are?', *Philosophy & Public Affairs*, 30, 4, Autumn.

Corlett, J. Angelo, 2010. 'Editor-in-Chief's Introduction', *Journal of Ethics*, 14, 3/4, September/December.

Cox, David, 2020. 'Canada's Forgotten Universal Basic Income Experiment', BBC, 24 June. https://www.bbc.com/worklife/article/20200624-canadas-forgotten-universal-basic-income-experiment

Crowder, George, 2012. 'In Defence of Berlin: A Reply to James Tully', in Bruce Baum and Robert Nichols (eds), *Isaiah Berlin and the Politics of Freedom: 'Two Concepts of Liberty' 50 Years Later*, London: Routledge.

Cureton, Adam, 2015. 'Justice and the Crooked Wood of Human Nature', in Alexander Kaufman (ed.), *Distributive Justice and Access to Advantage: G. A. Cohen's Egalitarianism*, Cambridge: Cambridge University Press.

Darwall, Stephen, 2006. *The Second-Person Standpoint: Morality, Respect and Accountability*, Cambridge, MA: Harvard University Press.

Davenport-Hines, Richard, 2022. *Conservative Thinkers from All Souls College Oxford*, Woodbridge: Boydell Press.

Deighton, J., 2017. 'Michael Seifert Obituary', *The Guardian*, 9 August.

Dowding, Keith, 2010. 'Luck, Equality and Responsibility', *Critical Review of International Social and Political Philosophy*, 13, 1.

Dworkin, Ronald, 1977. *Taking Rights Seriously*, Cambridge, MA: Harvard University Press.
Dworkin, Ronald, 1985. *A Matter of Principle*, Oxford: Oxford University Press.
Dworkin, Ronald, 2002. *Sovereign Virtue: The Theory and Practice of Equality*, Cambridge, MA: Harvard University Press.
Dworkin, Ronald, 2003. 'Equality, Luck and Hierarchy', *Philosophy & Public Affairs*, 31, 2, Spring.
Dworkin, Gerald, 2009. 'In Memoriam G. A. (Jerry) Cohen, *3 Quarks Daily*, 14 August. https://3quarksdaily.com/3quarksdaily/2009/08/in-memoriam-g-a-jerry-cohen-.html
Dunn, John 2001. 'Capitalism Kills the Soul', *Times Higher Education Supplement*, 12 January.
Edmonds, David, 2023. *Parfit: A Philosopher and His Mission to Save Morality*, Princeton, NJ: Princeton University Press.
Edmonds, David, 2023. 'Why Have So Many of the Giants of Moral Philosophy Been Jews?', *The Jewish Chronicle*, 28 April.
Edmundson, William, 2017. *John Rawls: Reticent Socialist*, Cambridge: Cambridge University Press.
Elster, Jon, 1980. 'Cohen on Marx's Theory of History', *Political Studies*, 28, 1.
Elster, Jon, 1983. *Explaining Technical Change*, Cambridge: Cambridge University Press.
Elster, Jon, 1985. *Making Sense of Marx*, Cambridge: Cambridge University Press.
Elster, Jon, 2003. 'Marxism, Functionalism, and Game Theory: The Case for Methodological Individualism', in Derek Matravers and Jon Pike (eds), *Debates in Contemporary Political Philosophy: An Anthology*, London: Routledge.
Encyclopedia Britannica, 'Divine Right of Kings', https://www.britannica.com/topic/divine-right-of-kings
Estlund, David, 1998. 'Liberalism, Equality and Fraternity in Cohen's Critique of Rawls', *Journal of Political Philosophy*, 6, 1.
Estlund, David, 2014. 'Utopophobia', *Philosophy & Public Affairs*, 42, 2.
Fabre, Cécile, 2008. *Whose Body is it Anyway?* Oxford: Oxford University Press.
Fabre, Cécile, 2021. 'Territorial Sovereignty and Humankind's Common Heritage', *Journal of Social Philosophy*, 52, 1, March.
Feltham, Brian, 2001. 'Introduction', in Brian Feltham (ed.), *Justice, Equality and Constructivism: Essays on G.A Cohen's Rescuing Justice and Equality*, Oxford: Wiley-Blackwell.
Fleurbaey, Marc, 2008. *Fairness, Responsibility, and Welfare*, Oxford: Oxford University Press.
Fording, Richard C. and Berry, William D., 2007. 'The Historical Impact of Welfare Programs on Poverty: Evidence from the American States', *Policy Studies Journal*, 35, 1, February.

Forget, Evelyn, 2011. 'The Town with No Poverty: The Health Effects of a Canadian Guaranteed Annual Income Field Experiment', *Canadian Public Policy*, 37, 3, September.

Forrester, Katrina, 2019. *In the Shadow of Justice: Postwar Liberalism and the Remaking of Political Philosophy*, Princeton, NJ: Princeton University Press.

Frankfurt, Harry, 1987. 'Equality as a Moral Ideal', *Ethics*, 98, 1.

Frankfurt, Harry, 2005. *On Bullshit*, Princeton, NJ: Princeton University Press.

Freeman, Samuel, 2001. 'Illiberal Libertarians: Why Libertarianism Is Not a Liberal View', *Philosophy & Public Affairs*, 30, 2, Spring.

Gaus, Gerald, 2010. 'Coercion, Ownership, and the Redistributive State: Justificatory Liberalism's Classical Tilt', *Social Philosophy and Policy*, 27, 1.

Geras, Norman, 1983. *Marx and Human Nature: Refutation of a Legend*, London: Verso.

Geuss, Raymond, 2003. 'Outside Ethics', *European Journal of Philosophy*, 11, 1.

Gheaus, Anca, 2022. 'Commentary' at *Freedom, Equality and Justice: G. A. Cohen's Lasting Relevance*, conference on Sypnowich book manuscript, Universitat Pompeu Fabra, Barcelona, 6 May.

Gilabert, Pablo, 2012. 'Cohen on Socialism, Equality and Community', *Socialist Studies* 8, 1, Winter.

Goldman, Emma, 2018 (1910). 'Anarchism: What it Really Stands For', in E. Goldman, M. Bakhunin, E. Malatesta, *Anarchist Classics*, Scotts Valley, CA: Createspace.

Gray, John, 2014. *Post-Liberalism: Studies in Political Thought*, London: Routledge.

Griffin, Robert, 1970. *The Politics of Fear: Joseph R. McCarthy and the Senate*, Boston: University of Massachusetts Press.

Harrington, Michael, 1985. *The New American Poverty*, London: Firethorn.

Harvey, David, 2013. *Rebel Cities: From the Right to the City to the Urban Revolution*, London: Verso.

Hazareesingh, Sudhir, 2015. *How the French Think: An Affectionate Portrait of an Intellectual People*, New York: Basic Books.

Hinton, Timothy, 2001. 'Must Egalitarianism Choose Between Fairness and Respect?', *Philosophy & Public Affairs*, 30, 1, Winter.

Hobsbawm, Eric, 1979. 'Points of Departure: Review of G. A. Cohen, *Karl Marx's Theory of History*', *New Statesman*, 2 February; reprinted in *Canadian Jewish Outlook*, April 1979.

Holtorf, Corneilius, 2017. 'Perceiving the Past: From Age Value to Pastness', *International Journal of Cultural Property*, 24, 4.

Honderich, Ted, 1982. 'Against Teleological Historical Materialism', *Inquiry*, 25, 4.

Honderich, Ted, 1991. *Conservatism*, London: Penguin.

Honderich, Ted, 2000. *Philosopher: A Kind of Life*, London: Routledge.

Horton, John, 2011. 'The Smartest Guys in the Room: Cohen and Sen on Justice', *European Journal of Political Theory*, 10, 3.
Hufe, Paul, Peichl, Andreas, Roemer, John and Ungerer, Martin, 2017. 'Inequality of Income Acquisition: The Role of Childhood Circumstances', *Social Choice and Welfare*, 49, 4, December.
Hume, David, 1751. *An Enquiry Concerning the Principles of Morals*, London: A. Millar.
Hurka, Thomas, 1996. *Perfectionism*, Oxford: Oxford University Press.
Hurley, Susan, 2003. *Justice, Luck, and Knowledge*, Cambridge, MA: Harvard University Press.
Hurley, Susan, 2006. 'Choice and Incentive Inequality', in Christine Sypnowich (ed.), *The Egalitarian Conscience: Essays in Honour of G. A. Cohen*, Oxford: Oxford University Press.
James, Simon P., 2015. 'Why Old Things Matter', *Journal of Moral Philosophy*, 12, 3.
Jamieson, Frederic, 2004. 'The Politics of Utopia', *New Left Review*, 25, January/February.
Johannsen, Kyle, 2016. 'Explanation and Justification: Understanding the Functions of Fact-Insensitive Principles', *Socialist Studies*, 11, 1, Winter.
Johannsen, Kyle, 2018. *A Conceptual Investigation of Justice*, London: Routledge.
Kamm, Frances, 2017. 'The Purpose of My Death: Death, Dying, and Meaning', *Ethics*, 127, 3.
Kandiyali, Jan (ed.), 2018. *Reassessing Marx's Social and Political Philosophy: Freedom, Recognition, and Human Flourishing*, London: Routledge.
Kandiyali, Jan. 2020. 'The Importance of Others: Marx on Unalienated Production', *Ethics*, 130, 4.
King, Loren, 2012. 'Concepts, Conceptions and Principles of Justice', *Socialist Studies*, 8, 1, Winter.
Knight, Carl and Stemplowska, Zofia (eds), 2011. *Responsibility and Distributive Justice*, Oxford: Oxford University Press.
Knight, Carl and Stemplowska, Zofia, 2011. 'Responsibility and Distributive Justice: An Introduction', in Carl Knight and Zofia Stemplowska (eds), *Responsibility and Distributive Justice*, Oxford: Oxford University Press.
Kolodny, Niko, 2013. 'Introduction', in Samuel Scheffler, *Death and the Afterlife*, Oxford: Oxford University Press.
Korsmeyer, Carolyn, 2016. 'Real Old Things', *The British Journal of Aesthetics*, 56, 3.
Krishnan, Nikhil, 2023. *A Terribly Serious Adventure: Philosophy and War at Oxford 1900–1960*, New York: Random House.
Kymlicka, Will, 2002. *Contemporary Political Philosophy: An Introduction*, Oxford: Oxford University Press.
Kymlicka, Will, 2006. 'Left-Liberalism Revisited', in Christine Sypnowich (ed.), *The Egalitarian Conscience: Essays in Honour of G. A. Cohen*, Oxford: Oxford University Press.

Labuhn, Beata, 2016. 'Breathing a Moldy Air: Olfactory Experience, Aesthetics, and Ethics in the Writing of Ruskin and Riegl', *Future Anterior*, 13, 2.
Lacey, Nicola, 2004. *A Life of H.L.A. Hart: The Nightmare and the Noble Dream*, Oxford: Oxford University Press.
Laslett, Peter, 1956. 'Introduction', in Peter Laslett (ed.), *Philosophy, Politics and Society*, Oxford: Blackwell.
Laycock, Henry, 1980. 'Critical Notice', *Canadian Journal of Philosophy*, 10, 2, June.
Lefebvre, Henri, 2003. *The Urban Revolution*, transl. R. Bononno, Minneapolis, MN: University of Minnesota Press.
Leopold, David, 2007. *The Young Karl Marx*, Cambridge: Cambridge University Press.
Leopold, David, 2022. 'Analytical Marxism', in E.N. Zalta (ed.), *Stanford Encyclopedia of Philosophy*, 5 September. https://plato.stanford.edu/entries/marxism-analytical/
Levy, Neil, 2002. 'Self-Ownership: Defending Marx against Cohen', *Social Theory and Practice*, 28, 1, January.
Levy, Paul, 2009. 'Professor Jerry Cohen: Maverick Philosopher who Subjected Marxism to the Rigours of Analytical Philosophy', *The Independent*, 12 August.
Lewis, David, 1972. *Louder Voices: The Corporate Welfare Bums*, Toronto: James Lorimer.
Lippert-Rasmussen, Kasper, 2001. 'Egalitarianism, Luck and Responsibility', *Ethics*, 111, 3, April.
Lippert-Rasmussen, Kasper, 2005. *Luck Egalitarianism*, London: Bloomsbury.
Lippert-Rasmussen, Kasper, 2018. *Relational Egalitarianism: Living as Equals*, Cambridge: Cambridge University Press.
Lloyd, John, 2009. 'Marxist Philosopher Famed for His Intellect and Wit', *Financial Times*, 21 August.
Locke, John, 1980 (1687). *Second Treatise of Government*, Indianapolis, IN: Hackett.
Lodge, David, 1984. *Small World*, London: Secker and Warburg.
Lukes, Steven, 1985. *Marxism and Morality*, Oxford: Oxford University Press.
Lukes, Steven, 2014. 'The Cold War on Campus', *Dissent*, Winter.
MacCarthy, Fiona, 1994. *William Morris*, London: Faber and Faber.
Mac Cumhaill, Clare and Wiseman, Rachael, 2022. *Metaphysical Animals: How Four Women Brought Philosophy Back to Life*, New York: Doubleday.
Mack, Eric, 1981. 'Nozick on Unproductivity: The Unintended Consequences', in Jeffrey Paul (ed.), *Reading Nozick*, Totowa, NJ: Rowman and Littlefield.
Mack, Eric, 2022. 'Robert Nozick's Political Philosophy', in E.N. Zalta (ed.), *Stanford Encyclopedia of Philosophy*, 21 April. https://plato.stanford.edu/entries/nozick-political/

Macleod, Alistair, 2012. 'The Domain of Distributive Justice: Personal Choices, Institutions, States of Affairs', *Socialist Studies*, 8, 1, Winter.
Macleod, Colin, 1998. *Liberalism, Justice and Markets: A Critique of Liberal Equality*, Oxford: Oxford University Press.
Macleod, Colin, 2012. 'If You're a Libertarian, How Come You're So Rich?', *Socialist Studies*, 8, 1, Winter.
Macpherson, C.B., 1962. *The Political Theory of Possessive Individualism*, Oxford: Oxford University Press.
Mandelbaum, Maurice, 1982. 'G. A. Cohen's Defences of Functional Explanation', *Philosophy of Social Sciences*, 12.
Marx, Karl, 1971 (1859). *A Contribution to the Critique of Political Economy*, London: Lawrence and Wishart.
Marx, Karl, 1975 (1846). 'Circular Against Kriege', in Karl Marx and Friedrich Engels, *Collected Works*, vol. 6, London: Lawrence and Wishart.
Marx, Karl, 1976 (1867). *Capital, Volume 1*, Harmondsworth: Penguin.
Marx, Karl, 1978 (1875). 'A Critique of the Gotha Programme', in Karl Marx and Friedrich Engels, *The Marx-Engels Reader* (ed. Robert Tucker), New York: W.W. Norton.
Marx, Karl, 1978 (1844). 'Economic and Philosophic Manuscripts', in *The Marx-Engels Reader* (ed. Robert Tucker), New York: W.W. Norton.
Marx, Karl and Engels, Friedrich, 1978 (1848). 'Manifesto of the Communist Party', *The Marx-Engels Reader* (ed. Robert Tucker), New York: W.W. Norton.
Matthes, Erich Hatala, 2013. 'History, Value, and Irreplaceability', *Ethics*, 124, 1, October.
Matthes, Erich Hatala, 2015. 'Impersonal Value, Universal Value, and the Scope of Cultural Heritage', *Ethics*, 125, 4, July.
Mayer, Thomas F., 1994. *Analytical Marxism*, London: Sage.
Meade, James, 1973. *Theory of Economic Externalities: The Control of Environmental Pollution and Similar Social Costs*, Leiden: Sijthoof.
Midgley, Mary, 2010. *The Solitary Self: Darwin and the Selfish Gene*, Durham, UK: Acumen.
Mill, John Stuart, 1875. *Principles of Political Economy with Some of Their Applications to Social Philosophy*, London: Longmans.
Mill, John Stuart, 1989 (1859). 'On Liberty', in *'On Liberty' and Other Writings*, Cambridge: Cambridge University Press.
Miller, David, 1989. *Market, State and Community: Theoretical Foundations of Market Socialism*, Oxford: Clarendon.
Miller, David, 1997. 'What Kind of Equality Should the Left Pursue?', in Jane Franklin (ed.), *Equality*, London: Institute for Public Policy Research.
Miller, David, 1999. *Principles of Social Justice*, Cambridge, MA: Harvard University Press.
Miller, David, 2013. *Justice for Earthlings*, Cambridge: Cambridge University Press.
Miller, David, 2014. 'Our Unfinished Debate About Market Socialism', *Politics, Philosophy and Economics*, 13, 2.

Miller, David, 2014. 'Political Theory, Philosophy and the Social Sciences: Five Chichele Professors', in C. Hood, D. King and G. Peele (eds), *Forging a Discipline: A Critical Assessment of Oxford's Development of the Study of Politics and International Relations in Comparative Perspective*, Oxford: Oxford University Press.

Miller, David, 2015. 'The Incoherence of Luck Egalitarianism', in Alexander Kaufman (ed.), *Distributive Justice and Access to Advantage: G. A. Cohen's Egalitarianism*, Cambridge: Cambridge University Press.

Miller, Richard, 1984. *Analysing Marx*, Princeton, NJ: Princeton University Press.

Miller, Richard, 2010. 'Relations of Equality: A Camping Trip Revisited', *Journal of Ethics*, 14, 3/4, September/December.

Morris, William, 1877. 'Manifesto, Society for the Protection of Ancient Buildings'. https://www.spab.org.uk/about-us/spab-manifesto

Morris, William, 1984 (1885). 'The Lesser Arts', in *News from Nowhere and Selected Writings and Designs* (ed. and intro. Asa Briggs), Harmondsworth: Penguin.

Murdoch, Iris, 1958. 'A House of Theory', in N. Mackenzie (ed.), *Conviction*, London: MacKibbon & Kee.

Murdoch, Iris, 1970. *The Sovereignty of Good*, London: Routledge.

Nagel, Thomas, 1970. *The Possibility of Altruism*, Princeton, NJ: Princeton University Press.

Nagel, Thomas, 1981. 'Libertarianism without Foundations', in Jeffrey Paul (ed.), *Reading Nozick*, Totowa, NJ: Rowman and Littlefield.

Nagel, Thomas, 2003. 'Rawls and Liberalism', in Samuel Freeman (ed.), *The Cambridge Companion to Rawls*, Cambridge: Cambridge University Press.

Narveson, Jan, 1978. 'Rawls on Equal Distribution of Wealth', *Philosophia*, 7, June.

Narveson, Jan, 1988. *The Libertarian Idea*, Philadelphia, PA: Temple University Press.

Narveson, Jan, 1996. 'Libertarianism vs. Marxism: Reflections on G. A. Cohen's *Self-ownership, Freedom and Equality*', *Journal of Ethics*, 2, 1.

Narveson, Jan, 2008. *You and the State: A Short Introduction to Political Philosophy*, Lanham, MD: Rowman and Littlefield.

Narveson, Jan, 2010. 'Cohen's Rescue', *Journal of Ethics*, 14, 3/4, September/December.

Narveson, Jan, 2012. 'Cohen on Rawls on Incentives and Equality', *Socialist Studies*, 8, 1, Winter.

Nebel, Jacob M., 2015. 'Status Quo Bias, Rationality, and Conservatism About Value', *Ethics*, 125, 2.

Nielsen, Kai, 2012. 'Rescuing Political Theory from Fact-Insensitivity', *Socialist Studies*, 8, 1, Winter.

Nietzsche, Friedrich, 2019 (1874). *The Use and Abuse of History*, Mineola, NY: Dover.

Noonan, Jeffrey, 2012. 'G. A. Cohen and the Ethical Core of Socialism: Equality or Life-Sufficiency?', *Socialist Studies*, 8, 1, Winter.
Nove, Alec, 1983. *The Economics of Feasible Socialism*, London: Routledge.
Nozick, Robert, 1974. *Anarchy, State and Utopia*, New York: Basic Books.
Oakeshott, Michael, 1991 (1959). 'The Voice of Poetry in the Conversation of Mankind', in *Rationalism in Politics and Other Essays*, Indianapolis, IN: Liberty Fund.
O'Brien, David, 2022. 'Conservatism Reconsidered', *Journal of the American Philosophical Association*, 8, 1.
O'Grady, Jane, 2009. 'Obituary: G. A. Cohen', *The Guardian*, 10 August.
Okin, Susan Moller, 1989. *Justice, Gender and the Family*, New York: Basic Books.
Okin, Susan Moller, 1993. 'Book Review, John Rawls, *Political Liberalism*', *American Political Science Review*, 87, 4.
Olsaretti, Serena, 2009. 'Responsibility and the Consequences of Choice', *Proceedings of the Aristotelian Society*, 109, 2.
Olsaretti, Serena, 2012. 'The Inseparability of the Personal and the Political: Review of G. A. Cohen's *Rescuing Justice and Equality*', *Analysis*, 72, 1, January.
Olsaretti, Serena, 2015. 'Rescuing Justice and Equality from Libertarianism', in Alexander Kaufman (ed.), *Distributive Justice and Access to Advantage: G. A. Cohen's Egalitarianism*, Cambridge: Cambridge University Press.
O'Neill, Martin, 2008. 'What Should Egalitarians Believe?', *Philosophy & Public Affairs*, 36, 2.
O'Neill, Martin, 2012. 'Free (and Fair) Markets without Capitalism: Political Values, Principles of Justice, and Property-Owning Democracy', in Martin O'Neill and Thad Williamson (eds), *Property-Owning Democracy: Rawls and Beyond*, London: Wiley-Blackwell.
O'Neill, Martin, 2023. 'The Radicalism of Equality of Opportunity', in *Is Equal Opportunity Enough?*, Cambridge, MA: Boston Review. https://www.bostonreview.net/forum/is-equal-opportunity-enough/
O'Neill, Martin and Williamson, Thad (eds), 2012. *Property-Owning Democracy: Rawls and Beyond*, Oxford: Wiley-Blackwell.
Online Etymological Dictionary, 'Conservative'. https://www.etymonline.com/word/conservative
Otsuka, Michael, 1998. 'Self-Ownership and Equality: A Lockean Reconciliation', *Philosophy & Public Affairs*, Winter, 27, 1.
Otsuka, Michael, 2002. 'Luck, Insurance, and Equality', *Ethics*, 113, 1, October.
Otsuka, Michael, 2003. *Libertarianism without Inequality*, Oxford: Clarendon Press.
Otsuka, Michael, 2007. 'Prerogatives to Depart from Equality', in Anthony O'Hear (ed.), *Political Philosophy*, Cambridge: Cambridge University Press.
Otsuka, Michael, 2009. 'Remarks at G. A. Cohen's Funeral', 11 August, All Souls College, Oxford.

Otsuka, Michael, 2010. 'Address at G. A. Cohen Memorial Service', 19 June, All Souls College, Oxford.
Otsuka, Michael, 2010. 'Justice as Fairness: Luck Egalitarian, not Rawlsian', *Journal of Ethics*, 14, 3/4, September/December.
Otsuka, Michael, 2011. 'Editor's Preface', in Michael Otsuka (ed.), *On the Currency of Egalitarian Justice*, Princeton, NJ: Princeton University Press.
Otsuka, Michael, 2013. 'Editor's Preface', in G. A. Cohen, *Finding Oneself in the Other*, Princeton, NJ: Princeton University Press.
Otsuka, Michael, 2013. 'Freedom of Occupational Choice', in Brian Feltham (ed.), *Justice, Equality and Constructivism: Essays on G. A. Cohen's Rescuing Justice and Equality*, Oxford: Wiley-Blackwell.
Otsuka, Michael, 2022. 'Commentary' at *Freedom, Equality and Justice: G. A. Cohen's Lasting Relevance*, conference on Sypnowich book manuscript, Universitat Pompeu Fabra, Barcelona, 6 May.
Otsuka, Michael and Williams, Andrew, 2004. 'Equality, Ambition and Insurance', *Aristotelian Society Supplementary Volume*, 78, 1, July.
Oxford, Bodleian Libraries, 1903–72. MS. Berlin 194, fols. 79, 114, 123, 164, 194; MS. Berlin 213, fols. 114, MS. Berlin 219, fol. 79, 'Papers of Sir Isaiah Berlin, 1897–1998, with some family papers, 1903–72'.
Oxford Socialist Discussion Group, 1989. *Out of Apathy: Voices on the New Left Thirty Years On*, London: Verso.
Parfit, Derek, 2002. 'Equality or Priority', in Matthew Clayton and Andrew Williams (eds), *The Ideal of Equality*, London: Palgrave Macmillan; shorter version previously published as 'Equality and Priority', *Ratio*, 10, 3, December 1997.
Parfit, Derek, 2006. 'Kant's Arguments for His Formula of Universal Law', in Christine Sypnowich (ed.), *The Egalitarian Conscience: Essays in Honour of G. A. Cohen*, Oxford: Oxford University Press.
Parr, Tom and Williams, Andrew, 2021. 'Fair Insurance Defended, Amended, and Extended', in David Sobel and Steven Wall (eds), *Oxford Studies in Political Philosophy Volume 8*, Oxford: Oxford University Press.
Pashukanis, Evgeny, 2003 (1924). *The General Theory of Law and Marxism*, New Brunswick, NJ: Transaction Publishers.
Paul, Jeffrey, 1981. 'Introduction', in *Reading Nozick*, Totowa, NJ: Rowman and Littlefield.
Phillips, Anne, 2021. *Unconditional Equals*, Princeton, NJ: Princeton University Press.
Phillips, Anne. 2023. 'Beyond Choice', in Deborah Chasman and Joshua Cohen (eds), *Is Equal Opportunity Enough?*, Cambridge, MA: Boston Review. https://www.bostonreview.net/forum/is-equal-opportunity-enough/
Piketty, Thomas, 2017. *Capital in the Twenty-first Century*, Cambridge, MA: Harvard University Press.
Plamenatz, John, 1960. 'The Use of Political Theory', *Political Studies*, 8, 1.
Pogge, Thomas, 2009. 'Cohen to the Rescue!', in Brian Feltham (ed.), *Justice,*

Equality and Constructivism: Essays on G. A. Cohen's Rescuing Justice and Equality, London: Wiley-Blackwell.
Pound, Ezra, 1996. 'Canto LXXXI', *The Cantos of Ezra Pound*, New York: New Directions.
Pugh, Jonathan, Kahane, Guy and Savulescu, Julian, 2013. 'Cohen's Conservatism and Human Enhancement', *Journal of Ethics*, 17, 4.
Pulzer, Peter, 1985. 'The Oxford Vote', *London Review of Books*, 7, 4, 7 March.
Quong, Jonathan, 2010. 'Justice Beyond Equality', *Social Theory and Practice*, 36, 2, April.
Rakowski, Eric, 1991. *Equal Justice*, Oxford: Oxford University Press.
Rawls, John, 1958. 'Justice as Fairness', *The Philosophical Review*, 67, 2, April.
Rawls, John, 1982. 'Social Unity and Primary Goods', in Amartya Sen and Bernard Williams (eds), *Utilitarianism and Beyond*, Cambridge: Cambridge University Press.
Rawls, John, 1985. 'Justice as Fairness: Political not Metaphysical', *Philosophy & Public Affairs*, 14, 3, Summer.
Rawls, John, 1993. *Political Liberalism*, New York: Columbia University Press.
Rawls, John, 1999. *The Law of Peoples*, Cambridge, MA: Harvard University Press.
Rawls, John, 1999 (1971). *A Theory of Justice*, Cambridge, MA: Harvard University Press.
Rawls, John, 2001. *Justice as Fairness: A Restatement*, Cambridge, MA: Harvard University Press.
Rawls, John, 2008. *Lectures on the History of Political Philosophy* (ed. Samuel Freeman), Cambridge, MA: Harvard University Press.
Raz, Joseph, 1988. *The Morality of Freedom*, Oxford: Oxford University Press.
Raz, Joseph, 1994. *Ethics in the Public Domain*, Oxford: Clarendon.
Reiman, Jeremy, 1989. 'An Alternative to "Distributive" Marxism: Further Thoughts on Roemer, Cohen and Exploitation', in Robert Ware and Kai Nielsen (eds), *Analyzing Marxism: Canadian Journal of Philosophy Supplementary Volume*, 15, Calgary: University of Calgary Press.
Riegl, Adolphus, 1996 (1903). The Modern Cult of Monuments: Its Essence and Its Development', in Nicholas Stanley Price, M. Kirby Talley and Alessandra Melucco Vaccaro (eds), *Historical and Philosophical Issues in the Conservation of Cultural Heritage*, Los Angeles, CA: Getty Conservation Institute.
Ripstein, Arthur, 1989. 'Rationality and Alienation', in Robert Ware and Kai Nielsen (eds), *Analyzing Marxism: Canadian Journal of Philosophy Supplementary Volume*, 15, Calgary: University of Calgary Press.
Roberts, Marcus, 1997. *Analytical Marxism: A Critique*. London: Verso.
Roberts, William Clare, 2017. *Marx's Inferno: The Political Theory of Marx's Capital*, Princeton, NJ: Princeton University Press.
Robeyns, Ingrid, 2008. 'Ideal Theory in Theory and Practice', *Social Theory and Practice*, 34, 3, July.

Roemer, John, 1982. *A General Theory of Exploitation and Class*, Cambridge, MA: Harvard University Press.
Roemer, John (ed.), 1986. *Analytical Marxism*, Cambridge: Cambridge University Press.
Roemer, John, 1996. *Egalitarian Perspectives*, Cambridge: Cambridge University Press.
Roemer, John, 1996. *Theories of Distributive Justice*, Cambridge, MA: Harvard University Press.
Roemer, John, 1998. *Equality of Opportunity*, Cambridge, MA: Harvard University Press.
Roemer, John, 1998. 'Socialism's Future: An Interview with John Roemer', *Imprint*, 3, 1.
Roemer, John, 2006. 'Impartiality, Solidarity and Distributive Justice', in Christine Sypnowich (ed.), *The Egalitarian Conscience: Essays in Honour of G. A. Cohen*, Oxford: Oxford University Press.
Roemer, John, 2010. 'Address at G. A. Cohen Memorial Service', 19 June, All Souls College, Oxford.
Roemer, John, 2010. 'Jerry Cohen's *Why Not Socialism?* Some Thoughts', *Journal of Ethics*, 14, 3/4, September/December.
Roemer, John, 2012. 'Ideology, Social Ethos and the Financial Crisis', *Journal of Ethics*, 16, 3, September.
Roemer, John, 2023. 'Designing for Outcomes', in Deborah Chasman and Joshua Cohen (eds), *Is Equal Opportunity Enough?*, Cambridge, MA: Boston Review. https://www.bostonreview.net/forum/is-equal-opportunity-enough/
Rondel, David, 2012. 'G. A. Cohen and the Logic of Egalitarian Congruence', *Socialist Studies*, 8, 1, Winter.
Ronzoni, Miriam, 2012. 'Life is Not a Camping Trip – On the Desirability of Cohenite Socialism', *Politics, Philosophy and Economics*, 11, 2.
Rosen, Michael, 2010. 'Jerry Cohen – An Appreciation', 3 June; unpublished talk given at Columbia University. https://scholar.harvard.edu/michaelrosen/publications/jerry-cohen-appreciation
Ruskin, John, 1921 (1849). *The Seven Lamps of Architecture*, London: J.M. Dent.
Ryle, Gilbert, 2000 (1949). *The Concept of Mind*, London: Penguin.
Ryle, Gilbert, 2009 (1971). *Critical Essays: Vol. 1 of Collected Essays*, London: Routledge.
Sager, Alex, 2015. 'Review of Jason Brennan, *Why Not Capitalism*', *Marx and Philosophy Review of Books*, 16 November.
Said, Edward, 2004. 'Thoughts on Late Style', *London Review of Books*, 26, 15, 5 August.
Sandel, Michael, 1982. *Liberalism and the Limits of Justice*, Cambridge: Cambridge University Press.
Sandel, Michael, 2007. *The Case against Perfection*, Cambridge, MA: Harvard University Press.

Sayers, Sean, 2000. 'Whatever Happened to Analytical Marxism?', *Radical Philosophy*, 104, November/December.
Scanlon, Thomas, 1981. 'Nozick on Rights, Liberty, and Property', in Jeffrey Paul (ed.), *Reading Nozick*, Totowa, NJ: Rowman and Littlefield.
Scanlon, Thomas, 1993. 'Value, Desire and the Quality of Life', in Martha Nussbaum and Amartya Sen (eds), *The Quality of Life*, Oxford: Clarendon Press.
Scanlon, Thomas, 1995. 'The Significance of Choice', in Stephen Darwall (ed.), *Equal Freedom: Selected Tanner Lectures on Human Values*, Ann Arbor, MI: University of Michigan Press.
Scanlon, Thomas, 1998. *What We Owe to Each Other*, Cambridge, MA: Harvard University Press.
Scanlon, Thomas, 2006. 'Justice, Responsibility, and the Demands of Equality', in Christine Sypnowich (ed.), *The Egalitarian Conscience: Essays in Honour of G. A. Cohen*, Oxford: Oxford University Press.
Scanlon, Thomas, 2010. 'Address at G. A. Cohen Memorial Service', 19 June, All Souls College, Oxford.
Scanlon, Thomas, 2018. *Why Does Inequality Matter?* Oxford: Oxford University Press.
Scheffler, Samuel, 2003. 'What is Egalitarianism?', *Philosophy & Public Affairs*, 31, 1, Winter.
Scheffler, Samuel, 2005. 'Choice, Circumstance, and the Value of Equality', *Politics, Philosophy and Economics*, 4, 1, February.
Scheffler, Samuel, 2006. 'Is the Basic Structure Basic?', in Christine Sypnowich (ed.), *The Egalitarian Conscience: Essays in Honour of G. A. Cohen*, Oxford: Oxford University Press.
Scheffler, Samuel, 2010. *Equality and Tradition*, Oxford: Oxford University Press.
Scheffler, Samuel, 2011. 'Valuing', in Jay Wallace, Rahul Kumar and Samuel Freeman (eds), *Reasons and Recognition: Essays on the Philosophy of T.M. Scanlon*, Oxford: Oxford University Press.
Scheffler, Samuel, 2013. *Death and the Afterlife*, New York: Oxford University Press.
Scheffler, Samuel, 2018. *Why Worry About Future Generations?* Oxford: Oxford University Press.
Schmidtz, David (ed.), 2022. *Social Philosophy and Policy*, issue on 'What Does Egalitarianism Require?', 39, 2.
Screpanti, Ernesto, 2007. *Libertarian Communism: Marx, Engels and the Political Economy of Freedom*, New York: Palgrave Macmillan.
Scruton, Roger, 2014. *How to Be a Conservative*, London: Bloomsbury.
Sen, Amartya, 1992. *Inequality Reexamined*, Oxford: Oxford University Press.
Sen, Amartya, 1999. *Development as Freedom*, Oxford: Oxford University Press.
Shapiro, Ian and Steinmetz, Alicia, 2018. 'Negative Liberty and the Cold

War', in Joshua L. Cherniss and Steven B. Smith (eds), *The Cambridge Companion to Isaiah Berlin*, Cambridge: Cambridge University Press.

Shelby, Tommie, 2021. 'Afro-Analytical Marxism and the Problem of Race', Presidential Address for 117th Annual Eastern Division Meeting of the American Philosophical Association, 16 January, *Proceedings and Addresses of the American Philosophical Association*, 95, November.

Sher, George, 2014. *Equality for Inegalitarians*, Cambridge: Cambridge University Press.

Sher, George, 2023. 'The Weight of the Past', *Australasian Journal of Philosophy*, 101, 1, July.

Shiffrin, Seana, 2010. 'Incentives, Motives, and Talents', *Philosophy & Public Affairs*, 38, 2, Spring.

Shoikhedbrod, Igor, 2019. *Revisiting Marx's Critique of Liberalism: Rethinking Justice, Legality and Rights*, London: Palgrave Macmillan.

Singer, Peter, 1972. 'Famine, Affluence, and Morality', *Philosophy & Public Affairs*, 1, 3, Spring.

Standing, Guy, 2011. *The Precariat: The New Dangerous Class*, London: Bloomsbury.

Statman, Daniel, 2023. 'Casting the First Stone: Did Cohen Have Standing to Condemn Israel's Condemnation of Terrorism?', *Critical Review of International Social and Political Philosophy*, https://doi.org/10.1080/13698230.2023.2239616

Stedman Jones, Gareth, 2016. *Karl Marx: Greatness and Illusion*, Cambridge, MA: Harvard University Press.

Steiner, Hillel, 1994. *An Essay on Rights*, Oxford: Basil Blackwell.

Steiner, Hillel, 2006. 'Self-Ownership and Conscription', in Christine Sypnowich (ed.), *The Egalitarian Conscience: Essays in Honour of G. A. Cohen*, Oxford: Oxford University Press.

Steiner, Hillel, 2019. 'G. A. Cohen, "Where the Action Was"', unpublished paper presented at G. A. Cohen's Political Thought Workshop, Halbert Centre for Canadian Studies at the Hebrew University, Jerusalem, 10 December.

Stemplowska, Zofia, 2009. 'Making Justice Sensitive to Responsibility', *Political Studies*, 57, 2.

Stemplowska, Zofia, 2011. 'Responsibility and Respect: Reconciling Two Egalitarian Visions', in Carl Knight and Zofia Stemplowska (eds), *Responsibility and Distributive Justice*, Oxford: Oxford University Press.

Stemplowska, Zofia, 2022. 'Commentary' at *Freedom, Equality and Justice: G. A. Cohen's Lasting Relevance*, conference on Sypnowich book manuscript, Universitat Pompeu Fabra, Barcelona, 6 May.

Stemplowska, Zofia, 2023. 'No Equality Without Liberal Equality', in Deborah Chasman and Joshua Cohen (eds), *Is Equal Opportunity Enough?*, Cambridge, MA: Boston Review. https://www.bostonreview.net/forum/is-equal-opportunity-enough/

Swift, Adam, 2003. *How Not to be a Hypocrite: School Choice for the Morally Perplexed Parent*, London: Routledge.
Swift, Adam, 2008. 'The Value of Philosophy in Non-ideal Circumstances', *Social Theory and Practice*, 34, 3, July.
Sypnowich, Christine, 1990. *The Concept of Socialist Law*, Oxford: Clarendon.
Sypnowich, Christine, 2003. 'Equality: From Marxism to Liberalism (and Back Again)', *Political Studies Review*, 1, September.
Sypnowich, Christine, 2006. 'Begging', in Christine Sypnowich (ed.), *The Egalitarian Conscience*, Oxford: Oxford University Press.
Sypnowich, Christine (ed.), 2006. *The Egalitarian Conscience*, Oxford: Oxford University Press.
Sypnowich, Christine, 2006. 'Introduction: G. A. Cohen's Egalitarian Conscience', in Christine Sypnowich (ed.), *The Egalitarian Conscience*, Oxford: Oxford University Press.
Sypnowich, Christine, 2012. 'G. A. Cohen's Socialism: Scientific but also Utopian', *Socialist Studies*, 8, 1, Winter.
Sypnowich, Christine, 2017. *Equality Renewed: Justice, Flourishing, and the Egalitarian Ideal*, London: Routledge.
Sypnowich, Christine, 2018. 'Liberalism, Marxism, Equality and Living Well', in Jan Kandiyali (ed.), *Reassessing Marx's Social and Political Philosophy: Freedom, Recognition, and Human Flourishing*, London: Routledge.
Sypnowich, Christine, 2020. 'What's Wrong with Equality of Opportunity', *Philosophical Topics*, 48, 2, Fall.
Sypnowich, Christine, 2021. 'Monuments and Monsters: Education, Cultural Heritage and Sites of Conscience', *Journal of the Philosophy of Education*, 55, 3, June.
Sypnowich, Christine, 2023. 'What's Wrong with Equality of Opportunity' and 'Why Equality Matters', in Deborah Chasman and Joshua Cohen (eds), *Is Equal Opportunity Enough?*, Cambridge, MA: Boston Review. https://www.bostonreview.net/forum/is-equal-opportunity-enough/
Sypnowich, Christine (forthcoming). 'The Demands of Equality', *Social Philosophy and Policy*.
Tan, Kok-Chor, 2004. 'Justice and Personal Pursuits', *Journal of Philosophy*, 101, 7, July.
Tan, Kok-Chor, 2012. *Justice, Institutions and Luck*, Oxford: Oxford University Press.
Tawney, R.H., 1979 (1931). *Equality*, London: George Allen and Unwin.
Taylor, Charles, 1980. 'Critical Notice' (G. A. Cohen, *Karl Marx's Theory of History: A Defence*), *Canadian Journal of Philosophy*, 10, 2, June.
Taylor, Charles, 1985. 'Atomism', in *Philosophy and the Human Sciences: Philosophical Papers II*, Cambridge: Cambridge: Cambridge University Press.
Taylor, Charles, 1985. 'Interpretation and the Sciences of Man', in Charles Taylor, *Philosophy and the Human Sciences: Philosophical Papers II*, Cambridge: Cambridge University Press.

Taylor, Charles, 1985. 'What's Wrong with Negative Liberty', in *Philosophy and the Human Sciences: Philosophical Papers II*, Cambridge: Cambridge University Press.
Taylor, Charles, 1994. 'The Politics of Recognition', in Amy Gutmann (ed.), *Multiculturalism*, Princeton, NJ: Princeton University Press.
Temkin, Larry, 1986. 'Inequality', *Philosophy & Public Affairs*, 15, 2, Spring.
Temkin, Larry, 1993. *Inequality*, Oxford: Oxford University Press.
Temkin, Larry, 2003. 'Egalitarianism Defended', *Ethics*, 113, 4, July.
Thomson, Judith Jarvis, 1981. 'Some Ruminations on Rights', in Jeffrey Paul (ed.), *Reading Nozick*, Totowa, NJ: Rowman and Littlefield.
Titelbaum, Michael, 2008. 'What Would a Rawlsian Ethos of Justice Look Like?', *Philosophy & Public Affairs*, 36, 3, Summer.
Tolokonnikova, Nadya and Žižek, Slavoj, 2014. *Comradely Greetings: The Prison Letters of Nadya and Slavoj* (transl. Ian Dreiblatt), New York: Verso.
Tomlin, Patrick, 2010. 'Survey Article: Internal Doubts about Cohen's Rescue of Justice', *Journal of Political Philosophy*, 18, 2, April.
Tonnies, Ferdinand, 2001. *Community and Civil Society* (ed. Jose Harris), Cambridge: Cambridge University Press.
Tormey, Simon, 2009. 'Simon Tormey Interviews Gerald Cohen', *Contemporary Political Theory*, 8, 3.
Trilling, Lionel, 1978 (1950). *The Liberal Imagination: Essays on Literature and Society*, New York: New York Review of Books.
Trotsky, Leon, 2005 (1925). *Literature and Revolution* (ed. William Keach, transl. Rose Strunsky), Chicago, IL: Haymarket Books.
Tucker, Robert, 1964. *Philosophy and Myth in Karl Marx*, Cambridge: Cambridge University Press.
Tully, James, 1980. *A Discourse on Property*, Cambridge: Cambridge University Press.
Tully, James, 2012. 'Two Concepts of Liberty in Context', in Bruce Baum and Robert Nichols (eds), *Isaiah Berlin and the Politics of Freedom: 'Two Concepts of Liberty' 50 Years Later*, London: Routledge.
Vallentyne, Peter, 2015. 'Justice, Interpersonal Morality and Luck Egalitarianism', in Alexander Kaufman (ed.), *Distributive Justice and Access to Advantage: G. A. Cohen's Egalitarianism*, Cambridge: Cambridge University Press.
Van der Vossen, Bas, 2019. 'Libertarianism', in E.N. Zalta (ed.), *Stanford Encyclopedia of Philosophy*, Spring. https://plato.stanford.edu/entries/libertarianism/
Van Parijs, Philippe, 1981. *Evolutionary Explanation in the Social Sciences: An Emerging Paradigm*, Totowa, NJ: Rowman and Littlefield.
Van Parijs, Philippe, 1989. 'In Defence of Abundance', in Robert Ware and Kai Nielsen (eds), *Analyzing Marxism: Canadian Journal of Philosophy Supplementary Volume*, 15, Calgary: University of Calgary Press.
Van Parijs, Philippe, 1991. 'Why Surfers Should be Fed: The Liberal Case for an Unconditional Basic Income', *Philosophy & Public Affairs*, 20, 2.

Van Parijs, Philippe, 2003. 'Difference Principles', in Samuel Freeman (ed.), *The Cambridge Companion to Rawls*, Cambridge: Cambridge University Press.
Van Parijs, Philippe, 2010. 'Address at G. A. Cohen Memorial Service', 19 June, All Souls College, Oxford.
Van Parijs, Philippe and Vanderborght, Yannick, 2017. *Basic Income: A Radical Proposal for a Free Society and a Sane Economy*, Cambridge, MA: Harvard University Press.
Vrousalis, Nicholas, 2010. 'G. A. Cohen's Vision of Socialism', *Journal of Ethics*, 14, 3/4, September/December.
Vrousalis, Nicholas, 2012. 'Jazz Bands, Camping Trips and Decommodification: G. A. Cohen on Community', *Socialist Studies*, 8, 1, Winter.
Vrousalis, Nicholas, 2013. 'Exploitation, Vulnerability and Social Domination', *Philosophy & Public Affairs*, 41, 2.
Vrousalis, Nicholas, 2015. *The Political Philosophy of G. A. Cohen: Back to Socialist Basics*, London: Bloomsbury.
Vrousalis, Nicholas, 2022. 'Commentary' at *Freedom, Equality and Justice: G. A. Cohen's Lasting Relevance*, conference on Sypnowich book manuscript, Universitat Pompeu Fabra, Barcelona, 6 May.
Vrousalis, Nicholas, 2022. *Exploitation as Domination: What Makes Capitalism Unjust*, Oxford: Oxford University Press.
Waldron, Jeremy, 1982. 'Ours by Right: Review of *Reading Nozick*', *Times Literary Supplement*, 19 November.
Waldron, Jeremy, 2006. 'Mr. Morgan's Yacht', in Christine Sypnowich (ed.), *The Egalitarian Conscience: Essays in Honour of G. A. Cohen*, Oxford: Oxford University Press.
Waldron, Jeremy, 2014. 'It's All for Your Own Good', *New York Review of Books*, 9 October.
Wall, Steven, 2009. 'Self-Ownership and Paternalism', *Journal of Political Philosophy*, 17, 4.
Wall, Steven, 2017. 'Perfectionism in Moral and Political Philosophy', in E.N. Zalta and U. Nodelman (eds), *Stanford Encyclopedia of Philosophy*. https://plato.stanford.edu/entries/perfectionism-moral/
Warren, Paul, 1994. 'Self-Ownership, Reciprocity, and Exploitation, or Why Marxists Shouldn't Be Afraid of Robert Nozick', *Canadian Journal of Philosophy*, 24, 1, March.
Warren, Paul, 2015. 'In Defense of the Marxian Theory of Exploitation: Thoughts on Roemer, Cohen, and Others', *Social Theory and Practice*, 41, 2, April.
Weinstock, Daniel, 2000. 'Review: G.A. Cohen, *If You're an Egalitarian, How Come You're So Rich?*', *Philosophy in Review*, 20, 6, December.
Weisbord, Merrily, 2022. *The Strangest Dream: Canadian Communists, The Spy Trials and the Cold War*, revised 3rd edn, Montreal: Vehicule Press.
Wente, Margaret, 2014. 'The Brave New World of 21st Century Learning', *Globe and Mail*, 28 June.

Wiggins, David, 2000. 'The Presidential Address: Nature, Respect for Nature, and the Human Scale of Values', *Proceedings of the Aristotelian Society*, 100.
Wiggins, David, 2001. *Sameness and Substance Renewed*, Cambridge: Cambridge University Press.
Wiggins, David, 2011. 'A Reasonable Frugality', *Royal Institute of Philosophy Supplement*, 69.
Wilde, Oscar, 1983 (1891). 'The Soul of Man Under Socialism', *Complete Works*, London: Hamlyn.
Williams, Andrew, 1998. 'Incentives, Inequality and Publicity', *Philosophy & Public Affairs*, 27, 3, Summer.
Williams, Andrew, 2008. 'Justice, Incentives and Constructivism', in Brian Feltham (ed.), *Justice, Equality and Constructivism: Essays on G. A. Cohen's Rescuing Justice and Equality*, London: Wiley-Blackwell.
Williams, Andrew, 2013. 'How Gifts and Gambles Preserve Justice', *Economics and Philosophy*, 29, 1.
Williams, Bernard, 1973. 'Critique of Utilitarianism', in J.J.C. Smart and Bernard Williams (eds), *Utilitarianism: For and Against*, Cambridge: Cambridge University Press.
Williams, Bernard, 1973. 'Egoism and Altruism', in *Problems of the Self*, Cambridge: Cambridge University Press.
Williams, Bernard, 1973. 'The Idea of Equality', in *Problems of the Self*, Cambridge: Cambridge University Press.
Williams, Bernard, 1993. 'A Fair State', *London Review of Books*, 15, 9, 13 May.
Williams, Bernard, 1995. 'Moral Luck: a Postscript', in *Making Sense of Humanity and Other Philosophical Papers 1982–1993*, Cambridge: Cambridge University Press.
Williams, Bernard, 1997. 'Forward to Basics', in Jane Franklin (ed.), *Equality*, London: Institute for Public Policy Research.
Williams, Bernard, 2005. 'Pluralism, Community and Left-Wittgensteinianism', in *In the Beginning Was the Deed: Realism and Moralism in Political Argument*, Princeton, NJ: Princeton University Press.
Williams, Bernard, 2008. *Philosophy as a Humanistic Discipline*, Princeton, NJ: Princeton University Press.
Williams, Bernard and Nagel, Thomas, 1976. 'Moral Luck', *Proceedings of the Aristotelian Society Supplementary Volume*, 50, 1.
Wolff, Jonathan, 1991. *Robert Nozick: Property, Justice and the Minimal State*, Cambridge: Polity.
Wolff, Jonathan, 1998. 'Fairness, Respect and the Egalitarian Ethos', *Philosophy & Public Affairs*, 27, 2, Spring.
Wolff, Jonathan, 2007. 'Equality: The Recent History of an Idea', *Journal of Moral Philosophy*, 4, 1.
Wolff, Jonathan, 2010. 'Fairness, Respect and the Egalitarian "Ethos" Revisited', *Journal of Ethics*, 14, 3/4, September/December.

Wolff, Jonathan, 2014. 'Editor's Preface', in G. A. Cohen, *Lectures on the History of Moral and Political Philosophy* (ed. Jonathan Wolff), Princeton, NJ: Princeton University Press.
Wolff, Jonathan, 2014. 'G. A. Cohen: A Memoir', in G. A. Cohen, *Lectures on the History of Moral and Political Philosophy* (ed. Jonathan Wolff), Princeton, NJ: Princeton University Press; previously published in *Biographical Memoirs of Fellows*, X, Proceedings of the British Academy, volume 172, Oxford, 2011.
Wolff, Jonathan, 2017. 'Review, Nicholas Vrousalis, *The Political Philosophy of G.A Cohen: Back to Socialist Basics*', *Marx and Philosophy Review of Books*, 14 August.
Wood, Allen, 1972. 'The Marxian Critique of Justice', *Philosophy & Public Affairs*, 1, 3, Spring.
Wood, Allen, 2004. *Karl Marx*, New York: Routledge.
Wood, Ellen Meiksins, 1995. 'Rational Choice Marxism: Is the Game Worth the Candle?', in Terrell Carver and Paul Thomas (eds), *Rational Choice Marxism*, University Park, PA: Pennsylvania State University Press.
Woodland Cultural Centre, 2024. 'Overview', https://woodlandculturalcentre.ca/about/
Young, Iris Marion, 1990. *Justice and the Politics of Difference*, Princeton, NJ: Princeton University Press.
Ypi, Lea, 2012. 'Facts, Principles and the Third Man', *Socialist Studies*, 8, 1, Winter.

Index

'Able' and 'Infirm' thought
  experiment, 69–70
acceptance of the given, 146, 148,
  159
actually existing socialism, 13, 21,
  23, 48–9
adaptive preference formation, 36,
  49, 118–19
advantage, access to, 23, 106,
  110–19, 130, 132, 134, 135, 160,
  168–9, 203n19, 203n29
age value, 149
agency, 44–5, 68, 118
Alfred Joyce School, 4
alienation, 75–7, 78, 118, 132–3
All Souls College, Oxford, 17–22,
  26–8, 107, 138, 154–6, 157,
  158, 163, 167, 170, 181n99,
  181n100, 212n83, 213n87,
  213n88
Althusser, Louis, 35–39, 42, 77; *see
  also* poststructuralism
altruism, 90, 99–100
Analytical Marxism, 1, 15–17, 21,
  30, 32, 45–7, 52–5, 71, 97, 98,
  105, 119, 122, 124, 134, 166–8,
  188n66, 188–9n71
analytical philosophy, 7–8, 10,
  13, 17, 30, 33–5, 38–9, 47, 52,
  55, 57, 64, 127, 133, 161–2,
  164, 165, 166–7, 169, 171–3,
  177–8n27, 182n126, 190–1n114
anarchism, 57–8, 168
Anarchy, State and Utopia (Nozick),
  58
Anderson, Elizabeth, 98, 129
anti-communism, 4, 8, 35, 47, 174
antisemitism, 3, 4, 6
Anti-Subversive Squad, 4
apartheid, 22
appropriation, 68–9, 72
Aristotle, 34, 170
Arneson, Richard, 134
art history, 149–50
artificial intelligence, 147
atheism, 29, 127, 162
attachment, 11, 141, 142, 162
authoritarianism, 2, 24
Ayer, A. J., 20

'Back to Socialist Basics' (Cohen),
  50, 101–2
Bardhan, Pranab, 15
basic income, 124, 207n86,
  209n141
basic structure, 89–94, 117, 127

Index

beauty, 112, 148, 150, 156–7, 162, 211n41
'Beliefs and Roles' (Cohen), 33
Berlin, Isaiah, 8–9, 14, 34–5, 47, 67, 170, 178n40, 178n42, 179n46, 190n104, 193n48
Berman, Marshall, 7, 28, 152
Bhargava, Rajeev, 185n180
Bible, 29, 162, 165
blame, 118, 119–21, 206n70; see also responsibility
B'Nai Brith, 5
Bolshevism, 2, 99
bourgeois ideology, 24, 30, 33, 44, 46, 53, 75, 108, 165
bourgeois social science, 44, 52, 166, 188n65
bourgeoisie, 6, 22, 25, 64, 151
Bowles, Samuel, 15
B.Phil., 6, 8, 33, 177n21, 179n47
Brennan, Jason, 58
Brenner, Robert, 15
brute luck, 106, 115–16, 121, 122, 128, 147, 165
bullshit, 15–17, 36–7, 38, 45, 46, 52–5, 60, 87, 128, 133, 134, 163, 167, 171, 173, 174, 180n76
Burke, Edmund, 138–9, 140, 144, 148
Burnyeat, Myles, 10

Callinicos, Alex, 42, 44
Canadian Communist Party, 3, 4, 11, 179n57
Canadian Jewish Outlook, 14
capabilities approach, 107, 109–12, 160
capitalism
  and alienation, 75–7, 78
  alternatives to, 48, 88, 136
  birth of communism from, 50, 56
  and commodification, 39, 76, 115, 153, 160
  and consumerism, 53
  and destruction, 151
  and exploitation, 13, 47, 51, 68, 70–6, 117
  and freedom, 13, 58–9, 62, 63–7
  and greed, 23, 29, 160
  and inequality, 15, 62, 67, 131
  and justice, 50, 51, 74, 87–8
  and labour, 40–1, 47, 51, 53, 63–7, 68, 70–8
  and libertarianism, 58–9, 62, 63
  Marcuse's critique of, 53
  Marxist critique of, 13, 24, 32, 39–42, 47, 51, 60, 74–7, 151, 153, 166, 168
  overthrow of, 76, 99
  and progress, 151–2
  and the state, 41–2
Capp, Al, 136
Carens, Joseph, 102
Carr, Sam, 11, 24, 179n57
Carter, Ian, 92
Casal, Paula, 26, 37, 45, 93–4, 157, 185n180
Catholicism, 4
change reversal, 145
charity, 28–9, 68, 128
Chesterton, G.K., 148
'Chesterton's fence' principle, 145
Chichele professorship, 17–18, 47, 167
choice, 23, 60, 62, 63, 77, 91, 93, 97, 107, 115–26, 128–9, 135, 159, 173–4, 204n48, 204–5n49, 205n53, 205n54, 206n73
citizenship, 82–3, 85–6, 88, 90, 93, 97, 129–30
clarity, 36–7, 53–4, 172–3
class struggle, 3, 44, 52, 76, 99
classless society, 49
Cohen, Bella (née Lipkin), 2–3, 4–5, 6, 11, 19
Cohen, David, 5
Cohen, G. A.
  activism, 22
  at All Souls College, Oxford, 17–22, 26–8, 107, 154–6, 157,

246 Index

Cohen, G. A. (*cont.*)
    167, 170; *see also* All Souls College
    awarded Isaac Deutscher Memorial Prize, 9, 14, 38
    background, 2–3, 118, 170
    charity, 28–9
    Chichele professorship, 17–18, 47, 167
    children and stepchildren, 10–11, 20, 24–5, 26
    competitive, 7, 10, 21, 22, 28, 182n122, 182n126
    death, 29–30, 164
    early life, 3–5, 170
    education, 3, 4, 6, 29
    humour, 2, 6, 9, 10, 11, 12, 14, 16, 19–20, 22, 27, 28, 37, 86, 163, 174, 181n101, 182n115, 182n117, 187n37
    legacy, 164–75
    at McGill University, 6, 19, 29, 33
    marriages, 10–11, 26
    at New College, Oxford, 6–9, 29, 33–5
    parents, 2–3, 5, 11, 14, 19, 24
    retirement, 29–30
    siblings, 2, 3, 5, 19
    teaching, 2, 20, 22, 27–8, 170
    travel, 13, 21, 26
    at University College London, 9–13, 19–20, 33, 76
    unpublished papers, 76, 183n133, 199n67
    visits to the Soviet Union, 21
    work ethic, 10, 21, 89, 172, 179n52
    works, *see individual titles*
Cohen, Gideon, 10, 20, 24, 29
Cohen, Joshua, 15, 45, 96
Cohen, Maggie (née Pearce), 10–11, 15, 19–20, 26
Cohen, Michael, 2, 3, 5, 177n12
Cohen, Michèle (née Jacottet), 26
Cohen, Miriam, 10, 20, 25
Cohen, Morris (Morrie), 2–3, 5, 11, 24, 139
Cohen, Sarah, 10–11, 20, 25, 29
Cold War, 8, 35–6
Cole, G. D. H., 17
collective ownership, 69–70
collective unfreedom, 65–7
colonialism, 156
comedy, 12, 19–20; *see also* Cohen, G. A., humour
commodification, 39, 76, 115, 153, 160
communism
    and analytical philosophy, 33, 38–9
    anti-communism, 4, 8, 47
    birth from capitalism, 50, 56
    Cohen's communist background, 2–4, 14–15, 24, 163, 166, 170
    and the Cold War, 35–6
    and conservatism, 139
    and democracy, 3
    and exploitation, 70–1
    inevitability of, 49–51, 56, 72, 189n91
    jazz band analogy, 71–2
    and justice, 51, 99–100
    and morality, 101
    and self-interest, 99–100
    and wealth distribution, 70–2
    see also Marxism; socialism
Communist Manifesto (Marx and Engels), 52, 151
Communist Party, 3, 4, 11, 35, 139, 179n57
community, 23, 29, 31, 71, 78, 80, 85–6, 96–102, 107, 117, 123, 128, 131–6, 160, 163, 165, 197n23
competition, 71–2
'Complete Bullshit' essays (Cohen), 36
conscription, 73
consensus, 86, 88, 97
consequentialism, 68, 74, 109, 141, 142, 143

conservatism, 25, 29, 31, 58, 136, 137–63, 164, 168, 169, 174
consumerism, 53
contracts, 40, 41, 59, 82, 193n50
'Contribution to the Critique of the Political Economy' (Marx), 39–40
cooperation, 82, 86, 92, 131, 134
cosmopolitanism, 89
culture, 37, 40–1, 48, 108, 109, 115, 117, 145, 147, 148, 150, 156, 167, 173, 182n126, 199n67, 205n56
'Currency of Egalitarian Justice, The' (Cohen), 22–3, 110–11
Czechoslovakia, 13, 23–4, 48

Darwin, Charles, 43
death, 142, 148
democracy, 3, 67, 86, 88, 93, 148
desert, 23, 59, 102, 132, 134–5
destruction, 150–2
Deutscher, Isaac, 9, 178–9n42
difference principle, 83, 84, 85, 86, 87, 112, 116
disadvantage, remedying of, 84, 89, 91, 106, 107–8, 115–17, 120, 128, 132, 164, 165
distributive justice, 70–2, 82–9, 93–4, 97–8, 107–12, 115–25, 129–35; see also wealth distribution
dogmatism, 30, 35, 46, 51–3, 54, 55
Dummett, Michael, 22
Duplessis, Maurice, 4
duties, 27, 86, 91, 93, 98, 125, 133, 143–4
Dworkin, Gerald, 13, 185n182
Dworkin, Ronald, 15, 20, 22–3, 25, 28, 31, 74, 107, 109–10, 113–17, 122, 161, 168, 183n127, 183n143, 204n33, 204n39

École normale supérieure, Paris, 35
Economic and Philosophic Manuscripts (Marx), 76

economic determinism, 6, 13, 32, 39–45
economic relations, 13, 39–42, 65
education, 58, 59, 66, 83, 108, 109, 121, 156
egalitarian conscience, 126–8
egalitarian plateau, 108–9
egalitarianism, 22–3, 31, 67–8, 70–1, 80–1, 83–99, 101, 106–36, 155, 158–63, 167–9, 173–4
Elster, Jon, 15, 16, 43, 44, 45, 46, 54, 76
Engels, Friedrich, 52, 53, 100, 151, 166
environment, 50–1, 72, 93, 96, 115, 152–3, 175
epistemological break, 35
equality, 1, 22, 23, 24, 29, 30, 34, 56, 59, 60, 61, 68, 70–3, 74, 76, 82–98, 100–2, 106–36, 204n33
Equality (Tawney), 101
equality of opportunity, 83, 87–8, 115, 122, 123, 128, 131–2, 133–4
equality of resources, 109–10, 111, 113
equality of welfare, 109, 111, 113
Estlund, David, 105
ethical investment policy, 22
ethics, 34, 103–4
evolution, 43
exchange value, 39
existentialism, 32
existing value, 31, 137–63
expensive tastes, 23, 28, 106, 113–15, 157–8, 168
exploitation, 13, 30, 47, 51, 67–8, 70–6, 78, 117, 167, 168

Fabre, Cécile, 27, 29, 37, 144, 185n180
fact-independent principles, 80, 87, 103–4, 105, 129, 157–9, 161–2
fairness, 82–3, 86, 87–8, 90, 92, 208n126

family, 90, 91, 94, 140, 168, 174, 199n63
fascism, 38
fatalism, 117–18
feasibility, 104–5
feminism, 10, 15–16, 23, 26, 28, 90, 91–2, 93–4, 96, 184–5n179, 210n12
fetishism, 39, 76, 109
feudalism, 40, 47
Finding Oneself in the Other (Cohen), 136
Fleuerbaey, Marc, 124
'Forward to Basics' (Williams), 101–2
Frankfurt, Harry, 36
Frankfurt School, 32
free markets, 49, 61, 62; *see also* market economy
free riders, 133, 167
free will, 117–18
freedom
  and anarchism, 57–8, 168
  and capitalism, 13, 58–9, 62, 63–7
  collective freedom, 65–7
  freedom of choice, 125, 127
  individual freedom, 17, 33, 57–63, 65–7, 74–5, 127
  and inequality, 57–60, 62
  and justice, 61, 88
  and labour, 57, 60, 63–7
  and libertarianism, 13, 30, 56–63, 68, 69, 168
  and Marxism, 17, 30, 60, 63–7, 68
  and morality, 62, 67
  positive freedom, 67
  and poverty, 62
  and private property, 30, 56, 57–63, 69, 168
  and social class, 63–7
  and social ethos, 125, 127, 135
  and the state, 57–60, 61
  unfreedom, 57, 60, 62, 63–7, 68, 74, 76, 168

French poststructuralism, 32, 35–7, 39
French Revolution, 138, 140
functionalism, 14, 41–2, 43, 45–6, 50, 54, 180n71

gambles, 116, 128, 132
gender, 10, 15–16, 19, 21, 28, 45, 82, 90, 91–2, 93–4, 96, 108, 156, 184–5n179
genetic modification, 147–8, 150, 152, 159
German idealism, 32
Gervais, Ricky, 20
Gifford Lectures, 162
Gilabert, Pablo, 93, 108, 132
global justice, 89
Goldman, Emma, 57
good life, 34, 89, 113, 160
goods fetishism, 109
Gordon-Solmon, Kerah, 185n180
Greece, 25
greed, 23, 29, 97, 98, 135, 160
green progressivism, 152–3

Hart, H. L. A., 177n24, 183n127
healthcare, 41, 58, 69, 122, 123, 156, 175
Hegel, G. W. F., 35–6, 37, 53–4, 190n107
heritage, 144, 145, 148–50, 151, 152, 155, 211n52
historical materialism, 8, 12–14, 32, 38–55, 56, 76, 92, 94, 152, 166, 168, 172
Hobbes, Thomas, 81, 82, 95, 170
Hobsbawm, Eric, 14, 42
Holiday, Tony, 22
holism, 45, 132, 161, 171
Honderich, Ted, 10, 138, 179n49, 179n52
housing, 109, 111, 144, 148–9, 155
human flourishing, 48, 100, 109, 111, 127, 130
human nature, 49, 77, 98, 105

Hume, David, 95, 101
Hungary, 38
Hurley, Susan, 19, 120

'If You're an Egalitarian, How Come You're So Rich?' (Cohen), 107, 161, 174, 202n2
immanent critique, 46, 79, 85, 168
impersonations, 19, 20
incentives, 23, 30, 80, 84–9, 90–1, 99, 113–14, 117, 120, 131, 196n11, 196n12, 196–7n15, 197n30
India, 21, 25, 26
Indigenous peoples, 156–7, 213n91
individual freedom, 17, 33, 57–63, 65–7, 74–5, 127
inequality, 15, 57–60, 62, 67–8, 70–3, 80–94, 102, 106–9, 115–22, 128, 130–2, 136, 147, 155–6, 165
injustice, 50, 51, 61, 68, 75, 87, 91, 95, 98, 140, 153, 158; *see also* justice
institutions, 23–4, 40–2, 57–8, 80–2, 88–94, 97, 98, 101, 108, 117, 125, 127, 128, 140, 168
insurance policies, 109, 123, 124
intrinsic value, 137, 140, 143, 150
Isaac Deutscher Memorial Prize, 9, 14, 38
Israel, 11, 120, 183n137

Jameson, Fredric, 49
Johannsen, Kyle, 87
joint ownership, 69–70
just inequalities, 106, 115–22
justice
  and the basic structure, 89–94, 117, 127
  and capitalism, 50, 51, 74, 87–8
  and communism, 51, 99–100
  and community, 80, 85–6, 96–7, 98, 99–102, 123, 128, 131–3, 165
  and conservatism, 158–9
  distinction of facts and principles, 103–5
  distributive justice, 70–2, 82–9, 93–4, 97–8, 107–12, 115–25, 129–35
  and egalitarianism, 80–1, 83–99, 101, 107–8, 131, 158–9, 165, 168
  and equality, 23, 31, 83–98, 107–8
  and exploitation, 70–3
  as fairness, 82–3, 86, 87–8, 90, 92
  and the family, 90, 91, 94, 168
  and freedom, 61, 88
  and gender, 82, 90, 91–2, 93–4, 96
  global justice, 89
  and incentives, 23, 30, 80, 84–9, 90–1, 99, 113–14, 117, 120, 131
  injustice, 50, 51, 61, 68, 75, 87, 91, 95, 98, 140, 153, 158
  and institutions, 23–4, 80–1, 82, 88, 89–94, 97, 98, 101, 117, 125, 127, 128, 168, 202n7
  and Marxism, 51, 57, 70–3
  and morality, 24, 51, 84–5, 86–7, 101, 103
  procedural justice, 82, 88–9
  Rawls's theory of, 23, 30, 80–94, 105, 107, 112, 117, 132, 167
  and rules of regulation, 87, 92, 94, 103, 129, 157, 161
  and social ethos, 29, 93, 95–9, 101, 125–9, 130–1
  social justice, 91, 95–8, 101–2, 127, 155–6
  and socialism, 88, 95, 97, 98–104, 105, 127–36
  and the state, 89–92
Justice as Fairness: A Restatement (Rawls), 88
justificatory community, 80, 85–6

Kahane, Guy, 147
Kamm, Frances, 142
Kandiyali, Jan, 78
Kant, Immanuel, 126, 143
Karl Marx's Theory of History (Cohen), 1, 12–15, 21, 30, 38–47, 50, 53, 56, 76, 163, 168, 172
Khrushchev, Nikita, 4, 13

Korsmeyer, Carolyn, 149
Kymlicka, Will, 14, 116, 135, 185n180

labour, 35–6, 40–1, 47–8, 51, 53, 57, 59, 60, 63–7, 68, 69, 70–8, 83, 97, 112, 114, 117, 125–9, 130, 151, 165, 168
labour movement, 50, 135
Labour Party (UK), 22, 50, 101–2, 132, 139, 167, 201n118
labour theory of value, 47, 75
laissez-faire economics, 56, 67
late style, 162
law, 5, 40, 90–1, 92, 100–1, 119, 126
Law of Peoples, The (Rawls), 89
Laycock, Henry, 43
Lefebvre, Henri, 152
left-libertarianism, 16, 62–3, 73
levelling down, 108
Leviathan (Hobbes), 81
liberal egalitarianism, 23, 61, 67–8, 78, 80, 107, 135, 161, 170; *see also* egalitarianism
liberalism, 31, 52, 58, 61, 67–8, 74, 80, 82, 85, 88–9, 95, 132, 137, 161, 169
libertarianism, 13, 16, 21, 30, 52, 56–63, 67–75, 78–9, 102, 108, 115, 132, 168
liberty, *see* freedom
Life magazine, 3
Lippert-Rasmussen, Kasper, 116, 185n180
Lithuania, 2
Little Boy and His House, The, 148–9
Locke, John, 58, 59, 68–9, 70, 73, 75–6, 82, 170, 191n15, 194n60, 194n70
locked room thought experiment, 64–5, 119
logical positivism, 34
London, 5, 9–13, 22
London Review of Books, 22
London School of Oriental and African Studies, 24

luck, *see* brute luck; luck egalitarianism; moral luck; option luck
luck egalitarianism, 23, 31, 115–24, 125, 128–36, 147, 159, 164, 167, 168, 183n143, 204n39, 204n47, 206n75, 208n111

Making Sense of Marx (Elster), 76
Mandelbaum, Maurice, 14
Marcuse, Herbert, 53, 190n104
market socialism, 99, 102, 133
markets, 49, 56, 61–2, 68, 85, 98–9, 102, 115, 122, 126, 130–1, 133–6, 152–4, 160, 163, 175, 196n11
Marxism
  and alienation, 75–7, 78, 118
  Analytical Marxism, 1, 15–17, 21, 30, 45–7, 52–5, 71, 96, 134, 166–7, 168, 187n50
  Berlin's views on, 8–9, 47
  Cohen moves away from, 49–51, 172
  Cohen plans thesis on, 8
  Cohen's articles and essays on, 14, 33, 38, 47–8, 50, 63–7, 76
  Cohen's book on, *see Karl Marx's Theory of History*
  and the Cold War, 35–6
  and conservatism, 139, 150–7
  critique of capitalism, 13, 24, 32, 39–42, 47, 51, 60, 74–7, 151, 153, 166
  and distinction of facts and principles, 103–4
  economic determinism, 6, 13, 32, 39–41, 45
  and equality, 23, 30, 70–3
  and exploitation, 13, 30, 47, 51, 70–6, 78, 167, 168
  and freedom, 17, 30, 60, 63–7, 68
  historical materialism, 8, 12–14, 32, 38–55, 56, 76, 92, 94, 152, 166, 168, 172
  and justice, 51, 57, 70–3

and labour, 40–1, 47–8, 51, 63–7, 70–8, 168
and modernism, 152
and morality, 101
and poststructuralism, 35–9
predictive aspects, 20, 49–50, 56, 167
and social change, 45, 49–51, 151–3, 168
and social class, 3, 5, 41, 44, 64–5, 60, 63–7
socialism without, 49–51
and the state, 41–2
and utopianism, 49, 52, 102, 105, 133, 166–7
see also communism; socialism
'Marxism After the Collapse of the USSR' (Cohen), 50
Mattes, Erich, 144
maximization, 141–2, 157
McCarthyism, 8–9, 178n36, 180n75
McGill University, 6, 8, 19, 29, 33, 34, 38
McMurtry, John, 11
means of production, 47, 70, 73–5
medical science, 146–8
metaethics, 103–4
methodology, 27, 32, 43, 44, 45–6, 78–9, 161, 166, 169–70
midfare, 111, 168
Midgley, Mary, 78
Mill, John Stuart, 26, 54, 135
Miller, David, 102, 104, 119, 133
Miller, Richard, 43, 132
modernism, 152
modes of production, 40, 43, 81
Montreal, 2–6, 19, 24, 170
moral equality, 123
moral luck, 119–20
moral philosophy, 8, 81, 100
morality, 24, 28–9, 51, 54, 62, 67, 84–5, 86–7, 101, 103, 109
Morris, William, 153–4
Morris Winchevsky School, 3, 4
motivation, 30–1, 82, 85–6, 95, 97, 98, 125

multiculturalism, 39
Murdoch, Iris, 35, 54, 78, 146
mutual justification, 85–6

Nagel, Thomas, 13, 67–8, 100, 119, 201n114
nanny state, 117
Narveson, Jan, 57, 58, 84, 140
natural lottery, 83, 116, 118, 205n56
needs, 23, 48, 59, 68, 71–3, 74, 96–7, 101, 106, 108, 114, 117, 131, 132, 133, 136
neutralism, 161, 169
New College, Oxford, 6–9, 29, 33–5
New Economic Policy, 2
New Labour, 139
New Left Review, 21
New Right, 58, 72, 135, 175
New Statesman, 14
Nielsen, Kai, 104
Nietzsche, Friedrich, 149, 170
No-Bullshit Marxism, *see* Analytical Marxism; bullshit; September Group
no-sucker socialism, 133–4, 167
Noonan, Jeff, 108
normative philosophy, 33–4, 50, 55, 105, 167
'Notes on Regarding People as Equals' (Cohen), 130, 133
Nozick, Robert, 13, 30, 57, 58–63, 67–70, 74–5, 78, 83, 115, 119, 144, 168, 191n6, 193n50, 193n56
nuclear disarmament, 22
nutrition, 109, 110–11, 160

Oakeshott, Michael, 148
occupational choice, 91, 112, 125–6, 173
Okin, Susan Moller, 15–16, 90, 91, 198n54
Olsaretti, Serena, 92–3, 122–3, 185n180
O'Neill, Martin, 87–8

option luck, 106, 115–16, 128–9
ordinary language philosophy, 7, 33, 34
original position thought experiment, 81–2
Orwell, George, 127
Otsuka, Michael, 37, 62–3, 73, 119, 136, 142, 154–5, 185n180
Outremont High school, 6
Oxford Academics Against Apartheid, 22
Oxford Socialist Discussion Group, 21, 183n132
Oxford University, *see* All Souls College, Oxford; New College, Oxford

Padlock Law, 4
Palestine, 120
Parfit, Derek, 18, 20, 25, 181–2n103
Paris, 5, 7, 15, 35
Parr, Tom, 123
particular value, 141, 143, 155, 156, 157
Pashukanis, Evgeny, 99–100, 101
paternalism, 29, 69, 209n142
patriarchy, 140
pensions, 58, 59
perfectionism, 21, 112–13, 115, 159–61, 168–9, 203n29, 213n108, 214n15
permissible inequality, 84, 86
personal, political nature of, 23, 91, 173–4
personal attributes, 111–12, 119
personal prerogatives, 96, 98, 125, 126–8, 200n93
personal responsibility, *see* responsibility
personal value, 141, 143, 144, 145, 155
philosophical anthropology, 48, 49, 78
Plamenatz, John, 35
plasticization, 146, 160, 211n41
Plato, 34, 81, 103–4, 170

poetry, 53, 174, 190–1n114
Pogge, Thomas, 103–4
Political Liberalism (Rawls), 88–9, 198n48
political participation, 67, 93
populism, 72
positive freedom, 67, 193n48
positivism, 34, 43, 81, 173
postmodernism, 32, 37
poststructuralism, 32, 35–7, 39, 92; *see also* Althusser, Louis
Pound, Ezra, 174
power, 41, 47, 51, 57–8, 61–2, 75, 90, 91, 108
Prezworski, Adam, 16
Princeton University, 13
priority of liberty principle, 83
prisons, 63, 156
Private Eye, 17
private property, 30, 40, 41, 56, 57–63, 67–70, 74, 88, 100–1, 144, 168
procedural justice, 82, 88–9
productivity, 23, 80, 84, 125
progress, 105, 151–2
proletariat, *see* working class
property rights, *see* private property
Protestantism, 4, 86
public justification, 83, 85, 86, 92
Pugh, Jonathan, 147
Pulzer, Peter, 18, 181n99

Quong, Jonathan, 93, 125

racism, 22, 91–2, 93, 199n66
Rastafarianism, 24
rational choice, 77, 117–18
Rawls, John, 15, 23, 30–1, 74, 80–94, 105, 107–9, 112–18, 124, 128, 130, 132, 161, 167, 168, 183n129, 198n41
Raz, Joseph, 88
Reagan, Ronald, 58, 72, 174–5
reciprocity, 74, 86, 92, 99, 131–4

Index

Reflections on the Revolution in France (Burke), 138–9, 140
reflective equilibrium, 83
relations of production, 39–40, 42, 50, 63
religion, 3, 5, 10, 29, 48, 127, 162, 165, 214n113; see also spirituality
Republic (Plato), 81
'Rescuing Conservatism' (Cohen), 137
Rescuing Justice and Equality (Cohen), 23, 80–1, 132
respect or relational egalitarianism, 98, 129–30, 208n111, 208n118
responsibility, 31, 85, 93–4, 96, 107, 113, 115–29, 132, 133–6, 159, 165, 173, 205n54, 206n73
responsibility-sensitive egalitarianism, 122–3
restoration, 145, 149–50
revolution, 20, 40, 44, 49–51, 72, 137, 138, 150–3
rewards, 23, 83, 102, 113–14, 116; see also incentives
Rhodes Trust, 22
Riegl, Adophus, 149–50
rights, 143–4
Ripstein, Arthur, 77
Roebyns, Ingrid, 105
Roemer, John, 15, 16–17, 28, 45, 74, 98–9, 122, 130, 180n75
Rosen, Michael, 21, 33
Rousseau, Jean-Jacques, 82
Ruskin, John, 149
Russian Revolution, 2, 50
Ryle, Gilbert, 7–8, 33, 34, 54, 78, 170, 173

Said, Edward, 162
Sandel, Michael, 132, 147
Satz, Debra, 16
Savulescu, Julian, 147
Scanlon, Thomas, 13, 92, 124, 142–3, 157

scarcity, 50–1, 71–2, 95, 101, 105, 136, 194n76
Scheffler, Samuel, 92, 118, 142, 143, 146, 157
scientific socialism, 52, 66, 166–7
Scruton, Roger, 153
Second World War, 3, 81, 95, 167
Seifert, Michael, 11
self-interest, 82, 85, 95, 97, 98, 99–100, 105, 130; see also selfishness
self-ownership, 13, 20, 30, 60, 62, 67–79, 191n4, 193n56, 193n57, 195n91, 195n106
self-realization, 36, 111, 130
selfishness, 23, 90, 92, 94, 99–100, 201n114; see also self-interest
Sen, Amartya, 17, 19, 20, 107, 108–9, 160, 169
September Group, 15–17, 26, 45, 73, 180n82, 181n89, 181n91, 188n59
sexism, 28, 45, 94, 199n66, 199n67
sexuality, 58
Shakespeare, William, 142
Sher, George, 120, 139–40, 159
Shiffrin, Seana, 16, 92, 185n180
Shmoo parable, 136
Singer, Peter, 91
slavery, 40–1, 74, 140, 155
social change, 31, 45, 49–51, 93, 105, 137, 138, 144–7, 151–3, 162, 168
social class, 3, 5, 38, 41, 44, 50, 61, 63–7, 76, 88, 99, 108, 114, 117–19, 168
social contract, 82
social ethos, 29, 93, 95–9, 101, 125–9, 130–1, 135
social justice, 91, 95–8, 101–2, 127, 155–6
social media, 147
social mobility, 64–7, 119
socialism
  actually existing socialism, 13, 21, 23, 48–9

socialism (*cont.*)
  camping trip analogy, 95, 130–1, 133, 134, 167, 208n119
  Cohen and Maggie's shared convictions, 10, 11
  Cohen's family background of, 3, 5, 11, 38–9, 46, 173, 210n6
  and community, 23, 29, 31, 99–102, 107, 117, 131–3, 136, 163
  and conservatism, 137–8, 139, 150–7, 163
  difficulty of realizing, 24, 101–5
  and equality, 106–7, 108, 124, 127–36
  inevitability of, 49–51, 56, 72, 167
  and justice, 88, 95, 97, 98–104, 105, 127–36
  and the market, 99, 102, 133
  no-sucker socialism, 133–4, 167
  Oxford Socialist Discussion Group, 21
  and responsibility, 31
  scientific socialism, 52, 66, 166–7
  and self-interest, 99–100
  in the Soviet Union, 13, 16, 21, 23, 24, 38, 48–9, 99, 101, 152
  utopian socialism, 49, 52, 102, 105, 133, 166–7
  without Marxism, 49–51
  see also communism; Marxism
socialized medicine, 41, 122, 123, 175, 180n74
Society for the Preservation of Ancient Buildings, 154
solidarity, 65, 86, 98–9, 124, 129, 130–1, 208–9n133
South Africa, 22
Soviet Union
  anti-Soviet sentiments, 4
  Cohen's visits to, 21
  collapse of, 16, 24, 48–51, 175, 181n89
  invasion of Czechoslovakia, 13, 23–4, 38
  invasion of Hungary, 38
  and justice, 99, 101

Khrushchev's 'secret speech', 4, 13
law, 101
New Economic Policy, 2
pro-Soviet sentiments, 5, 13, 24, 38
relations with the west, 3
Russian Revolution, 2, 50
socialism in, 13, 16, 21, 23, 24, 38, 48–9, 99, 101, 152
special role of in Marxism, 49–50
special burdens, 113–14
spirituality, 5, 10, 25, 29, 127, 162, 174, 214n113; *see also* religion
Stalin, Joseph, 4, 117, 131
'Star Wars' seminars, 20, 170
state, the, 41–2, 57–60, 61, 74, 89–92, 117, 144, 161
Steiner, Hillel, 15, 16, 19, 73, 119, 180–1n82, 181n83
stem cell research, 146–7
Stemplowska, Zofia, 123
stewardship, 144
Strathcona Academy, 6
'Structure of Proletarian Unfreedom, The' (Cohen), 63–7, 76
sufficiency, 107–8
summer camps, 2, 4, 5
superstructure, 6, 13, 40, 42
surveillance, 129
Sussex University, 9
Swift, Adam, 104–5

Tawney, R.H., 84, 108, 117
taxation, 23, 58, 60, 68, 69, 70, 77, 84, 93, 102, 128
Taylor, Charles, 17, 39, 42, 44, 54, 132
Taylor, Harriet, 26
technological development, 40–1, 44, 50, 147, 151–2
Thatcher, Margaret, 18, 20, 23, 58, 72, 84, 139, 153, 170, 175, 181n99
theodicy, 169

Theory of Justice (Rawls), 23, 81–2, 87–8, 89–90
Thomson, Judith Jarvis, 68
Tomlin, Patrick, 125
Toronto, 4
tradition, 140, 148–9, 157, 163
Trilling, Lionel, 138
Trotsky, Leon, 152
Tucker-Wood thesis, 51
Tuesday Group, 20–1

UK Commission for Social Justice, 101–2
Ukraine, 2
unborn, 61, 148
unchosen circumstances, 23, 31, 109, 117, 135
unemployment, 41
unfreedom, 57, 60, 62, 63–7, 68, 74, 76, 168; *see also* freedom
United Jewish People's Order (UJPO), 3, 4, 14
universal basic income, 124
University College London (UCL), 9–13, 19–20, 25, 33, 76
unjust inequalities, 106, 109, 115–22
unselfing, 77–8
utilitarianism, 63, 109, 127–8
utopianism, 49, 52, 71, 102, 105, 124, 125, 133, 166–7

value creation, 47
value pluralism, 52, 86–7, 105, 106, 135, 158–9, 163, 170
Van der Veen, Robert, 15
Van Parijs, Philippe, 15, 43, 124, 180n77, 187n37
veil of ignorance, 82, 85, 86, 90
Vietnam War, 22
Vrousalis, Nicholas, 7, 41, 43–5, 62, 67, 74–5, 98, 121, 129, 131, 153, 158, 169–70, 185n180

Waldron, Jeremy, 62
war, 95, 136, 167

wealth, 30–1, 57, 59–60, 61–2, 70–3, 80, 82–9, 93–4, 116, 121, 155
wealth distribution, 59–60, 70–3, 78, 82–9, 93–4, 97–8, 107–8
Weinstock, Daniel, 127
Weisbord, Merrily, 176n7
welfare state, 16, 20, 41, 58, 67, 68, 70, 72, 77, 87–8, 109, 123, 129, 135, 139, 198n42
wellbeing, 89, 97, 106, 111, 112–13, 114, 124–5, 128, 130, 132, 134, 160, 168
Why Not Socialism (Cohen), 23, 29, 95, 130–1, 132, 163
'Why Surfers Should be Fed' (Van Parijs), 124
Wiggins, David, 7, 152–3
Wilde, Oscar, 127
Williams, Andrew, 93–4, 123
Williams, Bernard, 100, 101–2, 120, 127–8, 130, 132, 147
Wilt Chamberlain thought experiment, 59–60, 61, 119, 191n6
Wittgenstein, Ludwig, 127
Wolff, Jonathan, 43, 97–8, 129, 131, 169–70, 185n180
Wollheim, Richard, 9–10
Wood, Allen, 51
Wood, Ellen Meiksins, 44
Wooden Acres summer camp, 5
Woods, Michael, 7
work, *see* labour
'Workers and the World, The' (Cohen), 38
working class, 3, 5, 38, 41, 44, 50, 53, 63–7, 72, 76, 153, 166
Wright, Erik Olin, 15, 17

Yiddish, 3, 29
Ypi, Lea, 103–4

Zionism, 4, 6, 11
Žižek, Slavoj, 153
Zuboff, Arnold, 12, 26, 180n71